A413

MISSIONS AND THE WORLD CRISIS

Books by Bishop Sheen

God and Intelligence
Religion Without God
The Life of All Living
The Divine Romance
Old Errors and New Labels
Moods and Truths
Way of the Cross
Seven Last Words
Hymn of the Conquered
The Eternal Galilean
Philosophy of Science
The Mystical Body of Christ
Calvary and the Mass
The Moral Universe
The Cross and the Beatitudes
The Cross and the Crisis
Liberty, Equality and Fraternity
The Rainbow of Sorrow
Victory Over Vice
Whence Come Wars
The Seven Virtues
For God and Country
A Declaration of Dependence
God and War
The Divine Verdict
The Armor of God
Philosophies at War
Seven Words to the Cross
Seven Pillars of Peace
Love One Another
Seven Words of Jesus and Mary

Preface to Religion
Characters of the Passion
Jesus, Son of Mary
Communism and the Conscience of
   the West
Philosophy of Religion
Peace of Soul
Lift Up Your Heart
Three To Get Married
The World's First Love
Life Is Worth Living — Volume 1
Life Is Worth Living — Volume 2
Thinking Life Through — Volume 3
Life Is Worth Living — Volume 4
Life Is Worth Living —Volume 5
The Life of Christ
Way to Happiness
Way to Inner Peace
God Love You
Thoughts for Daily Living
This Is the Mass (with Daniel-Rops
   and Karsh)
This Is Rome (with Morton and
   Karsh)
This Is the Holy Land (with
   Morton and Karsh)
These Are the Sacraments (with
   Karsh)
Go to Heaven
The Priest Is Not His Own

Missions
and the
World Crisis

Most Reverend Fulton J. Sheen, Ph.D., D.D.

NATIONAL DIRECTOR OF THE PONTIFICAL
SOCIETY FOR THE PROPAGATION OF THE FAITH;
AUXILIARY BISHOP OF NEW YORK

THE BRUCE PUBLISHING COMPANY
MILWAUKEE

NIHIL OBSTAT:

AUSTIN B. VAUGHN, S.T.D.
Censor librorum

IMPRIMATUR:

✠ FRANCIS CARDINAL SPELLMAN
Archbishop of New York
September 4, 1963

The nihil obstat and imprimatur are official declarations that a book or pamphlet is free of doctrinal or moral error. No implication is contained therein that those who have granted the nihil obstat or imprimatur agree with the contents, opinions or statements expressed.

Library of Congress Catalog Card Number: 63–17493

To
Mary
who
mothered the Divine Missionary
and all
those saintly souls
who
spend themselves and are spent
in the
Propagation of the Faith

Contents

Part I

The World Situation

1. *The Rhythm of the Missions*

The supreme business of a foreign missionary society is to put itself out of business as soon as possible. Since the aim of the missions is the establishment of the Church through the native clergy, foreign missionaries should strive to be self-liquidating. In theory, a day ought to come when the whole world would have had Christ preached to it and Africa, India, Japan, and Mongolia should have their own hierarchy, their own clergy, and be as free from the need of missionary imports as is the United States today.

Ebb and Flow

By the same token, there should be no purgatory. All who are baptized in Christ and have become partakers of His divine life ought to grow into perfection so that death would be the immediate flowering from grace to glory. But it is not so. Purgatory is an evidence of how practical God is, being a concession to human weakness. In theory, every doctor of theology ought to be a saint; but many would consider themselves fortunate if they "made" purgatory. So it is with the missions; though missionaries should diminish as time goes on, we happen to live in a practical universe, where there will always be necessity for missionaries, but not always in the same place. This ebb and flow of apostolic endeavors constitutes the rhythm of the missions.

Asia is presently almost a virgin missionary territory, only ¼ of one percent of Japan having the faith, and 1½ percent of India. In 500 years it is possible that Tibet and Burma may be sending missionaries to the United States. It must never be forgotten that the

3

Kingdom of God is presently on earth, but it is not thereby geographical. There is no assurance that any continent or nation will always
keep the faith though St. Patrick has assured the Irish that they will
never lose it. The gates of hell will not prevail against the Church,
but the gates of hell can prevail against Russia or England or any
other country.

France is the eldest daughter of the Church, but her faith has had
its vicissitudes. The French Revolution caused the number of religious to drop in twenty years from 26,774 to 16,235. The Abbey
of Igny alone which once counted 300 was reduced by revolutionary
terrorism to six. Today there are hundreds of parishes in France
without priests, and the number of ordinations is much less than it
was a century ago. Will a day ever come when France will have to
be repaid by America both in alms and in missionaries what it
once gave to this growing country? This is not very likely inasmuch
as France continues to be one of the greatest suppliers of missionaries
to the world and this indicates a tremendous inner vitality despite
a superficial decline.

The Balkan countries and Russia which were once totally evangelized and blessed with a native Church may, if Communism endures
for a century, become missionary countries again. On the other hand,
the whole of Northern Africa was once Christian. As early as 525
at the end of the Vandal invasion there were 180 sees. By 645 a
contemporary noted that "Catholic populations inhabit the oasis of
Djerid and penetrated the tribe of Aures and Zab." Over 800 bishops
were in Northern Africa when the Moslems appeared on the scene.
But in the year 1053 there were only five bishoprics left. The Church
must now move back into Northern Africa, though at one time Egypt
was in the fold of our holy faith.

In very few countries does the Church hold her gains, principally
because of persecution such as is now destroying the Church in
Eastern Europe, or from the decline of faith through worldliness.
The Judases go out, the Matthiases come in. The day Renan defected, Newman was baptized. What is true of persons is true of
nations. For those who go out some come in. Thus there will never
be an end to missionary activity. When the Church has succeeded

in giving the Cross of Christ to the people of India, it will be discovered that in some other part of the world the people will have taken it off their shoulders. Lands that were once evangelized will have to be evangelized again. Russia, which received the gift of faith in 988 and was in union with the Holy See, is now known as unholy Russia. But one day when the Red Cobra is killed, Russia will need to be taught all over again what Vladimir and his people once knew.

Channels and Shoals

In this rhythm, there will always be some great areas which will proclaim the power of the Incarnation with trumpetings of art, culture, and prosperity as Western Europe did in the thirteenth century. Asia's day is coming, and it will have philosophers who will do for Confucius and the glory of God what Aquinas did for Aristotle and Augustine did for Plato. "Gather ye up the fragments" is the Divine command; these fragments of Eastern culture will not be lost, but incorporated into the wisdom of the Church to reveal even unseen beauties of the Mystical Christ.

Our Lord seemed to suggest that at His Second Coming there would be a great decline in faith: "When the Son of Man comes, will He find faith left on earth?" Satan apparently will come very near his triumph as he did on Calvary, and then fall just short of it. If seven is the perfect number then it can be understood why Scripture says the sign of the Beast is 666 — one number short of perfection. So near and yet so far; Satan is ever winning the battle and losing the war.

Progress in a continuing spiral line is a pagan idea that does not suit either nature or grace. Youth opens and matures; the energy of the world is passing from potential to kinetic energy; the springtimes have their winters. Nothing is permanent in civilization here below except the Rock and the House which is built upon it, against which the winds and sea will rage and storm but not prevail.

As the rhythm of the missions oscillates between prosperity and adversity, persecution and peace, there is ever before the Church the immediacy of the Divine command: "Go teach all nations." We might even say, "Go reteach them." A refresher course is needed.

Faith is in souls and not in the earth. If it were of the earth, it would be permanent. But succeeding generations of souls which ebb and flow toward or from the Rock make it necessary to bring them back again to the Rock and Table of Life to relieve their starvation. The greatest guarantee of the continued faith in any land is the way it served the missions in the hour of its prosperity. If the rhythm ever affects the United States, please God, it too will have its rebirth in the glorious freedom of God, because it is now draining its resources to put rice in African and Indian mouths, turn pagodas into chapels, and supply the souls of Asia and Oceania and others who walk by the candles of Rama and Buddha, with the Divine Light of the Son of God, Christ the King of the World.

2. The Present Status of the Western World

To understand the missions one must consider the three tendencies of the modern world which will help to determine its future:

1. The decline of indifference
2. A world vacuum
3. An interregnum of barbarism

Indifference

Indifference means the denial of the distinction between the true and the false, right and wrong. Confusing charity and tolerance, it gives an equal hearing, for example, to speech which advocates the freedom to murder and to speech which advocates the freedom to live. Indifference is never a stable condition, but passes into polarization. As a crisis develops, the indifferent tend toward the opposite poles of good and evil, because a crisis creates the necessity of decision. The common tendency today to divide the world between Communism and Democracy, or God and chaos, Christ and anti-Christ, proves how quickly indifference has given way to the extreme opposites between which men must choose.

Few illustrate better than Pilate the transition which takes place in some minds from indifference to the polarization of evil. Educated under the Jameses and the Deweys of his time, when he absorbed Pragmatism, Pilate became totally indifferent to truth. As Truth stood before him in the Person of Christ, he sneered: "What is truth?" and then turned his back on it. Within a few hours this broad-minded *liberal* saw the degeneration of his indifference into a polarization

7

toward evil, which is still recorded in the Creed: "He suffered under
Pontius Pilate." Not in America alone, but throughout the entire
world, the Church is witnessing the shrinking of this "no man's land,"
where men refuse to make up their minds about God. The hour has
struck when every man in his conscience must suddenly realize the
truth of the words of the Savior: "He that is not with Me, is
against Me."

World Vacuum

The East and West may not be twain, as Kipling said, but they
meet in this common cultural experience: *both are living in a vacuum.*
The West is experiencing the death throb of the disintegration of
the secular culture initiated in the Renaissance, which stressed the
self-sufficiency of man. The East is feeling the decay of its centuries-
old ethical systems, such as Buddhism, Confucianism, and all the
other philosophies which sought to solve the problem of man. For
several decades this vacuum was temporarily filled by the materialism of the Western World, particularly in its industrial form as
adopted by the United States. It would seem that such a void would
create a vibrant opportunity for the missions of the Church. But the
egotist of the Western World is not necessarily ready for grace because he feels that inner void and "nausea" of which Sartre speaks.
Nor is the Eastern World ready for the plenitude of its historical
development simply because its house is being swept of its old
cultures and garnished.

Barbarism

This brings us to the reason why not too much must be expected
immediately in the way of conversion of the East and the West.
It is because, historically, between the end of any given era and the
beginning of the following, there is always an *interregnum of barbarism.* Between the Fall of Rome and the crowning of Charlemagne
there were the real *dark ages* of the Church. It is likely that with the
rapidity of communications and the effectiveness of war explosives
the interregnum of barbarism will be briefer in our time than in any
previous age. The barbarism which is filling up the void temporarily

is Communism. It is an *active* barbarism in the countries where there is a *strong* fifth column, and *passive* in the parts of Western Europe and the United States, where it has contributed to the decline of morals and the betrayal of intellectuals.

Communism is, indeed, intrinsically wicked, but it may very well be, from the Divine point of view, that Communism will play the same role in our world that Assyria played in the history of Israel. God made Assyria to chastise a people who had forgotten Him. The revelation of Our Lady of Fatima suggests that Russia has a punitive role to play in contemporary history. She warned that if men did not return to God, Russia would spread its errors throughout the world, inciting wars and revolutions. Communism, therefore, is the manure of our civilization; the fertilizer, which is a stench in the nostrils of good men, but which, in the eyes of God, may be the condition of a harvest, fiftyfold and a hundredfold. China, and the other countries of the East who have sampled Communism, err in thinking that it is the birth of a new order. It is rather the death of an old one: the last foul breath of the cheap Rationalism, Deism, and Agnosticism of eighteenth-century and nineteenth-century German thought, dynamized by Asiatic nihilism. As the modern man, bewildered by the anxieties and worries of life, becomes a split personality, so the modern world is gradually splitting into the polarized forces of Christ and anti-Christ.

One Humanity, Not Just One World

One of the primary purposes of the missions is to build not *one world* but rather *one humanity*. *One world* is a political and economic creation. *One humanity* is a Divine re-creation. The world is united from without; humanity is united from within. One cannot tie together twelve sticks without something outside of the sticks themselves. So one cannot tie up the nations of the world except by something outside of the nations themselves. International organizations assume that they not only pack the suitcase of the United Nations but that they also put themselves into it.

The Catholic point of view is that humanity is made one, as a body is made one, through a soul. When the Holy Spirit descended upon the Apostles, their discordant elements were fused into one body, and even one mind. The confusion of tongues was undone, and the poor divided speech, which men had "inherited from Babel's bricklayers," now became one language and one mind.

The purpose of the missions is not to unite the world in one political system, nor to make all countries believers in a particular form of democracy, but to allow them great political diversity with unity in the spirit. When the early Church received the Pentecostal outpouring her members shared their property in common. This was the creation of one economic world, but the spirit was first. The Communists assume that if men share property they therefore are one in Spirit. This fallacy assumes that if four men divide an apple they become brothers. Rather the Catholic position is that if they are first made brothers in Christ then they will share the apple. The Catholic who regards the Chinese, the Japanese, the Indians, and others, as his potential brothers will translate this act of faith into positive mission aid, that they may become actual brothers in Christ, to the end that there may be one world because there is one humanity.

There are dozens of periodicals with articles treating foreign affairs, international conditions, and world politics; but history to them is nothing but a succession of events without any definite purpose. Commentators judge today by yesterday and tomorrow by today. A well-known woman in our country very recently stated that those who believed Communism was right a few years ago are not to be condemned today because public opinion has changed. No! Right is right if nobody is right, and wrong is wrong if everyone is wrong. Murder does not begin to be right because many people practice it, nor does honesty cease to be a virtue even though Diogenes searched with a lantern for an honest man.

Few see world events in the light of eternity, and that every great crisis in history is directly related to God's holy will as regards His Kingdom on earth. The Fall of Rome in the beginning of the fifth century was so inexplicable to many Catholics that St. Augustine spent fifteen years writing and preaching the divine purpose behind it all. Some of his parishioners became so provoked that they said:

"Si taceat de Roma." But looking back, we see that the Fall of Rome was like the breaking of the shell of an egg. There was a nascent Christian life under the hard shell of Roman paganism. The barbarians broke that shell and Christianity emerged to conquer Europe. Communism could very well be the egg opener of the twentieth century, breaking the hard crust of materialism to allow the hidden Divine life to nourish the souls of men.

The hour has struck when those who believe in God and His providence in history are clamoring for a Divine view of world events. Who can better supply this than those in the Church who transcend parochial, diocesan, and national boundaries, whose vision is as universal as Christ who redeemed the world?

3. *The Basic Difference Between East and West*

Missionaries have long been conscious of the East as a dimension to be won for Christ. The West has only recently become conscious of the East — partly because of the East's rebellion against the imperialism of the West, and partly because Communism has wooed the East in order the better to challenge the West.

The East is now stirring like a giant aroused from sleep. The vast difference between the East and the West can be broken down into the elements of a *sentence*. A sentence is composed of subject, predicate, and the relation of existence between the two. The subject is something which is *determinable;* the predicate is that which determines it — for example, "the water is cold." "Water," the subject, is determinable; it can be hot or cold, pure or polluted. "Cold" is the particular determination in this instance.

The Eastern Stress

The thought of the East is, to a great extent, based on the subject, or the determinable. What is important to it is the great indetermined background of reality, which is like the ocean. Less important is every person born into the world, for he is a small determination of that indetermined mass, a little predicate added to the great subject. He comes into the world from this inchoate soul of the universe and then, when he dies, he goes back to it again. This universal, vague, indetermined something is the essence of the Brahman of Hinduism, Taoism, Nirvana of Buddhism, and even of Moslemism, in the sense that every person is of little significance before the great Allah. As a result, the person has little value; he must be content with his environ-

12

ment, the conditions in which he finds himself; and if he be a Moslem, he must resign himself to God and to His will which is sovereign and absolute.

Because freedom is related to the determining principle of life, it follows that the world which emphasizes the indetermined is never very much concerned with the problem of freedom as such, nor the sacredness of personality.

Now turn to the philosophy of the West. The great stress has been on the individual and his liberty. The *laissez-faire* of Capitalism and the new Liberalism stress this freedom to an extreme. When the nations met after World War I, the emphasis was on "self-determination"; after World War II, the emphasis is on "democracy," which means people's rule, and which is in essence the same thing. The stress of the West was, therefore, on the predicate, on human freedom, and on progress. While in the East the soul of the universe was all-important, in the West it was the individual who was all-important.

"Progress" became the soul of the West's religion, as the Brahman and Nirvana, or passive resignation, became the soul of the East's religion. The West *acted* because persons determined everything; the East *contemplated,* because the individual was only a sunbeam from the great sun, coming from it in the morning and returning to it at night in the great cyclic spin of the universe.

Which Is Right?

Neither is right, any more than a philosopher would be right who would define the cycle of twenty-four hours in terms of night exclusively. Each has split the sentence of reality in two. The East has taken the subject or the vague ethereal background of the universe; the West has taken the predicate or the self-determining, free, progressive principle within the individual himself.

Both are wrong. The future progress of the world is no more to be achieved by making the East imitate our technical progress and follow our democratic patterns than it is to be purchased by the East's forcing the West to absorb the free individuals into some vague, unconscious Nirvana. From a moral point of view, the East and the West are both sinners, for sin is deordination. Sin consists in taking one aspect of reality and making it stand for the whole; for example, equating prosperity with life (as does the Western view), or equating contemplation with life (as does the Eastern). The great sin of the East is in believing that *God does everything and man does nothing.* The great sin of the West is in believing that *man does everything and God does nothing.*

A Fixed Goal Needed

Each has a lesson to learn: The West, with its almost atheistic humanism, must learn, *"without Me you can do nothing."* All the free activities of man stem from the original endowment of the Creator. He must acknowledge that source of his energy, as the pendulum must acknowledge the clock. Man is independent only because he is dependent on God.

Furthermore, the best of human progress reaches a point of vagueness unless there is a reason for progress. As G. K. Chesterton once said: "There is one thing that never makes any progress, and that is the idea of progress." There must always be a fixed goal or destiny by which progress is measured. Otherwise, one never knows whether he is making any progress. Beyond this, there also comes a point where, to make further progress, the *higher must come down to the lower.* Before the chemical can enter into the plant, the plant must come down to the chemical and take it up into its system, with the chemical surrendering its lower nature to live the higher life. So, too, if man is to live a higher life, *life* must come down to man — and that is the Incarnation. Man then sheds off the old Adam of sin and egotism and selfishness and enters into the higher life, where he finds his freedom enlarged because there is spirit "and where the spirit is, there is liberty." He also finds himself more progressive, for he sees that real progress consists in the diminution of the traces of original sin.

The East has a lesson to learn, namely, the opposite one: that man can and must do something in cooperation with the Great Power of the universe. Its lesson is summarized in the words of Paul: "Nothing is beyond my powers, thanks to the strength God gives me." Man is not just a puppet in the hands of the Almighty. He came naked from his mother's womb but endowed with reason so that he could build a house for his shelter. God did not make a home for everyone but He gave men the skill to make tools. God made empty stomachs and men have to labor to fill their stomachs. The original order given in creation was to *"till the garden,"* and later on, *"Work while ye have the light."* The man who sits back, passive, on the assumption that God does everything is to be likened to the man who buried his talents in the ground. God will give him new strength only when he uses up the strength he already has. No one gets a second wind until he has used up the first. No one ever gets a second grace until he has spent the first, and particularly in the service of neighbor. Man must be energetic, active, progressive, must take the material things of the universe and make for himself a city — one that, though not lasting, will at least do credit to the mind that God has given him. The West has so much emphasized the material that it has become materialistic; the East has so much despised the material, in its contemplation of the Eternal, that to Western eyes it is reactionary.

No Scientific Progress?

The West is a scientific culture and civilization. And science is ultimately the discovery by man of the secrets that God locked in the universe when He made it.

The East has produced no technical science, and it was metaphysically incapable of doing so, for two reasons: (1) It lacked the kind of mental discipline which Christianity brought into the world, which was essential for the precision science demands. (2) It never saw the sacramental side of the universe, which Christianity introduced. God took water, and bread, and oil, and words, and a body, and made them material means for spiritual sanctification. He dignified matter by making it a channel for His grace.

It was only natural that, in the course of time, men should begin to see the value of the material universe and begin to unlock the Divine arcana contained therein. The possibility of science is inherent only in a culture already accustomed to seeing matter put to the *highest use possible,* namely, the sanctification of souls. From there on, it was easy to conclude that, if matter can minister to the spirit, then it can minister to the body of man.

The East scarcely learned that "nothing is beyond my powers, thanks to the strength God gives me"; that water, oil, steam, and fire, the great primitive forces of nature, can be harnessed and made to serve man on the way to God.

The Communists Teach the Missionaries

Communism is the *broom* which God is permitting the Soviets to use (*a*) to sweep away the cobwebs of Eastern thinking, and (*b*) as a judgment upon Western civilization for forgetting the role of the spirit in human culture.

Our blessed Lord said that the children of this generation were wiser than the children of light. By that He meant that they used a skill and a prudence to win people and wealth to themselves which His Apostles sometimes forgot to use in arousing men to the fellowship of Christ. Why is it that Communism can take over China in one generation — something which Christianity could not do in twenty centuries? There are obvious reasons, such as: Communism uses force, and Christianity depends on the free action of a will to grace; Communism caters to lower passions, Christianity disciplines passions; Communism has hordes of "missionaries," Christianity few.

But there is one technique which the Communists used that was right, and which was not generally used by the Christian missionaries. *The Communists made the Chinese believe that Communism came out of their own culture, was its flowering, and that in the philosophy of Communism was the fulfillment of the messianic hopes of the Chinese.* The Communists integrated themselves with the culture of the Chinese: sang their songs, danced their dances, and made them believe that they were flowering the buds of their culture. Actually they were like a freezing frost, giving them something alien to their culture, to their heart's desire, and to their great national traditions.

Despite the clever pattern of Communism in taking over a large part of the East, it is, nevertheless, much more than a philosophy or an economics. It is the *demonic* in history, in both the East and the West.

4. *Communism: The Demonic in History*

The human body rarely enjoys perfect health and composure in every cell and member; neither does the Mystical Body of Christ enjoy freedom from the trials and tribulations which are its lot as the prolongation of the Incarnate Life of Christ. Even at the very beginning of the Church, St. Paul made a distinction between the members of the Church that rejoiced and the members of the Church that suffered. He assumed a rhythm of suffering and peace when he urged that if one part of the Church suffered, the other part of the Church should suffer with it, and if one part rejoiced, the other part should rejoice. In the human body if the tongue tastes something sweet, the whole body rejoices, but when the head suffers from an ache, repercussions are felt throughout the entire body.

Applying this to the Church today, there are areas of peace and prosperity such as the Church enjoys in the United States and in certain parts of the missionary world. Progress is indeed slow in the missions but, at any rate, there are no overwhelming obstacles in certain localities. After a few hundred years of missionary apostolate, Africa is only 11 percent Catholic. The Moslems, indeed, are making more converts in Africa than the Church is. For every African converted to the faith of Jesus Christ, the Moslems convert two to Mohammed. The Church can rejoice that 40,000 priests have left their families and homes to bring the faith to the pagan world. Gratitude, too, is prayerfully expressed to God inasmuch as there are about a million souls a year added to the faith, either through baptism or conversion. Thus the Body of Christ grows again in "age and grace and wisdom before God and men."

17

But along with the reasons for rejoicing there is the depressing fact of sorrow, trial, and tribulation that need patience and hope. The Christian conscience is troubled by the growing Communist enslavement of the world. One person out of every three in the world today is under the domination of the Communist hammer and sickle. Included in this number are seventy million Catholics who are permitted to maintain their faith only under the possibility of exile, persecution, or martyrdom. Nor is there any sign that the Communist dehumanization is on the decrease. All China has been swallowed up by the Soviets. Out of our 8500 foreign missionaries practically none remains. The one million Catholics out of the six hundred million in China are today bearing witness to the faith under Communist persecution as nobly as did the faithful in the first three centuries of the Christian era.

Parables Prophesied This Condition

The parables of our blessed Lord reveal that the Church was to have its progress and its persecution, its hour when many fish would be gathered into the net, and also its moment when the powers of darkness would seek to destroy it. Along with the parables of the mustard seed and the leaven, which depict the Church as growing from small beginnings and yet in a hidden way working its mysterious influence on the world, there was also the parable of the tares or the cockle in which evil is pictured growing alongside of goodness. There were unclean animals in the Ark as well as the clean, bad fish in the same net with the good, chaff on the same barn floor as the grain, vessels of dishonor in the same house with vessels of honor. So, too, there is cockle growing in the same field with the wheat.

And yet this parable of the cockle is not a perfect description of what is happening in the world today, for it most likely referred to those who were in the Church, but not living according to its spirit. The visible Church has its intermixture of good and evil until the end of time, but in our time the evil is outside of the Church forming a "mystical" body all its own. It has its Peter and Paul in Marx and Lenin; its bible in *Das Kapital* of Karl Marx; its twelve apostles in the Soviet Presidium; its orthodoxy which is so sacred that if a devil comes from hell teaching any other doctrine he is not to be believed; its propaganda which sends out not missionaries but agents throughout the world in obedience to the command, "Teach Communism to all nations, infiltrating them in the name of Marx, Lenin, and Khrushchev." Its Rome is Moscow, to which pilgrimages are made to view the tomb of Lenin; it has its visible head and its invisible head, too terrible to be named.

St. Thomas Aquinas envisages such a "mystical" body of the Anti-Christ who would in simian fashion simulate the Church as the Body of Christ. The Risen Christ exercises a double influence on the Church: one internal by influencing its members, the other external by directing it to an end; so, too, says Aquinas, the devil as the head of the evil of the world exerts external influences for the achievement of his purpose, which is the turning of the rational creature from God. He explains that the satanic government does not mean that everyone is consciously subjected to his will; some are obedient to it consciously, others follow without much persuasion after the example of soldiers who march following their leader. But Satan is the head of all the evil ones because in him is the fullness of evil as in Christ was the fullness of Divinity.

The demonic in the world is different from the cockle in the field. It is more corporate, more unified, and in the technical language of philosophy has a "form" all its own. Communism seeks to dispossess the soul which is the form of the rational creature, and infuse a new form, as the Soviet-trained psychiatrists said over the body of Cardinal Mindszenty, "We will get rid of the soul that he has, and put in a Soviet soul. He will thus look like Mindszenty, talk like Mindszenty, but he will be a Soviet." Brainwashing, indoctrination, and other methods destined to destroy the intellect and the will of man, are resorted to until the victim is ready to be incorporated as a cell into the "mystical" body of the anti-Christ. As grace is deiform to the Christian, so the Soviet mentality is demonic-form to the member of the "mystical" body of the anti-Christ. Evil today is corporate, organic, "socialized." In the Gospel we meet cases of individual possession; in this disturbed civilization we meet socialized possession, in which nations and governments are under the empire of Satan. The Church is now facing a philosophy which organizes men outwardly into a completely controllable collective estate, and also organizes men internally into a totalitarian mode of thought and surrender of judgment.

No More Heresies

The Church probably will never again see a great heresy; nor, perhaps, will there ever be another great schism. Communism is the heir to all of the schisms and heresies of the centuries. It brings them all to a focal point and to their logical conclusion which is the setting up of an anti-God in place of God. The future struggles of the Church will not be from within but from without. The days of civil war, in which sect wars with sect, are over. From now on we face an invasion from outside culture, outside of religion, and outside of reason, namely, the enthronement of collective man in place of God.

No one better understands the nature of the present conflict than the priests of the Church behind the Iron Curtain and the missionaries of China, Korea, and Indochina. Both have seen in the language of Milton a phase of history where

> . . . eldest Night
> And Chaos, Ancestors of Nature, hold
> Eternal Anarchy, amidst the noise
> Of endless wars.

Those behind the Iron Curtain have seen how the established Church was wrecked by corporate evil. Those behind the Bamboo Curtain see how the missionary Church was destroyed by the same elemental force of barbarism. Both have learned what might be called the lesson of the Impossibility of Dialogue. With the infallible Vicar of Christ to guide the Church, the encyclical on Communism by Pius XI reminded the Catholic world that Communism was intrinsically evil.

Despite this guidance, there were a few behind the Iron Curtain who believed that it was possible to carry on conversations and to make compromises with Communism which would prevent it from becoming wholly wicked. We can recall that when we first became the National Director of The Society for the Propagation of the Faith in the United States, we wrote against the Communist persecution in China. A few letters came from China and a few from missionaries in the United States begging us not to accuse the Communists because, as they said, some compromise could be established with them and ultimate persecution avoided. But if we accused them of persecution, we would make a peaceful settlement impossible.

How easy it is to fall into the error of believing that Christ and Baal, God and Mammon can dwell together! Not to complain against a beast that claws off the right arm is no assurance that the left arm will be preserved. The futility and even stupidity of compromising with Communism and remaining silent during its persecution now becomes evident to all.

The philosophy of Communism is bent on the reversal of all human values, so that good becomes evil and evil becomes good. Indifference to this philosophy is the denial of the First Commandment. Those who held this compromising view, which is still held by some politicians of the Western World, have long since abandoned it. As the Communists imprisoned hundreds of our missionaries, murdered thousands of our faithful, dispossessed the Church of millions of dollars worth of property, it is universally admitted by the faithful that dialogue with Communism is impossible. No maneuver, no silencing of a word of condemnation will prevent Communism from achieving, if possible, the end that it has set for itself, namely, the destruction of the Mystical Body of Christ. There is so much at stake in the struggle that one has to have the courage to face the consequences. The Christian in these areas must resign himself to becoming a prey of relentless persecution. With dialogue ruled out, the Christian is condemned either to heroism if he lives, or to martyrdom if life is denied, but "those who are Christ's *must* suffer persecution."

Our blessed Lord said that those who denied Him on earth He would deny before His Father in heaven. He implied that every attempt to avoid commitment is commitment. That was His way of saying that dialogue was impossible. Even noncommitment leads the faithful in China to prison or to death, or else it serves the forces of evil. Nor is Communism satisfied with a mere denial of God; it demands defiance of God. There is a difference between the Titanism of Denial and the Titanism of Rebellion; the first is nihilistic; the second is demonic. Nietzsche was a Titan of Denial, for his nihilism was a jubilant acceptance of a world untrammeled by morality and God. As he put it: "The world lives on itself; it feeds on its excrements." But under Marxism, the Titanism of Denial has become the Titanism of Defiance, and Defiance becomes demonic when it imposes its own will upon the world or else proclaims its own divinity.

The Novelty of Our Crisis

We have had crises before, but never a crisis like this. Each reduplication of heresy has become more pathetic and more absurd. Here is not just a mere carrying over from generation to generation of a previous error; the twentieth century is a moment when the spirit of evil has come to a focus. What was spawned in successive revolts against the Divinity of Christ, the Trinity, the Eucharist, under such innocuous terms as Reformations, has become a sprawling giant. Marx once said that the Reformation of the sixteenth century destroyed the "outer priest." "It is our aim," he said, "to destroy the inner priest, that is to say, the spiritual nature of man." This is what the Church has come in contact with faintly in Eastern Europe, but which the missionary world has felt more deeply as it resists unto blood. Every spiral of error through the centuries has led the world into a profounder perversion and a more fundamental reversal of values.

The persecuted missionaries are dealing with exactly the same problem as the politicians in the UN. The difference is that the politicians believe dialogue is possible; the missionaries do not. The politicians refuse to see Communism as intrinsically evil; to them it is a political system that creates awkward moments for one who differs with it. Hence the spectacle of the persecutors sitting with the persecuted, the robber with the robbed, and the rapist with the raped. In no civil court would a thief be permitted to sit alongside the judge to judicate his own case, but in the international sphere it is often so.

Our missionaries who know better than anyone else are preserving for the world the view of the absolute incompatibility of Communism and civilization. While politicians tear up the photographs of justice, the missionaries keep the negatives for another day when justice dawns. Someone must proclaim to all the world the impossibility of dialogue and this role falls to our missionaries. When politicians learn from these persecuted defenders of freedom, justice will return, then peace, and finally charity.

A hopeful sign is that there has been an increase of missionary activity at the very moment when the prospect of missionaries is persecution or martyrdom. *Modern man wanted to be man without God; but God did not want to be God without man; therefore He became man; therefore His missionaries refuse to believe that men of good will in the world should be without God revealed through His divine Son, Jesus Christ.* One would think that an age such as this, from a human point of view, would be the one where missionary activity would be at its lowest ebb, not only because of the rising prejudices against missionaries in India, but also because a missionary to the rest of Asia must be prepared to die if need be for the Cross; yet these heroic men and women are multiplying to such an extent that in Ireland alone one out of every two priests is on the foreign missions.

Dialogue with Communism may be impossible, but martyrdom under Communism is not. The Western World is holding dialogues with Communism, and Communism in each instance comes off first with Poland, then a whole litany of nations. Our missionaries, like our politicians, go to the Communists, not to hold dialogue with them, but to be persecuted as witnesses of Christ; so that with Paul they can say to their glory: "I have toiled harder, spent longer days in prison, been beaten so cruelly, so often looked death in the face. Five times they scourged me and spared me but one lash in the forty; three times I was beaten with rods, once I was stoned. . . . What journeys I have undertaken, in danger from rivers, in danger from robbers, in danger from my own people, in danger from the

Gentiles; danger in cities, danger in the wilderness, danger in the sea, danger among false brethren. I have met with toil and weariness, so often been sleepless, hungry, and thirsty, so often denied myself food, gone cold and naked. And all this, over and above everything else which I do not count; I mean the burden I carry every day, my anxious care for all the churches; does anyone feel a scruple, I share it; does anyone's conscience hurt? I am ablaze with indignation. If I must need boast, I will boast of the things which humiliate me; but God who is the Father of our Lord, Jesus Christ, blessed be His Name forever, knows that I am telling the truth."

5. *Moslemism Is Also a World Force*

Everyone knows Communism is the great disturber of world peace. The general picture of the world drawn by politicians is that the world must choose between democracy and Communism, between America and Russia. There is still another sphere of influence, namely, Moslemism.

European Sphere of Influence

It used to be that the world outside of Europe was to a great extent influenced by Europe itself. The colonial expansion of the European powers, such as England, France, Germany, Portugal, Spain, and Holland, though it was primarily commercial and political, nevertheless did bring with it some remnant of Christian civilization. Unfortunately, much of the colonial expansion took place after Europe had lost its Christian unity. The principal interest of the European powers in their latter days was not the planting of the Cross of Christ in the colonies of Africa, India, Indonesia, Java, China, or elsewhere, but the acquiring of new markets, the annexation of territories, and the increase of wealth at home. But despite this fact, there was still the leaven of a Christian culture working in the mass of the Eastern World.

Russia and America

Today all this has changed. Two new powers or spheres of influence have risen to challenge Europe and to assert their right to dominate or at least influence the rest of the world, namely, Russia and the United States. Neither of these brings even an implicit defense of the Christian religion as did the European. One power, that of Russia, is definitely antireligious and anti-God. The other power, the United States — and here we speak not of its people but of its governmental policy — is definitely secular. It is totally indifferent to whether any part of the Eastern World has religion, just as it is indifferent to whether there should be raisins in a cake. Russia, on the other hand, is more logical. It says that you cannot be indifferent to religious values, you must either love them or hate them. Choosing for the moment to hate them, they begin their influence in the Eastern World with brainwashing through persecution, concentration camps, murders, and martyrdoms.

As a result, Asia is being courted by two lovers, one of which is anti-God, the other of which is Godless; one of which is materialistic, and the other of which is industrialistic, which is very often a fancy name for materialism.

The Forgotten Sphere of Influence

There is yet a third sphere of influence which neither the United States nor Russia considers sufficiently, and that is the influence of the Moslem people, who, though historically anti-Christian, are nevertheless firm believers in God. This gives the Eastern World a triple choice: a firm belief in God with a hatred of Christianity which is Moslemism; a secularism, or a total indifference to whether God is the source of rights, which is the policy of the United States; or the anti-God, anti-Christian tyranny of Russia.

In vain do we think that the struggle is between democracy and Communism, for when we put the conflict that way we assume that Asia must choose one or the other. Asia could reject both, for the Moslem sphere of influence still exists and may yet be the key to the solution of the world problem.

The Religion of the Moslems

Moslemism is the only great world religion which was founded subsequent to Judaism and Christianity and is made up of the elements of both. It was founded by Mohammed who was born about the year A.D. 570. During his travels he came in contact with Jews and Christians, many of the latter being in touch with Nestorian heretics. Mohammed claimed that the Angel Gabriel appeared to him and dictated to him the bible of Moslemism which is the Koran. There are five fundamentals in Islamism. The first is faith, which is public testimony that there is no God besides Allah, and that Mohammed is his prophet. Judaism placed the holiness of God in the foreground; Christianity, the love of God; and Islamism, the omnipotence of God. Islamism, however, denies any kinship between God and man which is essential to Christianity.

The second pillar of Islamism is prayer, which the people perform five times a day, at dawn, at noon, at 3 o'clock in the afternoon, at sunset, and one or two hours after sunset. Prayer is to be preceded by ablutions and without these ablutions prayer is sinful.

The third pillar of Islamism is almsgiving, which is free-will offerings to the poor.

The fourth pillar is fasting. The month of fasting is Ramadan which is the Moslem Lent. It is not an abstinence from certain kinds of food but from all food and drink including water and smoking and any stimulant.

The fifth and last pillar of Islamism is the pilgrimage. It is obligatory on every adult of either sex to make a pilgrimage to Mecca once in his life. This pilgrimage has kindled as nothing else the bond of Islam between peoples of all races and colors and made every pilgrim realize the vastness of the area that Allah rules.

The religion had its origin in Arabia, a country of deserts, a few oases, and few trade centers. It is primarily a religion of the desert, for the desert does help to form man psychologically in two ways: by impressing him first with the omnipotence of God and second with the nothingness and helplessness of man.

The stars of the desert seem so close that one could almost reach up into the heavens and pluck them out. There is no living creature, no animal, no greenery, no bush to arrest the eye. There is nothing to which the soul can cling within all of that vast expansive view except the heavens. Since in the desert one keeps his eye less on the sand than on the heavens, very naturally one becomes tremendously impressed with the omnipotence of God.

A second effect of the desert is the utter inadequacy of man. It is absurd to trust in oneself, in one's own power and cleverness and efficiency, for in the desert man is helpless. When the water gives out, only God can lead one on a path to the oasis. God's sovereignty is everything and before Him one is nothing.

The result is that the Eastern peoples have built up their great sin that God does everything and man does nothing.

The Conversion of the Moslems

The conversion of the Moslems is *presently* almost impossible, for several reasons which are considered here.

1. Conversion to Christianity is punished by severe social ostracism.

2. Because the Moslems believe that Christ was not the Incarnate God and Redeemer of the world, but only a kind of John the Baptist announcing Mohammed, it follows that for a Moslem to become a Christian is like a Christian becoming a Jew. It is a reversion from the substance to the shadow, from the reality to that which prefigured it.

3. It is to be granted that Moslemism has a deep prayer life, a rich cultural inheritance, a firm belief in the sovereignty of God, and that it has been a benefactor to Western civilization. The five pillars of the religion, which consist in faith in God, prayer, alms, fasting, and pilgrimage, have made Moslems a devout people which secularism has been slow to destroy.

But their religion has the same incompleteness as all natural religions: first, the direction of religion is from man to God, instead of from God to man, which is the nature of Christianity. Man quickly reaches his limit in ascending toward God. God Himself must descend in order to lift man up to a state where he could not be by his own nature. This denial of any essential kinship between God and man, on the part of the Moslems, this transcendance of God to a point where human freedom is to some extent weakened, makes the acceptance of a God-man on earth almost impossible. This intellectual misunderstanding of the inner life of the one God has made the Moslems difficult to lift to a supernatural life.

4. Added to these are historical reasons for bad feelings in the past between Moslems and Christians. Both have something to forgive and forget. Christians must forgive and forget how the Moslems snuffed out the Church in Northern Africa; Moslems must forgive and forget how we treated some of them at the time of the Crusades.

5. Finally, the overemphasis on the person Mohammed makes him almost a barrier to a deeper understanding of the one God who creates as Father, redeems as Son, and sanctifies as the Holy Spirit, rather than a mere man bringing blessings to mankind. A Dutch writer, Abraham Kuyper, discovered how very much even the name of Mohammed usurped the place of God or Allah in prayer. Having made a study of 1800 to 2500 prayers, which were offered each year by the Moslems, he discovered that homage was paid four to five times in each to Mohammed. The Communists have made inroads among the Moslems precisely on this exaggerated cult of Mohammed. By allowing them to keep Mohammed they take away their belief in God. In theory, Moslemism should be the strongest natural rampart against Communism in the world. That Russia can win over Moslem governments to its atheistic totalitarianism would never be possible if they attacked or denied Mohammed; but the Communist denial of God has not made such alliances impossible.

Cardinal Lavigerie, the founder of the White Fathers, who have more missionaries in Africa than any other mission society, said it would be one hundred years before a convert would be made among the Moslems.

The apologetic question which confronts those who have the divine mandate to teach all nations is: what method or approach should be used? Our answer is twofold: the intellectual and the spiritual, the wisdom of scholars and the simplicity of saints. "Be ye wise as serpents and simple as doves."

The intellectual approach should be that of a scientific study of the Koran and its Islamic tradition, such as Christians have made of Scripture. With no bias, prejudices, or ill-will, there should be an appeal to the reason of the Moslems such as Thomas Aquinas' in the Contra Gentiles, which he wrote to convert them. The Moslems, he said, will not accept Scripture, therefore, we must find a common denominator and it is this — *that we both can think.* The four books of the *Contra Gentiles* use this intellectual approach. A development of the rational in the way of internal criticism is most imperative. Unfortunately, little of it has been done. And yet Moslem students in Egypt have been known to laugh in class at some of the incidents mentioned in the Koran.

A two-volume work has recently been written by Hanna Zacharias, on *L'Islam, entreprise jeune.* The thesis is simple: Islamism is Judaism explained by a rabbi to the Arabs; the Koran was written by a Jew, not an Arab; the primitive Koran was lost. The thesis is based on parallels between the Old Testament and the Koran which are many. But tradition does not sustain the theory of Zacharias, nor the New Testament references in the Koran. Furthermore, it forgets that when Mohammed came to Medina he was ignored and ridiculed by the Jews, who regarded him as a Gentile. Though Zacharias is one-sided, she does point up the borrowings of Mohammed from the Old Testament and, more important, the authenticity of many texts in the Koran. Furthermore, such experts as Noldeke, Blanchere, Lammens, and others point out the confusion of the names of the scribes who were supposed to have taken down the presumed revelation to Mohammed. Tradition is unanimous that at the death of Mohammed there was no written Koran, but only an oral tradition. The first successor of Mohammed, Abou Bekr, with his successor Omar, made the first copy. But there were also others who wrote down the traditions; that is why there is no fixed canon concerning authenticity. M. Gaudefroy-Desmombynes in his scholarly work on Mohammed (Albin Michel, 1956, 708 pp.) states that if one chose to use only controlled and certain texts from the Koran and Tradition, one would have no life, for there is "practically nothing" that could be admitted. Western scholars have developed the science of philology which enables them to scrutinize and evaluate alleged authorship through comparison of texts, editions, and translations. The corporate conclusion is that the language of the Koran is not the language Mohammed used to communicate the oral tradition.

As education broadens among the Moslems, as they frequent Western universities and learn the objective scientific approach to documents, as the women begin to be educated, the Moslems themselves will recognize borrowings from Judaism and Christian heretics. This will be their introduction to Christianity. Then will they see that not all is false in Moslemism, but that the segment of Divine Truth which they possess is to be complemented by the fullness of the circle. Where there is truth, there is love. Not in bitterness, not with a desire to evacuate Moslemism of its many naturally good elements, but rather with calmness and intellectual accuracy let the scholars complement the good our missionaries are doing for the Moslems by educating and healing them. The Moslems have had a great intellectual tradition especially in the Middle Ages; let them now welcome scholarship once again and they will not be the losers.

The Proper Attitude Toward Islamism

Our attitude should be (1) to forget unhappy relations in the past and (2) to look for what is good.

1. Those who have come to the fullness of the revelation of God in Christ should forget that the Moslems have been one of the great enemies of Christianity. It is true that they practically extinguished it in Northern Africa, reducing within two hundred years the number of Christian bishops from 855 to 5; it is true that they almost submerged the Christian West, at one time coming within 125 miles of Paris and several centuries later coming to the very walls of Vienna; it is true that those who do become Christians are ostracized and sometimes martyred; it is true that no one in human history ever dared to match himself with Christ except Mohammed, who declared himself the superior of Christ saying that Christ was only a prophet announcing Mohammed as the latest and greatest of all the prophets; it is true that Christians can be saved, according to the Moslems, only by becoming Moslems or by accepting the humiliation and defeat in the payment of tribute; it is true that the only religion which has clashed with Christianity and conquered a large part of its territory, without ever surrendering any except Spain, has been Moslemism.

But the historical clashes between Moslemism and Christianity in the past must not impede reconciliation and affection among peoples. At the present time Russia is an enemy of all believers in God and human rights, but if the day ever comes when this anti-God Soviet government vanishes, we will accept the Russian people to our hearts. As it would be wrong to harbor any hatred against the Chinese because of the way they are persecuting the missionaries of the present time, so it would be wrong to harbor any resentment against the Moslems because of the past attitude of Christians toward them or of them toward Christians.

The Crusaders did not make a very profound influence on Islam as a whole, but to a great extent widened the gulf.

Then there was only one voice raised in warning; it was the voice of a great Catalan scholar and poet Raymond Lull. He promulgated the idea of a peaceful crusade. He selected groups of monks for the study of the Arabic language to prepare them for the work of preaching and martyrdom among the Saracens. He wrote: "whence it seems to me that the conquest of the Holy Land ought not to be attempted except in the way in which Thou and Thine apostles acquired it, namely, by love and prayer and pouring out of tears and blood." When advanced in age, he went to North Africa and died preaching as a Christian martyr, stoned to death by an angry crowd. But it is the spirit of Raymond Lull that we would invoke as the proper attitude toward the Moslems today. There is never any substitute for charity.

2. Find what is good.

The Moslems are firm believers in God. Mohammed did bring his country and his people out of polytheism into monotheism and to a recognition of the sovereignty of God. Creation to the Moslem exists only to affirm the uniqueness of God. Very often this belief in God results in a kind of abandonment to fatalism as against the Christian doctrine of cooperation of man with God, but at least there is a recognition of a great power above man which many in the Western World have forgotten.

To the credit also of the Moslems, it must be said that they are a prayerful people. It may very well be that there is more prayer in the Moslem world to God than there is in the post-Christian civilization of the Western World. It may be that Iran prays more to God than France, that Pakistan has a higher average of prayer to God than the United States. There is no judgment about the quality of the prayer, or the value of the intercession, but merely of the number of people who at least five times a day do bow to God.

Associated with Moslemism have also been great spiritual movements such as Sufism which pays great attention to God, purity of heart, sincerity of intention, fear and love of Him who will introduce them into the ways of heaven.

Finally, there has been great development of philosophical thought in the Moslem world. Thanks to Moslems Aristotelian philosophy was brought into the Western World and became the foundation of Western philosophy. St. Thomas himself was familiar with the thought of many of the Moslem philosophers.

The Mystery of Moslemism

The Moslems are destined to play a providential role in the world of the future, and the full mystery of their existence upon the earth has not yet been grasped. The mystery of Moslemism revolves around three important elements in their religion:

1. The relation they claim to Abraham
2. Their recognition, in a vague sort of way, of Christ
3. Their devotion to Mary

1. THEIR RELATION TO ABRAHAM

Pope Pius XII once said that all Christians were "spiritual Semites," because we were descended spiritually from Abraham. God called Abraham to be the father of the living, and our kinship with Abraham in the flesh became the kinship with Christ in the spirit. Thus we trace our continuity with Abraham.

The Moslems also go back to Abraham and bear him great devotion, but it is interesting that they trace their lineage not through Isaac, as do the Jews and the Christians, but through Ishmael.

Abraham had two sons, one was born of a mother who was a slave, named Agar, and the other who was born of a free woman, Sarah. St. Paul commenting upon the fact in Galatians 4:23 says that the two women and their sons stand for the two dispensations. The slave woman Agar stands for Mount Sinai which St. Paul puts in Arabia. The free woman who was Sarah stands for the earthly Jerusalem and its spiritual development through the Messias.

St. Paul makes the two sons to stand for law and grace. Isaac born of Sarah stands for the unfolding of Abraham through the Jewish law into grace, and Ishmael born of Agar stands for bondage and slavery without the grace of any part in the blessings to be given to Abraham and his progeny.

The Moslems trace their genealogy through Ishmael and not through Isaac. They quote the Book of Genesis which says of Ishmael: "I will bless thee and render thee fecund and will multiply thee and I will make thee a great nation." The Arabs say that this refers to themselves who were the founders of Moslemism. They are the children of Ishmael and God promised to make them a great nation. They even go so far as to point out that there is the same number of letters in the Hebrew word for great nation as in the word Mohammed in Arabic. This argument, however, means nothing, for the number of the beasts in the Apocalypse corresponds exactly to the Greek letters in the word Mohammed.

St. Paul states that there will always be a war between Ishmael and Isaac. This does not necessarily mean between the Moslems and the Christians; it merely means between those who are still in the natural order of the flesh and those who are in the order of grace. St. Paul's idea is: "Now, as then, the sons of Ishmael born after the course of nature persecute the sons of Isaac who were born after the spirit."

The Moslems, therefore, on their own admission represent a belief in God which refuses to come to a flowering in the fuller revelation of God in Christ. They do, however, tie themselves up with the revealed contents of God in the Old Testament; they have carried over into Christian history some of the profound elements of belief in God found in pre-Christian Judaism and in Orthodox Judaism. We are one with the Moslems in recognizing the Old Testament picture of Abraham as the father of the people who would one day receive the fullness of the revelation in Christ. We differ in that they break off the lineage by choosing Ishmael who would not be heir to the promises of God. But Ishmael was the brother of Isaac, and they are one with us in their belief in God. If they are not yet ready to receive the spiritual heritage, we must keep and guard it for them, that in a day not too distant they may claim it. May Abraham, whom we salute each day in the Mass, heal the breach between the brothers and bring them to the fullness of the Light!

2. THE FIGURE OF CHRIST

Moslemism is the only great religion of the Eastern World that acknowledges Christ. Hinduism with its millions of gods has not recognized Him in its post-Christian history and is the only religion in the world without a personal founder. Buddhism never recognized Him even in its later history during Christianity; its major concern has been with getting out of the wheel of fate. No other world religion has a very clear concept of God, and none has come to know Christ even during Christian history, but the Moslems do know Christ. Islamism accepts Christ, His supernatural birth, His ability to work miracles, His flawless life, but it denies his Divinity, His eternal relationship to God the Father, the Trinity, and His death and resurrection.

Our Blessed Lord to the Moslems is only another of the prophets announcing Mohammed. He was the latest of all the prophets. Our Lord was not crucified but was taken up into heaven and He now is in the second heaven, but there are others much higher than He; for example, Joseph the foster father of our Lord is in the third heaven, Aaron is in the fifth, Moses is in the sixth, Abraham is in the seventh.

Though He is exalted in a kind of exceptional miraculous way and endowed with great powers never given to any human, nevertheless, having fulfilled His prophetic mission announcing Mohammed, He left the world in a miraculous way. He is living now in a quasi-angelic state until the time when He returns to this earth to complete His tasks and die like other human beings.

Though Christians may complain, and rightly so, that Moslems have a distorted notion of our blessed Lord, nevertheless it can be said that our blessed Lord has one foot in the door with them. And it must be our aim and our purpose through charity and kindness to give them a fuller understanding of our blessed Lord which was impossible to their founder who knew religion only from a confused concept of it. They have at least touched the hem of the garments of Christ, and a healing power will flow out from Him as it did to the ailing woman of the Gospel.

3. MARY

The nineteenth chapter of the Koran has 41 verses on the Blessed Mother. The Moslems believe in the Virgin Birth of our blessed Lord; they also believe that Mary was preserved free from the stain of original sin; therefore, they have a vague concept of the doctrine of the Immaculae Conception.

The Koran says this of the Annunciation:

> . . . she retired from her family to a place towards the east, and took a veil to conceal herself from them; and we sent our spirit Gabriel unto her, and he appeared unto her in the shape of a perfect man. She said, I fly for refuge unto the merciful God, that he may defend me from thee: if thou fearest him, thou wilt not approach me. He answered, Verily I am the messenger of thy Lord, and am sent to give thee a holy son. She said, how shall I have a son, seeing a man hath not touched me, and I am no harlot? Gabriel replied, So shall it be: thy Lord saith, This is easy with me: and we will perform it, that we may obtain him for a sign unto men, and a mercy from us: for it is a thing which is decreed. Wherefore she conceived him: and she retired aside with him in her womb to a distant place.

The Nativity scene in the Koran makes Jesus speak in defense of His Mother:

> So she brought the child to her people, carrying him in her arms. And they said unto her, O Mary, now hast thou done a strange thing: O sister of Aaron, thy father was not a bad man, neither was thy mother a harlot. But she made signs unto the child to answer them; and they said, How shall we speak to him, who is an infant in the cradle? Whereupon the child said, Verily I am the servant of God; he hath given me the book of the gospel, and hath appointed me a prophet. And he hath made me blessed, wheresoever I shall be; and hath commanded me to observe prayer, and to give alms, so long as I shall live; and he hath made me dutiful towards my mother, and hath not made me proud, or unhappy. And peace be on me the day whereon I was born, and the day whereon I shall die, and the day whereon I shall be raised to life. This was Jesus, the son of Mary; the Word of truth, concerning whom they doubt.

It is our firm belief that the revelation of Our Lady of Fatima portends the conversion of the Moslem. In years to come we will see that our Lady's appearance marked a turning point in Moslem history. Why did the Blessed Virgin choose a tiny, insignificant village like Fatima, so that she who is the Mother of God would be called "Our Lady of Fatima"? The daughter of Mohammed, the founder of Moslemism, bore the name of Fatima. Writing after her death, Mohammed said: "Fatima is the most holy of all women in paradise, next to Mary."

The Moslems occupied Portugal for centuries. When they were finally driven out, the last Moslem chief in the locality had a beautiful daughter by the name of Fatima. A Catholic boy fell in love with her, and she not only stayed behind when the Moslems left, but even embraced the faith and became a Catholic. Her young husband changed the name of the town where he lived to Fatima; thus the very place where our Lady appeared in 1917 has an historical connection with Fatima, the daughter of Mohammed.

The Moslems gave an enthusiastic reception in Africa and India and elsewhere to the pilgrim statue of Our Lady of Fatima. Moslems attended Church services in honor of Our Lady of Fatima; they allowed religious processions and even prayers before mosques. In Mozambique the Moslems who were unconvertible began to be Christians as soon as the statue of Our Lady of Fatima was erected. Many are now coming into the Church. Devotion to Our Lady of Fatima seems very natural to them, and also a tribute to their own Fatima.

Missionaries in the future will more and more see that their apostolate among the Moslems will be successful in the measure that they give them Our Lady of Fatima. Mary is the advent of Christ. She brings Christ to people before Christ is born as she brought the unborn Christ to Elizabeth.

Conclusion

The East is already dissatisfied with Russia because of its tyranny and with America because of its materialism. Into the break Moslemism may step.

Already their prejudices are fading away, three of their solidly Moslem countries maintaining representatives at the Holy See. Our missionaries are educating their children, the parents wanting the moral upbringing which our Christian teaching brings; our missionaries are turning some of their desert places into valleys through irrigation, are caring for their sick and healing their diseases. May the sons of Ishmael one day embrace the sons of Isaac who have rescued the heritage; may the Christ, whom like the Greeks they know as the Athenians knew the unknown God, and may Mary, whom they love and whose purity they venerate, not change their belief in God, but deepen it, until they see that mystery hidden from the ages, that God walked this earth in the form of man and died for us — the Ishmaels as well as the Isaacs.

6. A Syllogism Is Sorry Rhetoric to the Oriental

The Eastern World does not have the same respect for Aristotelian logic as does the Western World. The Oriental mentality stresses totality, or the whole personality. From one point of view, it seems to come close to what St. Thomas Aquinas describes as the "whole personality, doing the thinking, the willing, and the feeling." The entire psyche is at work, though the *localization* of this "total" attitude is not in the head, but in the *center of the body,* or what we would call the heart. The head is the symbol of Western mentality; the heart or a similar center, the symbol of the Oriental. The Westerner regards thought as a separate function most representative of the "rational animal." The Oriental does not so much "think" as we do; he "ponders"; i.e., he fuses all his thinking, loving, feeling experiences into an inseparable unity.

As a result, the Westerner knows the world better than man; the Easterner knows man better than the world. The first tames nature; the latter tames himself. The former is an extrovert and thus produces a scientific, technical civilization in which nature is turned into industry; the latter is an introvert and seeks to deepen that inner peace through the fusion of all those human experiences which constitute contemplation.

If, for the Oriental, not the head but the totality of experience constitutes what we call "reason," then what is the Oriental symbol for this centrality and fusion? One Japanese scholar says it is the heart. Writing for the Buddhists, Daisetz Suski explains, "Different though the teachings of Shintoism, of the poetic art, and of Confucius may be, they all aim ultimately at the comprehension of a Single Heart." The Chinese word *sin,* and the Japanese word *shin,* though meaning "heart," do not seem to mean exclusively the physical heart. If such were the case, we would not have the "totality" which is so representative of Eastern thought. Rather the heart means "feeling," "consciousness," or "center." Hence the tendency in Asia to speak of "bowels" or "entrails." Here again, this is not to be understood as a definite organ, but rather a symbol like the one we use in saying: "My heart bleeds for you." "Thinking and feeling, which in the West exist as separate entities, here operate as a single force," writes the Japanese Kitayania. Another Japanese writer, Yoshiro Nagayo, explains that, "if we put our whole emphasis on the brain in the sense of the word 'intellect,' the lower portion of the body would float in the air, our feet would become separated from the earth, our ideas would become abstract and our nerves would break down."

The Western World has a fondness for the "Thinker" of Rodin. Though he is not the "primitive" just having his first idea, he is still a "thinker." But in the many statues we see of Buddha, where does the center of human gravity seem to be, if it is not in the navel? Why do Japanese wrestlers seek to cultivate a paunch? Why do they stand facing and staring at one another, if it is not to develop full concentration of body and soul? Why in one of the Chinese books of meditation is it said that one "must first subdue the intellect" and proceed from "conscious action to unconscious inaction"? In India, too, the sentiments of joy, sorrow, and anger in the Tamil language are related to the viscera. Why is there a system as coherent as a cathedral in Thomas Aquinas, but no related reflections in Confucius? The Zen contemplations dispense with dogmas, books, and teachings, so as to reach the "confluent experience of universal oneness." A monk once asked the master Ummon, "What is the purest form of truth?" Ummon answered, "The hedge around the closet." This meant that universal truth is beyond all divisions and distinctions of what is pure or filthy.

Western Logic

The Western mind proceeds in reasoning from the major premise to the minor premise to the conclusion.

Rationalism is strictly of the head; feeling, sentiment, and desire must necessarily be excluded, if the conclusion is to be logically drawn. The Western mind traditionally has sought to be "logical"; hence the ultimate in inconsistency is to be accused of "contradicting yourself." But with the introduction of Machiavellian politics, the repudiation of ethical norms, the Western mind is no longer so afraid of being "illogical." I remember once arguing with an Englishman in Jerusalem, and saying to him, "Sir, you have just contradicted yourself." He answered: "What of it?" I was completely dumbfounded, for to a Western mind, contradiction is intellectual suicide, just as cutting one's throat is physical suicide. The English colonial system was not based on principle, but on expediency and, therefore, has a flexibility which defies all logic. American Pragmatism, which identifies the true with the useful and the good with the pleasurable, also spurns the Western tradition of rationality. Despite these aberrations, however, the Western mind does take pride in consistency. "Think" has become a common sign in our industrial civilization. Western thinking is based on ideas, judgment, and reasoning — all products of the intellect. A judgment is made up of ideas, and syllogistic reasoning is made up of judgments.

Science is based on the principle of causality, and causality is one of the basic principles of reason. A thing which has not the reason of its being in itself, must have it in another. A triangle has within its definition and nature the quality of three-sidedness. But a "yellow" or "red" triangle is extrinsic to its nature; hence one must seek the source of "yellowness" or "redness" in something else; in other words, it is caused. Science became possible because nature was assumed to be rational, consistent, and universal in its operations. Mind, being logical, could, therefore, unwrap the laws of nature and bend them to the service of man. Thought was basically "reasonable, or logical," because behind the universe was the "Logos" which is the Basic Ground of all consistency, both in nature and in man.

Eastern Totality

The Eastern mind, setting store more on centrality than on rationality, may be illustrated in this fashion:

If experiences multiply to a point where like arrows, they seem to converge to one central point, then the conclusion is "true." At first, all these arrows may fly in different directions as they do in a mind which cannot decide where to go for a vacation. When a sufficiently large number of reflections or arrows seem to concentrate in a given place, then the conclusion becomes true. The head does not draw the conclusion but the total consciousness, in what we would call thinking, willing, feeling, and living. The Western mind is, therefore, often bewildered by Eastern diplomacy; it seems as unpredictable as a Pearl Harbor. This is because non-head factors are influencing the thinking. While the Westerner is going from idea to idea, the Oriental is going from mood to mood. Lily Abegg, who has given much enlightenment on these points, says this of the Western mind: our brains are good for constructing machines, but not for understanding human affairs. Witness the inability of the Western mind to understand India which juggles Communism in one hand, democracy in the other. The Hindu mentality which allows for an indefinite number of gods, regardless of their nature, also allows for political positions which are equally contradictory.

Such a mentality does not produce a highly industralized civilization or even science. Only Western civilization with its background of intellectual discipline, which Christianity gave it, could produce a logical transformation of the logic of nature.

Science and technology can be developed in the Eastern World, but this is only because they are apprentices and imitators of the West.

The Eastern mind puts little value on causality. The science of I Ching is not based on causality, but on relationship, or coexistence, or relative simultaneity, or the fact that certain experience began to coalesce or "jell." A conclusion is not reached by the head, but perceived by the whole "psyche." Feelings affect the mind, resolutions affect sensations in a vast interplay of physical, conscious, unconscious, psychic, volitional elements, and all seem to concentrate in some mysterious center which is not the head. This does not make for science, but it certainly does make for the confusion of Western scientists and politicians.

The Missionary Approach

From the above, the following pedagogic suggestion is offered to the missionaries of the Western World who seek to bring Christianity to the Eastern World.

Works in apologetics written in France, Italy, or Germany are too "logical" in the Western sense for the Eastern World. Rather, the approach should be to gather up the good religious aspirations of Eastern people, as they are manifested in their natural religions, and point them as so many arrows converging on Christ, the Savior of the world. Then the word of God is not just something "proven" to them, but rather it is what the Council of the Vatican defined as the third motive of credibility, namely, the satisfaction of the decent aspirations of the human heart. In other words, Confucius is relatively just as good as or even better as a starting point for some minds than Aristotle. It must not be forgotten that not even the Western World accepted Aristotle until the Middle Ages, and St. Thomas was rapped on the knuckles for being so "modern," or "reactionary" as the case may be. Augustine in his *Confessions* has many beautiful pages on Plato and affirms his superiority over Aristotle.

Why not, then, start with what is naturally good in any Eastern religion, as our Lord started with a drink of cold water in converting a Samaritan, as Claudia began with a dream in understanding Christ more than her rational husband, as Paul began with an inscription to a pagan deity in converting the senators of Athens?

In like manner, the concept of the *Nirvana* should not be swept away utterly, but purified, as Clement of Alexandria purified the pagan concepts of God held by men and women in the market place. The *Nirvana* probably does not mean absolute annihilation, but rather the consummation of the sacrifice of the ego. Buddhism goes too far in saying that all pain ends with the extinction of desire; but we do not go far enough in teaching that to the point where we extinguish all carnal desires and desire only what Christ desires we ever attain peace. Was Buddha so far away from seeing that through the death of Christ all men are saved, when he said, "Let all the sins that have been committed in this Kali age of the world fall on me, and let the world be delivered"? True, to some Buddhists there is no God, no worship, or sacrificial priesthood, but if Buddha is honored, there is at least one little arrow with which to begin their elevation.

The multiple solutions of the Eastern mind for the problem of suffering must not be cleared away as rubbish before one preaches Christ. Rather they already have the horizontal and the vertical bars of the cross to express the contradiction of life and death, Yin and Yang, darkness and light. It is only the person of Christ that can resolve their contradictions by showing that death does lead to life. Mencius was unconsciously pondering the Cross when he said: "When heaven is about to confer a great office on any man it first exercises his mind with suffering." The Upanishads in the same spirit reflect, "Suffering is the ransom the son of man has to pay if he would attain his glory."

Pope Gregory told Augustine not to destroy the pagan temples of England, but to purify them, as his own beloved Rome did in dedicating pagan temples to our Lady. "I came not to destroy, but to fulfill" has a wider application than to the Jewish Law. It refers to every pagan contemplative who ever groped through the darkness to the light of God. Our Western logic, being so rigid, is apt to concentrate on the fallacies of Eastern thinking, rather than seeking, to use the language of Pius XI, "to find gold in gold-bearing rocks." Would not a modern Paul see the "unknown God" in the inability of the Indian mind to find rest in the abstract idea of the unity of Brahma? Because of this, various Divine workings were gathered up by the Brahmanic teachers and assigned to distinct persons; Vishnu was the Divine Preserver; Siva the Divine Destroyer, and all three, Brahma, Vishnu, and Siva, were regarded in epic poems as constituting a Trinity, three forms or *trimurti*. Better still, the Indian name for the Supreme Being is a component of the three names of our transcendentals, Ens, Verum, and Bonum. Reason cannot know the Trinity, but reason can ask as Plato did: "If God is one, whom does he love, and to be happy one must love." To liberate their crude religious concepts from the dross is not easy, nor is the teaching of the Cross easy, but one wonders if there is not a more natural readiness for the Cross in India than there was in Greece. With Browning we may say to them: "How hard it is to be a Christian! Hard for you and me."

One wonders how many missionaries in the Far East ever read Buddha or Confucius or Lao-tze, and how many in India ever read the great Epic poems? Yet if our missionaries were a-courting, they would study poetry to win a poetess and music to win a musician. Then why not, when they go a-courting for souls, study the traditions and the religious aspirations of the people to win them to Christ? These Oriental hearts have stretched out lame hands of faith, and groping, have gathered up both wheat and chaff. The missioner must not see the chaff, but the wheat; the wheat is not yet the Bread of Life, but the wheat of any such Eastern religion can be used to point to Christ as Christ Himself used the wheat to tell the Greeks of his death and resurrection.

We must not be too hateful of what is good in ancient Eastern thinkers, otherwise we shall find ourselves unhappy in heaven. I expect to find Socrates, Aristotle, and Plato there, and also Buddha, Confucius, Tao, Lao-tze, and some of the unknown writers of early Indian hymns. All these and many others are certainly God's gift to the East to keep burning some remnant of Divine Truth. They are not on the level of Isaias and Jeremias, but they are certainly what Paul has called "witnesses" to the pagan world.

What a tragedy, too, that the Indian, Chinese, and Japanese students who study in our Western seminaries, and even some of the African students taught by professors educated in Rome, Fribourg, and Louvain, hear of the errors of Hegel, Kant, and Hume and nothing of Buddha or Confucius!

There is a possibility that we may have occidentalized Christ. Our task as teachers is to do more than make Aristotelians with yellow skins or Platonists with brown skins. This teaching prevails because we do not know Oriental thinking; we have not seen that any of the great national Eastern religions is a *Preparatio Evangelica*. Paul quoted Greek poets to the Athenians, but if he were in Peiping he would have quoted Buddha or Confucius.

The Oriental philosophers have no supernatural system, but they do have a natural system, and we can use it as a stepping-stone to Christ. The same is true of the dim gropings of the African people for God. These systems are like cedars of Lebanon that can be cut and carved by revelation and compacted into the edifice of charity; they are the quivers from which we can gather arrows to shoot from the bow of Christian revelation, to a target which may not be an Aristotelian head, but is a Sacred Heart.

Part II

Foreign Policies, Foreign Aid, and the Missions

1. Foreign Policies and the Missions

The two major foreign policies of the world which seek to bring other nations under their ambit are those of the United States and the Soviets. Unlike either is a third major influence: the Missions.

The Foreign Policy of the United States

American foreign policy has largely been directed to a concentration of a *defense* against Communism with Europe as the bastion of that defense. The nations of Western Europe have been invited by the United States to accept its military aid and to become perimeters of defense against the Soviet assault on the world. The strength and the failure of American foreign policy has to a large extent fluctuated with the acceptance or the rejection of its plan of European Defense. As the European nations fail for one reason or another to cooperate with the program of the United States, the latter turns toward the army of its former enemy, Germany, to arm it against the Soviets. The important point is that the foreign policy of the United States sees Europe as the best defense against Communism.

The Foreign Policy of the Soviets

The United States concentrates on *defense;* the Soviets on *offense*. But the Soviet thinking has completely altered concerning the nature of this offense.

The first stage represented by the philosophy of Marx and Engels applied dialectical materialism to world affairs. The revolution which would produce Communism, it was predicted, would take place in a highly capitalistic or advanced industrial country. Marx said that just

49

as there were dialectics in matter so that it produced its own motion without the need of God, so there was a dialectic in all capitalistic productions: capitalism would eventually increase the mass of the exploited; this, in its turn, would produce the Communist revolution or the "expropriation of the expropriators." Stalin himself once boasted that this immanent law of economic determinism enabled the Soviets to foresee the course of history.

But it happened that history did not follow Communist theory. First of all, instead of the rich growing richer and the poor becoming poorer, there arose in highly developed countries a large middle class; the class lines between capital and labor, instead of becoming more rigid, became more loose; the most highly industrialized country of the world, namely, the United States, failed to produce a Communist proletariat; and finally, the development of technology, the spread of popular government, and social reforms completely disproved the Communist expectation that the revolution would come first in the so-called capitalistic countries. Marx himself was so convinced of his own theory that he completely discounted Russia as a nation that would one day become Communist, simply because it completely lacked industrialization and, therefore, the raw material for the unfolding of the immanent law of dialectical materialism.

Marx ignored the revolutionary struggle in the so-called economically underdeveloped areas of the world. But now there has been such a shift in Communist thinking that Russia is expecting the world revolution, not in the area where Marx expected it, but rather in the so-called backward areas of the earth. Lenin himself seized power in one of the least developed countries of Europe, and it is very likely that, if it had been highly industrialized, he would never have seized power. Furthermore only in underdeveloped countries has Communist revolution been successful. Since Communism has not *developed* the way Marx expected it, namely, in the highly industrialized nations, the Soviets are now concentrating on the underdeveloped countries of the world; hence the spread of Communism in Korea, Venezuela, Malaya, Indonesia, Burma, India, Iran, Guatemala, and the present terrific concentration on Africa. Marx would turn over in his grave if he saw how his theory of revolution failed to operate in capitalistic countries. But his followers were wise enough to scrape the theory for the fact that the most vulnerable areas of the world for Communism are the underdeveloped.

Even Lenin himself at times was wrong about revolution in capitalistic countries. He argued that the less advanced peoples of the world or the underdeveloped areas would increasingly become the tools of capitalistic exploitation. When Karl Kautsky argued that capitalistic imperialism was not a necessary phase of capitalism, Lenin severely criticized him. In 1947, Eugene Varga, the Soviet economist, was disciplined by the Soviets for saying that some underdeveloped areas may be breaking away from capitalistic domination. Facts proved that Varga was right. There has been a drop of about four hundred million people under colonialism in the past few decades. India and Pakistan have become fully free from Great Britain; Indonesia is free from the Dutch; Britain's African colonies are taking steps toward self-rule; and France has already lost an area in Africa equivalent in size to the United States. Kautsky and Varga are now recognized to be right. But since capitalism does not necessarily produce the exploitation of the underdeveloped areas, the Soviets were realistic enough to know that it is to those areas that they must go in order to establish world revolution.

Despite the error that Lenin made concerning Kautsky, he did see that the masses of people in the underdeveloped areas were the potential allies of the Communists, as he wrote:

> In the colonial countries, millions and hundreds of millions, in fact the overwhelming majority of the population of the globe, are now coming forward as independent, active, revolutionary factors. It is perfectly clear that in the impending battles in the world revolution, the movement of the majority of the population of the globe, which at first is directed toward national liberation, will turn against capitalism and imperialism and will, perhaps, play a much more revolutionary part than we expect.

The Communist policy in the Far East has been to transform its society by skipping the phase of capitalism which Marx said was absolutely essential for the development of Communism. Now the Soviets see that in the underdeveloped areas it is possible to seize power through propaganda against "capitalistic and imperialistic" nations and then exploit their resources in the manner in which it accuses capitalism of doing.

There is no point in elaborating the shift in Communist policy. What is important is to note the vast divergence between the foreign policy of the United States and the foreign policy of the Soviets. The United States concentrates its *defense* against Communism in Europe; the Soviets, on the contrary, concentrate their *offense* against Europe and the United States in the underdeveloped countries of the world. As Lenin once said: "The shortest route to Paris passes through Peiping."

The Missions

The missionaries with their roots in Western Christian civilization have this in common with the Soviets: they, too, concentrate on the East and the underdeveloped areas of the world. Two hundred thousand missionaries are presently fulfilling the Divine mandate to what the foreign policy makers of the world call the underdeveloped areas, but which, to the missionaries, are the yet un-Christ-ed areas. The East to the missionaries is a vast door about to be opened to the Gospel. There is an appointed time for every nation and it could well be that we are witnessing what Spengler called "The Decline of the West." The moment has now come for the curtain to roll up on the East. The prohibition to Paul not to pass into Asia has now been rescinded by the Holy Spirit!

The missionaries and the Communists are meeting head-on in the underdeveloped areas of the world. To anyone interested in the missions, it would seem that the Soviet foreign policy is wiser than the foreign policy of the United States, and that if the United States had concentrated on the underdeveloped areas of the world instead of on Europe, there would have been less danger of Soviet imperialism. While the United States was building up defenses in Europe, the Communists were on the *offensive* in the East. So were the missionaries, but for a totally different purpose; the Soviets to crucify human personality, the missionaries to crucify egotism to make room for the Spirit and the unfolding of personality.

Communism knows that it cannot tyrannize man except through

the destruction of the spirit — hence the denial of the soul and God in its philosophy of dialectical materialism. The missionaries, on the contrary, know that wherever God is exiled, man is tyrannized; hence the basis of their teaching is that man is endowed with inalienable rights by God and, therefore, has powers transcendent to any State. Since man did not receive his rights and his liberties from the State, no State or tyrant can ever take them away.

A second point of conflict is that the Soviets utilize the individuals in any area as a means to an end. Persons are like grapes who have their life squeezed out of them in order to produce the wine of totalitarianism. The missionaries, on the contrary, believing in the sacredness of personality, insist that as soon as possible a native clergy must be established, for under no circumstances, not even in religion, must the people be subservient to any other nation or power.

The conflict of the missions and Communism in any part of the East, for example, in Korea, or Vietnam, is a cameo of the world situation. The real problem today is not the conflict of democracy and totalitarianism, for democracy with a loss of morality and belief could vote itself into totalitarianism. The real struggle is between two contrary philosophies of life: one submerging man to the collectivity, the other elevating man to spiritual solidarity in Christ. The center of the stage is occupied by the Communists and the missionaries because both concentrate on the underdeveloped areas. The foreign policy of the United States is offstage and off-center because it thinks primarily of defense in Europe but not among the socially disinherited peoples of the East. The violent persecution of the missionaries by Communists is an evidence of how much Communism knows them to be their real enemy; before man can be tyrannized, God and the soul must be exiled. The struggle is unequal because the Communists use the sword while the missionaries must drink the Cup — the Cup which the heavenly Father giveth them to drink. As Simeone Weil has said: "He who takes not the sword will perish on the Cross." The missionaries cannot use Peter's sword against Communist hordes; therefore, they must take the Cross and become "witnesses" or martyrs. But in heaven's scales their Cross will outweigh Soviet swords.

2. The Hand That Gives or the Hand That Receives

Missionary groups make no distinction between giving to a Chinese, a Christian, a Moslem, a pagan, or an atheist. All that is necessary is that they be in need, for if the hand that receives is *human,* regardless of race, color, or religion, then to the missionary the work is humanitarian.

But philanthropic, governmental, and other such political agencies, as well as foundations, judge whether a work is to be humanitarian by a totally different standard; to them what is humanitarian is determined by the hand that *gives,* not the hand that receives. To such agencies, the work is Protestant if a Protestant organization does it; it is Catholic if a Catholic organization does it, regardless of who is helped. When the UN or a foundation or a philanthropic organization is asked to aid the ten million lepers in the world, they answer "No! You are a Protestant organization," or "You are a Catholic organization, therefore you are sectarian, and we cannot help sectarian agencies."

The word "sectarian" has been sometimes associated with narrowness, though often unjustly. A truly religious person or organization should never be narrow, for his love should embrace Samaritans and enemies. Today, however, sectarianism has moved entirely away from the religious field into the political and secular domain; particularly noticeable is it in the case of philanthropy, charity, grants, and subsidies. As an example, notice the difference in what constitutes "humanitarian service" as practiced by missionaries, whether Protestant or Catholic, and as envisaged by governments and philanthropic

54

foundations in their grants or financial aid. *What is the determinant of humanitarianism to missionaries? The hand that receives. What is the determinant of humanitarianism to governments and philanthropic associations? The hand that gives.*

Which is the more logical way to consider aid to the two thirds of the population of the world who go to bed hungry every night — the missionary way which helps everyone regardless of religion, or the political and foundation ways which hold that if a religious hand gives to the nonreligious or the human the work is "sectarian"? If the colored hand gives, does that make it Negro charity? If the white gives does that make it European charity? If the yellow hand gives does that make it Asiatic charity?

Suppose a Jew, a Protestant, and a Catholic chance upon a family being evicted from the slums. Without ever inquiring whether the family being evicted is Catholic, Protestant, or Jew, they pay the rent, buy food and clothing, and nurse the sick in the family. Was it Jewish charity, because the Jew paid the rent? Was it Protestant charity because the Protestant brought food, and was it Catholic charity because he paid a doctor's bill? No one would say that what makes any work humanitarian is *the hand that gives.* Since no distinction of religion, race, or color is made, the work is humanitarian.

Apply this to the great humanitarian agencies of the Protestant and Catholic missions throughout the world. In addition to their specifically religious works, they both do a tremendous amount of humanitarian work, such as caring for lepers, building trade schools, digging wells, teaching agriculture, erecting hospitals, and establishing mobile hospital units. There is not a single one of these works that is restricted to race, color, or religion. Whether the needy be Moslem or Christian, Hindu or Taoist, anti-Christian or Communist, it makes not the slightest difference to these missionaries. They are all human beings, and not one of them may be permitted to sink below the level of the human. Dr. Eugene Kellersbeger and his wife pay frequent visits to the Protestant leper colonies throughout the world. Spiritually minded as they are, they never reject any leper that comes to them because he is of a different sect or because he is a Communist or a pagan.

When the Catholic missionaries dig a well for the Moslems in the desert, the well is not thereby a Catholic well; it is a people's well because they drink from it. The work is humanitarian because there is no distinction between the recipients of the charity. When it comes to humanitarian service there is no one less "sectarian" than the missionaries. Many Catholic Sisters in jail in China nursed back to health the Communist judges who tortured them. Communism is an evil but the Communists are potential children of God. Helping humanity is not sectarian — it is humanitarian.

Governments, foundations, and philanthropic organizations say that the hand that gives is the one that determines the work; if a Negro gives aid, it is Negro aid; if a Presbyterian nurses a Catholic Sudanese, it is a Presbyterian work; if a Catholic shares his bread with a Methodist missionary in China, it is a Catholic work. This way of measuring aid by the distributor rather than by the consumer could cause gross misunderstanding. Does a Quaker in the government of the United States make government aid Quaker charity? Is it Mormon aid because a Mormon in the Cabinet distributes relief to flood areas? Is it Catholic postage because a Catholic sells stamps? Or is it American because Americans receive aid and postage independently of race, color, or religion? It is the *consumer* or the *receiver* who is the determinant of the nature of the aid and not the giver or the distributor. Since humanity receives, the aid is humanitarian. This is the standard of all religious groups.

Where does sectarianism begin? It begins when the agency holds that the giver must be nonreligious, that is, not tied up with any organization that is a religious group even though it aids humanity. Such an attitude is fraught with dangers. If the standard be that the hand that distributes must not be religious, it will not be long until it is said that the hand that distributes must be antireligious and such is the essence of Communism. As Molotov once said: "Bread is a political weapon." By this he meant that bread will be given only to those who think Communism — the rest have to starve. There is prejudice, bigotry, and unfairness in the view that the hand that gives must be devoid of religious affiliations; it is even more narrow to say that because the giver is religious he will not help humanity. As a matter of fact, it is only those who really know how to love God that ever serve their neighbor well. Those who are devoid of that spirit of love will be found most lacking in the truly humanitarian outlook.

The government of the United States has given millions of dollars in aid to the Eastern World, but we have not won the sympathy of the Eastern people. This may be because we have placed more emphasis on the distributor than on the consumer. We lost good will because we stressed the giver rather than the receiver. Even in our civic appeals for community needs, a man who gives is supposed to wear a red feather in his cap — "Look, Mom, see what I did?" The stress has been on the giver, not on the receiver. No wonder the good Lord said that when we gave charity we were not to blow trumpets or wear red feathers. Whenever the emphasis is on the giver, there is pride, publicity, egotism, and its resultant selfishness. "When thou givest alms . . . do not sound a trumpet before thee . . . to win the esteem of men." If the aim of the United States is to aid humanity we cannot stress the fact that it is American aid and ask an armful in return. Such aid is given not to aid but to buy. We have the red feather in our cap but the white feather in our heart because we are afraid to forget the hand that gives. We should concentrate solely on the hungry who receive, giving to stomachs because they are empty and to men because they are human. Good will is a by-product of our disinterested service. If we put "America first" in giving, we find "America last" in good will; but if we love hungry people as missionaries do, we will find that America will be loved, simply because we did not buy our love and thereby insult the dignity of those we aided. We may be richer than they are, but we are not necessarily nobler. That will depend upon the motives behind our giving.

Missionaries in Asia and Africa, regardless of their creed, never make it a rule that no sulfone will be given to lepers who are antireligious or bigoted; but if we who are associated with a world organization aiding all missionary societies and peoples, ask the UN or a foundation for money to aid the lepers or to feed hungry Hindus or care for the sick with mobile hospital units, we are told, "No, you are sectarian."

Is it not rather the political group or the foundation that is sectarian because it watches the hands that give the coin rather than the putrid flesh that takes it? The more religious a man is the more he loves humanity; the less religious a man is the more prejudiced and sectarian he is, the more he sets up false standards for aiding the needy. Cannot a man love baseball without parading in a Yankee uniform? Must no hungry stomach be aided, no festering body healed, no leper cured, unless a giver wears the uniform of "No Religion"? Why is the Red Cross supported by all religious groups? Because it aids humanity. Suppose the religious people said that, inasmuch as the Red Cross workers in a flood area are mostly Methodists, the Congregationalists and the Catholics would no longer support the Red Cross. That would be using the standard of the giver instead of the receiver, and death to all humanitarian work.

The missionaries of all faiths who labor out of love, without salary, who know the customs and habits of people because they live with them, are penalized by government and philanthropic agencies because they happen to have a prayer book in their back pocket. Does that make them less worthy of being good Samaritans than the man who has none? Is a man necessarily more liberal to humanity because he is a liberal, and less liberal because he is a Christian? It immediately becomes evident that we get into prejudices of the worst kind when we ask to see the hand that distributes the aid, as if hands folded in prayer are thereby rendered unfit to love the world. When our Lord saw the five thousand in the desert, He said that they should not be sent away hungry. The more universal the love, the more universal the charity; the narrower the love, the narrower the giving. What would happen if religious people in the United States judged automobiles by the hands that made them rather than by the universal intent of all automobiles — to serve for transportation? We trust that government agencies and philanthropic organizations in the future will avoid narrowness and sectarianism and be concerned with whether or not the agencies help everyone regardless of creed or race or color. They need not build Catholic churches or Protestant churches or rectories. But they could aid religious groups in humanitarian work, and at the same time do a far better job.

3. *Proselytizing by Foreign Aid*

After World War I, England gained much new territory as colonies; after World War II, Russia annexed by force even an empire. But America gained nothing in either war. On the contrary, the United States has attempted to raise standards of backward countries in keeping with a principle enunciated by Woodrow Wilson in 1918: "The principle of native welfare that colonies should be governed in the interest of native peoples."

In keeping with this moral attitude, a Point IV Program was developed in 1949 "for making the benefits of our scientific advances and industrial progress available for the improvement and growth of underdeveloped areas."

The new arrangement with the underdeveloped countries is what might be called a "package deal"; that is to say, aid is tied up with military and security assurances. Aid formerly was divorced from any political considerations, but now what was humanitarian has become harnessed to national considerations of security. Voluntary assistance is linked to military assistance. The two are called "companion, rather than opposite approaches." The pantry now has a gun in it, and the horse that pulled the plow must now also clear an airfield. In other words, America has gone in for proselytizing, and proselytizing is always bad where the people are poor. Any good missionary could tell the government of the evils of tying up the gift of food with a requested favor.

The errors of proselytizing are twofold:

1. It smacks of the philosophy of Molotov who said: "Bread is a political weapon," except that here bread is an economic or a

military weapon. Bread to the poor must have no strings tied to it, not even a wrapper advertising the giver. Hot soup cannot be mixed with cold war. It is both an insult to the people who receive it and an undignified gesture on the part of those who offer it. Our blessed Lord said: "What man is there among you, of whom if his son asks bread, will reach him a stone?" This might be paraphrased to mean: "What nation is there among you, of whom if the hungry ask for bread, will reach him a tank?" The essence of prostitution is the tying of money to love, or of mixing a military alliance with bread. Many a young woman has said to a rich man: "So that's why you offered me a mink."

Whenever government agencies or foundations refuse money to those who labor with the poor, the refusal is "justified" on the grounds: "We cannot help a proselytizing group." This, of course, is not the real reason. The real reason is a refusal to aid religion. But now we have governments proselytizing.

Missionaries know very well that proselytizing is ineffectual. No one is ever converted to God by a bowl of stew, much less is anyone ever won over to a government policy by government aid. Our Lord fed the multitudes and they followed Him across the lake for more bread. He knew that allegiance was only stomach-deep and not soul-deep, for He said: "You did follow Me, because you ate and were filled." From that day on the true missionaries have never tried to proselytize through aid. We are, for example, maintaining hundreds of schools, dozens of hospitals and nurseries in Moslem countries, but we know that because we bind up wounds and enlighten minds, we cannot win them over to our way of thinking. They are to be helped because they are human; there is to be no "package deal." As a matter of fact, we have discovered in China that, where some religious agencies, not our own, won over many Chinese because of "social centers," almost all of the Chinese thus aided defected to Communism under pressure.

America's aid to the needy peoples will never convert the people to "mutuality of interests." Despite the billions paid out by our government, there is a growing hatred of America. This is in part due to Communist lies: but it is also due to the fact that we give with an ulterior purpose. As one man said when told someone hated him: "Why should he hate me? I never did him a favor."

We are a rich nation and the rest of the world is poor by our standards. Many poor resent receiving from the rich, because it increases their sense of inferiority. No missionary would attempt to proselytize an Ibo with a new pair of overalls, not only because faith is not vendible — Simon Magus once thought it was — but also because true religion does not necessarily bring prosperity. Proselytizing destroys missionary activity whenever it is attempted, and few are the missionaries who ever used it. *A fortiori,* it will be a complete debacle when governments try it. Anyone who knows Irish history is familiar with the evils of "Souperism." When England persecuted Ireland, it starved the Irish in an effort to win them over to English ways of thought, particularly in religion. The English offered the Irish bowls of soup if they would give up their faith. It was a "package deal." My great grandfather was the leader of "Anti-Souperism," it being his business to tell the Irish people to die rather than be "proselytized by a bowl of alphabet soup that lacked all the "H's."

With such a heritage it is only natural to be opposed to a government policy that links armies with artichokes and cabbages with cavalry. A leader of Protestant missionaries, Dr. Walter van Kirk, executive director in the National Council of Churches, knows that missionaries should never proselytize through aid. He has pointed out the weakness of such a position: "There is genuine concern among many people of our churches that United States technical assistance programs, for maximum acceptability and effectiveness abroad and for continuing support at home, should be kept as clear as possible from political and military involvements of security measures and from economic involvements of loans and grants-in-aid."

A second reason why proselytizing on the part of a nation fails is that it treats vital problems in terms of the abstract instead of the concrete. This is in general one of the effects of the modern sociological approach. It is not interested in the criminal, but in the problem of the crime; not in the bad boy or girl, but in juvenile delinquency. The nomenclature may seem unimportant, but actually it hides the gross error introduced by the French Revolution. The latter unfurled a love of humanity, but humanity in the abstract. Charity loves the neighbor who may be the enemy; the materialists love humanity which is nobody. From that time on it became possible to profess the greatest love of humanity without showing the least concrete love of the poor individual. Communism carried this to the extreme when it glorified the "masses." With this professed affection for an entity that does not exist, the Soviets conducted the liquidation of those persons whom they choose to call the "enemies" of the masses. Biology supplanted charity, with the result that the individuals were allowed to perish if only the species remained.

The proselytizing on the part of foreign aid was to win the less favored nations over to the democratic point of view by presenting the problem of aid in the abstract, for example, "to develop under-developed areas, to stimulate profitable and fair trade and to assist people in free production." This is economic language, not humanitarian language; it stresses problems rather than personalities and will fail as a proselytizing approach. Underdeveloped areas, business and free trade are incapable of psychological reaction. Problems do not suffer; only human beings have a pain in the pit of their stomachs. People are not saved by the barrelful.

The government could learn from our technical experts, the missionaries who deal with people in these underdeveloped areas. Missionaries deal with the concrete, the personal, the individual. Christianity does not begin by reforming society; it begins by regenerating men.

The Christian point of view is that the poor are the more honorable members of Christ's Body. The only reason the poor need those who "have" is in order that they may have a roof over their heads, clothes on their backs, food in their stomachs, and a crib for their children. The reason, however, why those who "have" need the poor is in order that they may have grace in their hearts and the blessing of God on their whole being. The missionaries know that people are never won from *above,* but from *below.* If good will results it must be a by-product and never something directly sought. If the body is healthy, the cheeks will glow; beauty is a by-product of health. So, too, the good will of others is not directly sought, otherwise it is like rouge on the cheek.

But if missionaries do not proselytize, that is "make" a package deal of bread and Bible, pepper and Pontiff, then what do they do? They evangelize. To proselytize is to make use of outward aid and helps to convince a person *externally* to embrace a certain position. To evangelize is to present motives of credibility, which allow the individual to decide for himself whether he will assent to a truth in cooperation with the grace of God. Proselytizing is like advertising; it is an attempt to make one come to a point of view by reiterated appeals; evangelization works upon a truth already perceived by the mind that other truths consonant with it may be accepted.

In our missionary work no one is asked to give up his religion because he becomes a member of our leper colony, or because he received aid from our hospitals. Last year we aided millions and millions of children, lepers, and victims of disease, most of whom were pagans. Neither a bandage nor a loaf of bread nor a sulfa injection nor a hospital bed was used to change the human spirit of the recipient. Regardless of what they are and what they may become, they must be helped, for it is God's will that no one ever be allowed to sink below the level of the human.

We want to win all the socially disinherited people of the world to the free way of life, in contrast to the slavery of Communism. But we who have been conducting missionary treks for twenty centuries know that it will never be done through proselytizing. Rice Americans and nylon democrats are not worth the having. The people are poor, and God knows they are; for example, no peasant in Asia has a coal fire or a gas oven; only in Japan and India has electricity been taken to the farm. The inequality of America is the inequality of wealth; in the rest of the world, it is the inequality of poverty, most of them more or less starving.

These people should be helped by our government but not to win them to *our* way of life; rather to let them be free to live *their* way of life. Our missionaries will take care of Moslem teeth even though Moslem hearts remain Moslem hearts. If they want to change their belief, that must not be because their teeth were filled, but because their hearts were filled with the grace of God.

It is, therefore, our suggestion that the government begin using Protestant and Catholic missionaries in these poor lands. We mean those who have labored among the people for fifteen years or more and have developed technical aid, such as schools in New Guinea where the trades are learned, agricultural farms such as those opened in Assam, and irrigation projects such as those in operation in the Sahara, or mobile medical units such as are circulated in India.

These Protestant and Catholic missionaries will not sell America, nor will they win military pacts. But America will gain by it in the end. Just as a man does not really love a woman unless he loves virtue more, so no one will really help the poor nations unless he loves the poor more.

1. *The Universities and the Missions*

Politics is ahead of education, but education should be ahead of politics. It has been generally true through the history of education, that the classroom and the books of the intellectuals were the forerunners of political trends. Liberalism and Marxism were first academic, then later came into the arena of public life. But in our contemporary world, education has lagged behind politics in its vision and its world consciousness. The United Nations has done more to make the people cognizant of their world neighbors than all the courses in our universities. When courses are introduced in world affairs in universities, they are often nothing but reflections upon international political trends already developed in the United Nations. This lag is further accentuated by the fact that very few universities have given much attention to the thought of great religious movements of the Eastern World, such as Moslemism.

Though leadership has passed to politics, it has, nevertheless, been guilty of one serious lacuna, or perhaps even a deliberate omission. Politics has ignored the influence of the missions in world affairs. Typical of this is the report published by the Civil Education Section of the United Nations Civil Assistance Command, Korea. In 1954 it published a 32-page mimeographed booklet which deals with the history of Christian missions in Korea. The booklet says "as regards the Church itself, organized Protestant Mission work was begun in Korea in 1884. The earliest date at which the Catholic population in Korea is mentioned is 1912." Actually, the modern beginnings of the Catholic faith in Korea go back to 1770. The first missionary in Korea was a Father Tchu who was executed in 1801 and by that time there were already several thousand Catholics in the country. The first Korean priest was ordained in 1845 and martyred in Seoul in 1846. Catholic Sisters opened an orphanage in Seoul in 1888.

Two conclusions emerge: (1) Politics has gained ascendancy over education in alerting citizens to world problems. (2) Politics generally overlooks or completely ignores the works of the missions in foreign lands. The problem now is: How can education keep up with world affairs and reassert its primacy over politics? It can do so by introducing courses into universities which will discuss the world *ex parte aeternitatis*. Here we must record the startling and tragic fact that there is not a single Catholic university in the United States which gives a fully equipped course on Missiology.

Reasons for the Omission

There are three possible explanations for the want of a course in Missiology in Catholic universities. One is due to the psychology of the people who, up to the present time, have regarded the missions as a work of supererogation or a "pious extra." It is only natural, though it is never supernatural, for a nation to believe that only after the Church is completely established in its own country should one be interested in establishing it in other countries. This indeed forgets that the Divine decree "Go, teach all nations" was given when there were only 120 Christians in Jerusalem. Neglecting the world missions in universities has meant that Church history deals more with what happened than what is happening; the Church was presented with an archaeology rather than with a mission.

The second reason for the omission of a course in Missiology is due to standardization. Though Catholic universities should have their own standardizing agencies, they generally submerge them and give the primacy to the standards set by secular agencies. Since the latter have never considered courses on Missiology, partly because they do not consider religion as falling under the measurement of standardization, Catholic universities have been reluctant to present such courses. From a Catholic point of view it is extremely difficult to justify a university having twenty or more courses on Abnormal

Psychology and not one on the soul, as it is to justify an omission of a course on the Mission of the Church to the modern world. When, however, one realizes that the secular agencies will standardize only courses like the former and not the latter, it can readily be understood why they are not considered for credit in education.

A third reason for the absence of the courses is that the missionaries themselves have been considered only as zealous and heroic souls who love the romance of the foreign missions, or in fewer instances as "misfits" for the home missions. Now, only the ignorant would hold such a view, for it is recognized that practically all of the missionaries are technicians in the strict sense of the term. There are few at the desks of the State Department in Washington who have the knowledge of the countries of Asia such as is enjoyed by some of our missionaries. It is regrettable, for example, that the UN will take a technician from Iowa and send him to Pakistan, though he has never been in Pakistan before; or that they will take an agricultural expert from Oklahoma and send him to Africa, though he knows nothing about Africa. The Church has tens of thousands of experts who have been living in these countries for twenty, thirty, or forty years; who speak the languages of the people and know their psychology; who have already built experimental farms for natives, such as the large one in Assam; who have taught irrigation to the Moslems, such as is now being done in the Sahara, and who have opened technical schools in New Guinea. The UN can be excused for not appreciating the technical knowledge of the missionaries, but there is less excuse for Catholic universities who have a better knowledge of the missions than the officials of the UN. Not until the universities see the missionaries as scholars and technicians instead of religious with feet itching to travel will the universities incorporate their great wisdom into courses.

Reasons for Courses in Missiology in Universities

The first reason for a Catholic university having a course in Missiology is to keep up to date with the present shift of the world from the West to the East. Our education for centuries has been Western, with its roots principally fixed in the Grecian and Roman world. Practically no attention was given to the thought of the Eastern World, such as the philosophy of Confucius or the Hindus or Buddhism. Education and culture have revolved about three cities: Athens, Rome, and Jerusalem — the city of the beautiful, the city of the law, and the city of the good. It is not without interest that the languages of these three civilizations proclaimed the death of Christ.

In our day, however, the axis for civilization is moving to three other cities: Peiping, Moscow, and Delhi. American political thought at present believes that the military defense of the world should revolve around the old axis of Western civilization, hence the NATO or the military defense of Europe. Moscow, with greater foresight, sees that the East is more important and concentrates on China; and for that reason Lenin said that the old political axis of Europe would fall after Asia had been conquered.

If then the shift to the world is from the West to the East, if the East is like a great giant aroused from slumber, if Communism has chosen the East as the vestibule to its conquest of the West and the world, it follows that the universities should give more attention to the philosophy and to the culture of the East, and recognize that the scepter of future political world power will one day shift to the lands of the Rising Sun. For the past two decades, everyone familiar with the missions has stressed the importance of Africa as a world power. In vain did one attempt to educate the secular forces to its importance. Only recently did a popular picture magazine seem to realize that Africa might possibly hold a balance of power for the future.

Given this transition from the West to the East, it is important that Catholic universities keep apace with the culture of these lands that were once thought worthwhile only as colonies of Western powers. The great struggle of the present world is not for new colonies; the great struggle is for minds and for souls — even Communism is interested in them. In the training school of the foreign diplomats in Moscow, courses are given on the missions in the lands that Communism one day hopes to devour. This fact alone should alert the Catholic universities of the Western World to the importance of a course on Missiology which would stress the movement of Christianity among the peoples of the East.

A second reason for a Catholic university having a complete course in Missiology is because this seems to be the fullness of time for the enrichment of the East in the Gospel of Christ. The historical fact is that the Gospel, after Pentecost, did not go eastward, but westward. St. Paul at one time stood on the borders between the Eastern and the Western Worlds. He was induced to pass into Europe where his first convert was Lydia. He expressly says that he was prohibited by the Spirit from going into Asia. The philosophical question arises why the providence of God should have chosen that the Gospel go westward rather than eastward. Probably there were two reasons for it.

Why the Gospel Went Westward

First, faith is grounded on reason. The Grecian world developed reason to its utmost; in fact, it was fitting that reason should be developed as far as it possibly could, before there would be an Incarnation. St. Thomas tells us that one of the reasons for the Incarnation was to supplement reason which had exhausted itself and still did not come to the summa of natural truths. God willed that faith should be grounded on reason, and since the Grecian world had reason, it was fitting that faith go to the land where the rational foundations were already laid. If the faith had gone eastward, there would not have been the development of dogma and doctrine that there was in the Western World; Eastern thought was more immediate and intuitional and, hence, could not have given those formulations which were so essential for the complete unfolding of the Logos who became Incarnate.

A second reason why the Gospel went westward was that only in the Grecian world was nature respected as such. The science of physics was held by Aristotle to be the third noblest science of the human mind. Inasmuch as the life-giving power of the Incarnation was to be communicated through sacraments, it followed that the Western World which held nature in high repute was a better raw material for the development of sacramental theology than the East.

In the East, nature was never considered apart from theology. Most of the religions were pantheistic, which meant a confusing and a merging of nature and God. Only in the Greek world, where matter was regarded as something quite distinct from the substance of God, could the Church best develop the theology of the sacraments in which matter is made a channel for the communication of God's grace.

Now that the theology of the Church has been developed on the solid basis of reason and nature, so that faith has a rational introduction and sacraments have a matter, the time seems ripe for the Gospel to pass into the East, and for the Holy Spirit to lift His prohibition. The West has completed its apprenticeship; now philosophy and theology are ready to pass to the Eastern World. In vain do we think that our theology has already reached the peak of its development. There is a principle in philosophy *quidquid recipitur, recipitur per modum recipientis.* Water poured into a blue glass looks blue; water poured into a red glass looks red. Christ poured into Western civilization naturally will take on a Western coloring, but when the theology of Christ passes through the Eastern mind, we will see certain aspects of Christ revealed, which the Western World has not yet perceived. It is very likely that to the East is reserved the development of what might be called the "Theology of the Spirit of Christ." There is no tract in our theological seminaries explicitly on this subject and yet this constitutes the burden of many of the Epistles of St. Paul.

Which country of the Eastern World will be given the privilege of developing the hidden aspects of the Spirit of Christ remains to be seen. It is possible that the honor may fall to India because of its naturally mystical current. It is safe to predict that once our Catholic doctrine goes eastward there will be a development of theology that will be just as great as was the development during the medieval synthesis or the development of the De Ecclesia Tracts after the Reformation. No Catholic university in the world can ignore a study of the enrichment of its philosophy and theology as Christ's presence becomes magnified in the East. A professor of psychology in a university would feel ashamed not to know the latest development in his field; then let not the universities blush at the developments and unfoldings of faith in that part of the world where live the major portion of the population redeemed by the Blood of Christ.

A third reason for a course in Missiology could be found in the fact that the whole world today is missionary. The term "propaganda" once was exclusively Catholic. It referred solely to the propagation of the faith. Today the term has been taken over by governments and refers to the control of minds through the repetition of slogans and formulae. Hitler once said that the modern mind would never believe a small lie but that it would believe a big one. (Such is often the purpose of political propaganda.) Advertising influences minds to buy things; propaganda influences minds to accept ideas; evangelization influences souls to surrender to God. The whole world is in a state of mission. What is at stake today is not physical colonialism or the conquest of new lands, but mental colonialism or the conquest of new minds. The alternative presented to the modern world is to choose between an ideology and the Logos. The Communist success in brainwashing indicates the high price they put upon the subjection of personalities to their narrow ideology. Never before in history was the whole human race subject to conversion as it is at the present time; or perhaps, better still, so exposed to either conversion or perversion. No university can ignore these facts, and in no other department or course could they be as adequately treated as in courses in Missiology.

Nature of a Course on Missiology

St. Thomas says that the reason for any science is to perfect a rational being. In general, the science of Missiology will be concerned with theological, historical, canonical questions, as well as pastoral problems, methodology, or psychology of presenting Catholic truth to peoples of other lands. In addition to these and other courses, there would be auxiliary sciences such as ethnology, linguistics, geography, psychology, history of colonialism, sociology, tropical hygiene, medicine, agriculture, ethnography, history, pedagogy, architecture — most of which were enumerated in the encyclical *Evangelii Praecones*. These would constitute the matter of the science, or its material object. The formal object of Missiology would be the activity of the Church considered under the very special aspect of implanting the Church to differentiate it from the action of the Church in areas where it is already established. Missiology is not a science apart but a scientific specialization stressed by the Sovereign Pontiffs because the implantation or the reestablishment of a Church is of primordial urgency in virtue of the missionary imperative of Christ Himself.

If the urgency of world affairs did not dictate a course in Missiology, then certainly obedience to the ordinances of the Church would suggest it. In 1777 the Congregation of the Propaganda gave the following instruction: *Haec autem (doctrinae subsidia) petere illos oportebit ex probatis auctoribus, iisque maxime qui de rebus ad missiones pertinentibus pertractarunt. . . . Imprimis vero respicere nusquam desinant in decreta et rescripta Sedis Apostolicae. . . ."* Benedict XV, in an Apostolic letter, added: *"omnino eos (missionarios) in omnibus disciplinis, tum sacris tum profanis, quae Missionariis opus sint, erudiri oportebit."* Later on, the Holy See declared officially that Missiology was one of the "special disciplines" of theology which was repeated in the *Deus Scientiarum Dominus* of 1933. Pope Pius XII did not excuse the diocesan clergy from such a knowledge of *"exquisita ac solida missionalium rerum cognitio."* Complete courses in Missiology are already taught in Rome, Nimejan, Ottawa, Fribourg en Suisse, and Münster in Westphalia. Fordham University has a few courses on Missiological subjects, but there is no Catholic university in the United States which has a course in Missiology which fulfills the requirement of the Holy See.

The Relevance of Certain Courses

In addition to the courses which are already mentioned as essential to Missiology, there are other branches in universities which could be made much more interesting, if they embrace the Eastern as well as the Western World. If one selects a course which would seem to be most irrelevant to the missions, it would be Logic. And yet how interesting Logic would be if we compared the Logic of Aristotle with the Logic of the Eastern people! For example, why the Chinese syllogism has five terms and the Aristotelian three terms. This would test the skill of any professor. Equally absorbing would be why

Aristotelian Logic would use a universal to tie together two propositions and the Arabic Logic substitute two visions from which would flash a new insight never before calculated. For example, Arabic Logic would combine a peculiar formation of clouds in the sky which would suggest a Gothic tower; from both of these visions would flash a notion of the goodness of God.

Hindu Logic might be compared to our modern mathematics or symbolic logic. Modern Logic is the logic of indeterminateness. Propositions are so widened and definitions so broadened, as to escape completely the alternatives of true or false. That is why Hinduism is very willing to accept Christ as long as He is put in the Pantheon with the 365 million other deities. After comparing these two logics, it would also be helpful to indicate why Aristotelian Logic will perhaps always remain the logic of the Church even in foreign lands, because Aristotelian Logic leads to decision and, therefore, to action. It elicits decision because it gives the alternatives of true or false. Hinduism with its indeterminateness makes for indecision. Possibly that is why the Eastern World, which has not been as dedicated to Absolute Truth as the Western World, has also made less material progress. Whitehead, it will be recalled, argued that experimental science could have arisen only in the Western World, which in turn had been perfected by Christian discipline and by exactness of Grecian Logic. Aristotelian Logic will never be outmoded in the missions, because men will have to act and the infinite choice of a Hindu Logic makes for indecision.

Through no intentional pun, the semantics of the Semites is vastly different from the Aristotelian. The Aristotelians use words to express nature; for them what is intentionally in the mind is fundamentally in things. Both universality and extratemporality are the earmarks of Aristotelian ideas; but for the Semitic world there is less stress on universality and extratemporality. Aristotle asks: "What is a man?" and answers it by saying that man is a rational animal. The Semitic world is not concerned with the universal nature, but rather asks: "What is man that thou art mindful of him?" Here there is concern with destiny, with history, with deeds, and with temporal unfolding. Here probably is to be sought an explanation for the fact that the Old Testament, quite apart from its revealed character, is actually the first philosophy of history. The Greeks had no philosophy of history, because they were concerned with universals. The Jewish world had a philosophy of history, because for them history was the unfolding of a Divine plan, a concept which ought to be equally true for us who are the heirs of Israel.

Another auxiliary science that seems difficult to refer to missions is that of economics. But here we discover that the stress on Missiology would make the study of economic trends much more interesting. The inroads of Communism in the East give the student an opportunity to study the difference between the colonial imperialism of Capitalism and the colonial imperialism of Communism. They are the same, inasmuch as both emphasize the primacy of the economic, both assume a materialistic philosophy and the use of technological and industrial advances. They are different, however, inasmuch as Communism gives an explanation of the changes that take place in the culture and civilization and religion of a country, while Capitalism is rather thoughtless and indifferent about an explanation.

A further and very important difference is that when Capitalism enters into a country it takes charge of things, for example, the mechanics of the state, raw materials, politics, civil and material administration. When Communism enters a country, it leaves the country as it finds it; it does not immediately take over things; it takes over men or minds. It sets up trained minds in certain positions; these minds are to act as cells or spheres of influence to Communize labor unions, politics, economics, and military life. For that reason, Communism is much more insinuating than Capitalism. Capitalism looks for benefices; Communism looks for submission of minds. The latter also has a greater potency to stir up people of the East, not only because it has the advantage of a protest against existing conditions, but also because it thrives by promises, which can always smack of the Infinite because they are not yet realized.

The character of the world today is ecumenical. The world is one, not because every city in the world is forty-eight hours from our airport; it is one because all men are made of one blood to dwell upon the face of the earth; and because all men have a right to share in the fullness of the earth. No one people or race exists for itself alone. The imperfections of one are supplied by another. Each nation of and by itself is imperfect. Relative perfection exists in the ensemble or the community. As Dr. Mulders once asked himself: "Can a Catholic university demonstrate its catholicity and universality in better fashion than by consecrating *ex professo* a part of its labor to the missionary apostolate?" We trust that our Catholic universities that already find time for courses in obedience to secular standards will also find time, in obedience to the standards of the Holy See, to give learned courses on Missiology, or the expansion of the Church, to the one billion five hundred million unbelievers throughout the world.

2. Laity and the Missions

"The devil is the ape of God." Communism is the ape of the Church. It secularizes each detail of the Mystical Body: it has its visible head; and it has its invisible head — the dark enemy of Christ. It has its hierarchy, its orthodoxy, its Peter and Paul in Marx and Lenin; it has its Holy Office which judges heresy and "deviation"; but above all — and this is what concerns us here: it has its *mission*. Its mission is to the world: "Going therefore make disciples of all nations, teaching them to obey all things whatsoever *mission* has commanded you."

Its mission is not the Soviet Union; its mission is the world. It covers the same area as the Gospel. It makes no distinction between "home" missions and "foreign" missions. The Congo is its field as much as the Ukraine. Whence came this sense of universal mission? From the Gospel! Just as Commmunism would have no concept of sacrifice if there had been no Cross, so it would have no concept of mission had there not been the Divine mandate: "Make disciples of all nations." Does it not, therefore, behoove us to restore the Catholic idea of *mission* as referring to the entire world?

The term "foreign mission" evidently implies the division of civilization into two parts, one of which is Christian, the other of which is not. A "foreign" missionary was one who moved out of the Christian dimension into the lower level of what was called the pagan or non-Christian civilization. But does this condition exist today?

For centuries, the civilization of the Western World was Christian; that is to say, its fabric, its mass, its political-economic-moral body was governed by Christian principles. The individual was stabilized by this Christian environment. Today, all of this is changed:

1. The great mass of Western civilization is not Christian in its political, economic, and social structure.

2. The very atmosphere which surrounds our Western civilization is pagan.

3. In the days of Christian civilization, it was the individual who had to be saved; today it is society in its totality that has to be saved.

Christian civilization was once considered as "inside" the reservation, and non-Christian civilizations as "outside"; but today the fence has been broken down with the result that the distinction between "foreign" and "Christian," or Christian and pagan, is practically eliminated. It is the world of mass civilization which has to be reconciled to God. The hierarchy of France has spoken of the "mission" to France. Germany in 1936 called itself a "mission" land. So too is the United States. There are really no "foreign" missions. The Church is *missionary*.

Wherever there are sheep that are not of the fold — there is a mission. The distinction between the Oriental Congregation, the Consistorial Congregation, and the Congregation of the Propagation of the Faith exists for purely jurisdictional reasons. From the evangelic and apostolic point of view all have laid upon them the double burden to "teach" and "baptize," to apply jurisdiction and sanctification.

Our blessed Lord did not tell each of His Apostles to restrict himself solely to one area. As He ascended into heaven, He said to them: "Go into the world." After His Ascension, the angel said to the Apostles: "Why stand ye here looking into the heavens?" There was work to be done in the world. Every bishop is appointed first to the world, and then to his diocese, and then only for jurisdictional reasons. The entire world, therefore, is the mission of the Church, and those who think in terms of the world have the "Catholic sense."

Communism Is Not Only a Mission: It is a Lay Apostolate

Almost all of the great doctrinal decisions of the Church were made when she was under attack. As the Crucifixion led to the glory of the Resurrection, so too, in a lesser degree, heretical assaults paved the way for doctrinal development. An example of this is to be found in the emphasis on the hierarchy and the priesthood in the Council of Trent, and the emphasis on the laity by the Pontiffs of the present time and in the Second Vatican Council.

When we come to the twentieth century with its militant atheism, we find a new kind of heresy, namely, that of the mass civilization of Communism. Karl Marx, its founder, described in one single line the relationship between the Reformation and Communism: "The Reformation destroyed the interior priest: Communism must destroy the external priest." By this Marx meant that as the Reformation had destroyed Holy Orders, so Communism will destroy the spiritual nature of man and reduce him to a mere cog in the economic automation of the State. Communism is, therefore, a "lay" movement — in the sense that the secular takes the place of the sacred. The kingdom of God becomes the kingdom of the laity.

The Lay Apostolate Is the Answer to Communism

Communism as a "lay" movement must be answered by the lay apostolate. The very instrument that would defeat us must be the instrument that will save us. Such was the plan of Redemption: original sin came through a disobedient man, a proud woman, and a tree; Redemption came through an obedient New Adam, a humble maiden Mary, and the tree of the Cross.

If Communism gives the laity a sense of mission, then the Church must reaffirm the mission of the laity. Communism has the zeal, but no truth; we have the truth, but not sufficient zeal. They have the heat and the passion, but not the light; we have the light, but we are carrying candles instead of firebrands. Up to this stage in the world's history it has been common to say: "The devil take the hindmost." Now there is danger of the devil taking the foremost, particularly if the laity are not summoned to the reconciliation of the world to Christ.

The Laity in the Apostolic Church

At Pentecost, the laity were described by the following characteristics:

1. "They occupied themselves continually with the Apostles' teaching,

2. Their fellowship in the breaking of bread, and

3. The fixed time of prayer" (Acts 2:42).

They were under the hierarchy. The Apostles and the bishops received a *Divine mission* to build up the Mystical Body: the laity receive a *mandate* or a *Canonical Mission* to do so. The full acceptance of Catholic teaching is, therefore, the first condition of the lay apostolate.

It was the laity, in the persons of Aquila and his wife Priscilla, who completed the instructions of Apollo (Acts 18:26) and later on became the helpers of Paul (Rom 16:3). Apollo, who never seemed to have received any ministerial consecration, was a vigorous preacher of Christ (Acts 18:27, 28). St. Paul calls Philemon one "who shares our labors" (Phlm 1:1), or in more modern English, "our much loved fellow worker." St. Paul also mentions Appia, whom he calls "a dear sister in Christ."

To the credit of the laity it must always be kept in mind that our Lord first appeared after the Resurrection to the women, that is to say, to lay people. They were first at the Tomb, but their testimony as such did not have great weight without apostolic affirmation. That was why they were told to warn Peter. It may be said, with tongue in cheek, that they really started the hierarchy moving.

The Mission of the Laity Then and Now
Is to the World

It is not the United States, it is not Latin America, it is not Korea, it is not Hungary, it is the world that is in the state of mission. Isaias looking into the future said that God would not "be content with the tribes of Israel whom he summoned . . . nay, I have appointed thee to be the light of the Gentiles, and I will send my salvation to the furtherest corners of the earth." The summons to the laity is not because we wish the sufficiency of the laity to make up for the insufficiency of the clergy, but rather because our present world situation is one in which the Mystical Body of Christ is confronted with the mystical body of the anti-Christ. While the priest is between the sanctuary and the altar, the laity will be between the sanctuary and the world that as yet knows not Christ. The Communion rail is not a barrier between the laity and the apostolic body of the Church. The Communion rail is the place where "all who eat One Bread are One Body" and the purpose of the Body is the reconciliation of the *world* to Christ.

Obstacles to the World Missionary Character of the Apostolate of the Hierarchy and Laity

There are three kinds of narrowness which militate against this Catholic sense of world missionary apostolate: (1) geographical contraction, (2) religious frontierism, (3) jurisdictional egotism.

Geographical narrowness assumes the *exclusiveness* of one country or one continent as the object of missionary zeal and alms. For example, a very important area of mission activity today is Latin America. It would be geographical narrowness to assume that there must be a concentration of all missionary activity on that particular area to the neglect of others, or on Formosa to the neglect of Thailand. The Church, because it is a Body, must grow gradually in all places. The human person would be grotesque if he had an abnormally large head, or if the right arm was longer than the left, or one leg shorter than the other; so would the Body of the Church. As St. Paul reminds us, "We are to follow the truth, in a spirit of charity, and so grow up, in everything, into a due proportion with Christ, who is our Head" (Eph 4:15).

Religious frontierism is the identification of the mission work of the Church with the mission activity of a particular society or institute. A graduate of one of the large Catholic universities in the United States once asked the writer what was the nature of his work. When the writer told him that it was to serve the missions in all areas of the world, and all missionary activities, he remarked: "You mean to say that there are other foreign missions in the Church besides India?" He heard only about India in his college!

There are about 639 religious societies in the Church. No one of them can serve the world, but all together do serve the world beautifully. Their spirit of unity is increasing every year. It is now ardently to be hoped that there will soon be a missionary exhibit in which, instead of having separate booths for each missionary group, all will merge to demonstrate their mission activity in the *world,* e.g., the area of Africa, the area of Latin America, Asia, etc.

Jurisdictional egotism is not very common, but when it does appear, it manifests itself in this form: the ordinary of a diocese decides for himself where most of the missionary alms of his diocese will be first and principally spent, rather than subordinating his judgment to the Vicar of Christ who serves the general instead of the particular good. "Charity seeketh not her own." One of the reasons why St. Paul was so very anxious to have Bishop Timothy with him was because he had the "interest of everyone at heart." In contrast, he said of those who arrogate to themselves their own interest: "One and all have their own interest at heart, not Christ's" (Phil 2:21). A recent letter of John XXIII on the missions stated that those who aid a particular work do *well,* but that those who aid him to aid all do *better.*

Peter hesitated even after Pentecost about receiving Cornelius, a Gentile, into the Church, but the Holy Spirit urged him on until Cornelius was received without any connection to national Israel. The temptation is strong to make oneself the judge of where alms shall go. This is allowable, even praiseworthy, within the limitations expressed by the Holy See, namely, that the Holy Father should be "first and principally aided." As John XXIII said more recently, the Holy See is best equipped to equalize the distribution to all areas and all missionaries. We are not to help Americans simply because they are Americans nor the French because they are French nor the Irish because they are Irish. We are to help them only because they are Catholic. Maybe this is the reason why the vision of Cornelius is related no less than three times in Scripture, in order to show that the universal principle of Redemption that was introduced at Golgotha had now become an historical reality.

Concrete Suggestions

1. *The laity should be recruited from high levels of intellectuality and spirituality.* Because there is no strict and long novitiate for the laity, there is the temptation for many to be would-be followers as the three that came to our blessed Lord. No young woman should

be permitted to enter any kind of lay organization because she cannot find a husband, or because she thinks that mission work for the Church might be "interesting." No man must be induced to do so because he was moved by a sermon, or is dissatisfied with his present "boss," or would like to leave his wife. The laity must learn that if incorporation to the mission of the Church promises them more happiness, it also by the same token demands greater sacrifices. In our modern world young men and women rush into marriage without considering its seriousness; they must not flock to an apostolic commitment without considering whether or not they can finish the tower they started to build.

2. *Lay organizations in direct apostolate require an explicit mandate from the hierarchy.* What makes a lay organization Catholic is not the fact that it is organized by Catholics, but that it has received a canonical mission or a mandate from the hierarchy. It is this mandate from the hierarchy which gives to the lay organization the right to witness to Christ. The bishops of France in March, 1946, declared that the mandate of Catholic Action is not conferred on the members of any group, but on the movement itself. In Belgium, *the Council of Malines* prescribed that leaders on the national, diocesan, and even regional levels should be installed by the respective bishops themselves. Pius XII said in his encyclical *Mediator Dei* that the hierarchical priesthood does not derive from the people. The priest as such acts *in persona Christi capitis.* The laity derive their mission from the hierarchy, through whom they share in the complete life of the Mystical Body, and thanks to whom they are equipped to quicken the world.

3. *The Holy Spirit does not necessarily begin with money.* The new lay organizations do not take their start with what might be called the American spirit, or the immediate need of money, but from the Holy Spirit. Recently, we heard of someone in a diocese who was asked to organize the laity. He immediately asked the bishop for $20,000! Starting any lay organization on the basis of material sufficiency is often the way to assure its greatest spiritual inefficiency. We are living in a world in which the contrast between economic sufficiency and poverty is more glaring than ever before. Two thirds

of the people of the world go to bed hungry every night. One wonders if a sharing in that hunger is not one of the essential conditions of beginning a lay organization.

We may ask ourselves why it is that there are so many more conversions to the faith in Africa and Asia than there are in the United States. It could very well be because there is a greater spirit of poverty among the missionaries in those lands. Relying more upon God and His grace, and less upon Madison Avenue techniques, there is a greater receptivity on the part of souls. In the encyclical on Communism Pius XI stated that in the present condition, the virtue that is needed above all others is a humble, disinterested poverty in which there is a faithful copy of the life of the divine Master who could say: "The foxes have their holes and the birds their nests, but the Son of Man has nowhere to lay his Head."

The Holy Father then went on to say that a priest who is evangelically poor and disinterested will work miracles in the midst of his people. What applies to the priesthood applies also to the laity. Our blessed Lord when He came down from the Mount of the Transfiguration was asked by His Apostles why they could not drive the devil out of a certain young man. The answer of our Lord was: "That kind of a devil is driven out only by prayer *and* fasting." The reason our blessed Lord stressed both was because prayer is that which *attaches* us to heaven, while fasting is that which *detaches* us from the earth; the two are inseparable. Living out the first beatitude of the "poor in spirit" is a proof that we love. Without this spirit, the laity will not be strong. That is why the laity have done much for the Church in some countries while failing in others. As Cardinal Newman wrote: "In all times the laity have been the measure of the Catholic spirit; they saved the Irish Church three centuries and they betrayed the Church in England."

4. *The Apologetic of Sanctity.* The most important consideration of all, for any form of the mission of the laity, is sanctity. Holiness is the only apologetic that touches the modern world. It has heard our arguments, it has listened to our sermons, and it tells us: "I have heard of all that before." But there is something that it has not seen, and that is that all-possessing Christian spirit which without words

leaves impressions on auditors similar to the innocence of a child. Without deep, profound unity with the glorified Christ, we are like high-powered electric wires that have no contact with the dynamo. As Cardinal Suhard wrote: "The Christian is not called upon to destroy or villify the world, but to assume it, to sanctify it, to offer it in homage to God." The Christian apostolate is always a crucified apostolate.

When the wealthy senator Paulinus asked Jerome how he could serve the Church, Jerome said he either had to serve it in the priesthood or as a monk. Today, it would be said with Chrysostom (who was one of the greatest believers in lay apostolate among the Fathers of the Church) that you serve God in the world. There is no new form of sanctity required; it is only the old sanctification working through a new engagement, namely, the mass of our contemporary civilization. It is in our day that will be fulfilled the words of our Lord:

> I am not asking that thou shouldst take them out of the world, but that thou shouldst keep them clear of what is evil (Jn 17:15).

This new mission of the laity in the world has a double aspect: one *personal,* the other *social.* The *personal* aspect requires *penance, asceticism, holiness;* the *social* aspect requires the application of this holiness to the world. The ascetical principle is not the denial of temporal values; it is rather their affirmation. Pius XI ordered that the feast of Christ the King should be celebrated on the Sunday before All Saints, thus emphasizing that in this life the reign of Christ is in the souls of His holy ones.

When Pius XII addressed the new cardinals that he made on February 20, 1946, he said: "The faithful and, more precisely, the laity are stationed in the front ranks of the life of the Church, and through them the Church is the living principle of human society. Consequently, they must have an ever clearer consciousness not only of belonging to the Church, but of *being the Church,* that is, of being the community of the faithful on earth under the guidance of their common leader, the Pope, and the bishops in communion with him. *They are the Church,* and therefore, even from the beginning, the faithful with the consent of the bishops have united in associations directed to the most approved diverse types of human activity. And the Holy See has never ceased to approve and to praise them."

Our present hour takes us back to the very first Council of the Church in Jerusalem when St. James arose and said:

> Simon has told us, how for the first time God has looked with favor on the Gentiles, and chosen from among them a people dedicated to his Name (Acts 15:14).

In this particular passage the word "people" is *laos,* which means that the honorary titles of Israel had become the right of the faithful in Christ, namely:

> You are a chosen race, a royal priesthood, a consecrated nation, a people God means to have for himself; it is yours to proclaim the exploits of the God who has called you out of darkness into his marvelous light (1 Pt 2:9).

3. *The Woman in the Missions*

The time has come for all good women to come to the aid of the missions. Up to the present time, the role of woman has been almost completely ignored in the expansion of the Church. Schmidlin, who has written so learnedly of the heralds of the Gospel, never once in his works of theory mentions women. In contrast, the inspired writers of the Gospel felt it was worth noting for posterity; though there was only one faithful man at the foot of the cross, there were three women. There are many records of men failing at the crisis of the Crucifixion, but there is not a single record of a woman failing. As the Divine Missionary went to the consummation of His life, a woman braved the rigors of the Roman law, entered the supreme court of Pilate, and pleaded as the first Portia for the Divine Prisoner. On the way to the crossroads of Calvary, a man is forced to carry a cross, but a woman freely offers a cleansing towel while women water the dust of His road with their tears. Once on the Hill there are three women present and their name is Mary: Mary the contemplative, Mary the Mother, and Mary the salvaged sinner. It is very likely that the lone man would not have been there had it not been for the women, and in particular for the Woman. On the day when the Spirit took visible form as tongues of fire, as before when the Word has taken visible form as a man, we find the same Woman presiding at both, the first time to give birth to the Head of the Church, the second time to preside at the birth of His Mystical Body.

The Gospels were written by men who were inspired by God; therefore, they mention women; history has been written by men who were not inspired, so they rarely mention women. An excuse for this may be that men are the makers of history, but women are the makers of the home; this is true, but, were it not for the homes, there would be neither history nor historians.

Two hundred and seventy years ago, one of the first treatises on Missiology was incorporated into a commentary on the theology of Duns Scotus. Typical of the attitude toward women in the missions was the reasoning process of the author who excluded them from the missions. His argument was:

> Missionaries must preach;
> But preaching is the work of wisdom;
> But wisdom belongs to man — not to woman.
> Proof: Aristotle said that women have no brains: *Sapientia non viget communiter in mulieribus.*
> Since women have little wisdom, they must not be missionaries.

This prejudice against women was directed not only to the missions but to works of healing. In 1849 when the first woman M.D., Elizabeth Blackwell, received her degree, she was refused permission to lecture in any medical school in the British Isles. The Germans said that a woman was to be attached to the three K's, "Kinder, Küche, und Kirche"; she had no other mission than to the kids, the kitchen, and the kirk.

There were few with the insight of De Tocqueville who wrote in his *Democracy in America,* finished in 1840, against the current attitude toward women: "If I were asked to what the singular prosperity and the growing strength of the American people ought to be attributed, I should reply to the superiority of their women."

Our thesis is that women must play a more important role in the missions. This thesis is not defended on the basis of equality, for that is a mathematical concept which ignores the difference in function of man and woman. Rather it is based on psychology and history.

The Psychology of Womanhood

Man was made by God; woman was made by God from man. Man coming directly from God, has initiative, power, immediacy of authority. Woman coming from God through the ecstasy of man, has intuition, response, acceptance, submission, and cooperation. Man's mission is to rule over the external world and subject it; woman's mission is to prolong life in the world and rule it in the home. Man fashions things, having come from the dust; woman fashions life, having come from both the life of God and man. Man gives reasons why he loves; woman loves more for love's sake. Man conquers and builds and invents; woman tends, devotes, interiorizes. Man gives; woman is a gift.

Analogically, the woman in the missions plays the same role that Eve did to Adam, and the same role that Mary did to Christ. Eve was Adam's helpmate: the man is for the Lord and the woman is for man, St. Paul tells us. As Genesis put the relationship, "It is not well that man should be without companionship; I will give him a mate of his own kind." A helpmate does not imply inferiority, but rather a complement, like a bow to a violin, a cup to a saucer. When we come to our Lord and His Blessed Mother, we find that her role was to supply Him with a manhood. The Son of God needed lips with which to teach, hands to bless, feet to search for wandering sheep, and a heart whereon John might lean. He who is the Shepherd bade her make Him a lamb, that He might be the sacrifice for our sins. She was His natural eucharist for she gave Him body and blood to "consecrate," or more accurately to unite with His Divine Person in the Hypostatic Union.

Uniting both Genesis and the Gospel, the role of women in the missions is first to be a helpmate to the missionary by making human natures supple and ready and receptive for the continuation of the Incarnation by grace. As Mary supplied the human nature for Christ, so women are to supply human natures for the missionaries. This is not done corporally through generation, but socially through medical assistance, the feeding of the hungry, the binding of wounds, the teaching of catechism, and the thousand and one tasks a woman can do better than a man. As the sacristan prepares bread and wine for the priest at the altar, so the woman prepares the raw material of human nature for sanctification which can be done only through the priest. She functions primarily *ex opere operantis;* he, when a priest, functions primarily though not exclusively *ex opere operato.*

Once it is granted that the psychology of a woman is different from that of a man, it follows that the missions must utilize both the one who is closest to the body and its ills, and the one who as a priest is closest by Divine appointment to the soul and its ills. If He whose name is *Qui mittendus est* chose as the gateway to the missions a woman, and then put her in the midst of the missionary Church when He sent His Spirit to the world, it follows that we who dare speak in His name, may not ignore the necessary role of woman in the evangelization of the Gentiles.

Historical Reason

Our missionary work today is principally in Asia and Africa. Before inquiring how we are to convert them, it might be well to see how Europe was converted. About twenty years after the Resurrection, there was still no Christianity in Europe except a few scattered Roman soldiers or Jewish merchants, who wandered into Europe. Paul and Silas now find their path into Asia blocked, for "the Holy Spirit prevented them from preaching the word in Asia." The Spirit willed first that the Gospel be preached in Europe. Paul obeyed the vision of the Macedonian who said: "Come into Macedonia and help us." Traveling inland to Philippi, Paul preached at the river's edge and made the first convert in all Europe, *and she was a woman: Lydia*. It was in her house that Paul and Silas established their headquarters for the preaching of the Gospel to Europe.

Missionary activity in Europe begins with a woman and a woman's hospitality to missionaries. Let not Europe now, which is growing old, ever forget, as the Spirit opens Asia to the Gospel, that Lydia was the midwife to the birth of the faith in Europe. If Paul had been so shortsighted as to refuse the role of a woman in his missionary activity, the faith would have suffered. Nor let the missionaries of Africa, China, Japan, and Korea forget the role of their Lydias.

The subsequent history of the faith in Europe also records the importance of women in the missions. St. John Chrysostom in summarizing the missionary activities of four centuries said that though men excelled in the political life, when it came to patience in "persecution and labors, women surpassed men in courage." Both for evil and for good, woman can win a man. The devil tempted a woman and a man fell. God went to a woman and man was restored. Clovis was converted through Clotilde, a Catholic wife. In England, Ethelbert of Kent was converted through Bertha who later on received a letter of commendation from Gregory the Great. The Bohemians received the increase of the faith through Ludmilla and Hungary had its St. Stephen remotely through Sarolta and Aldaide. Lioba helped Boniface evangelize Germany. It was a recognized principle among the missionaries in Europe that the way to convert a pagan sovereign was through his wife. Of all the missionaries of this period, none seemed to be as emphatic in using women as missionaries as Boniface, while Gregory the Great in his letters urged the conversion of women as a means of bringing husbands to the faith.

Those who scruple about the role of women in the missions should not forget that the Church officially and pontifically has its own mission society. The Society for the Propagation of the Faith, which was founded by a woman, Pauline Jaricot. Let not the missionary dioceses and vicariates which receive aid from the Holy See ever forget that aid now comes to them because of the sublime insight of a woman. Men have had visions before of the world as a unit, such as Alexander the Great, who after conquering Asia in the name of Europe said, "God is the common Father of all men." But here is a woman of a bourgeois family who saw the need of a world revolution before Marx and who dreamed and yearned to reverse the conquest of Alexander by pouring out the blessings of Europe to Asia. Her cause has already been introduced for beatification, and may God hasten the day when missionaries will see a woman with a world mission honored by the faithful of the East and the West.

Another Pontifical Society, that of St. Peter, the Apostle for Native Clergy, was founded by Stephanie and Jeanne Bigard. The thousands of native seminaries throughout the world are supported to a great extent by the indomitable courage of this mother and daughter. During World War I Benedict XV transferred the society to Rome.

But from an entirely different point of view, the missions need women because of peculiar conditions prevailing in these non-Christian lands. The woman missionary has a function other than to do chores for the men missionaries. The woman of Islamism, who is kept hidden as the slave of man, is awaiting the Christian woman of the missions who will liberate her. In India, while no husband was ever supposed to commit *suttee*, some wives were expected to commit suicide on their husband's funeral pyre. The women of the West who are the lineal descendants of the Lady who sang *Magnificat* are under missionary summons to relieve their sisters of the East.

Added to this is the fact that a woman missionary as a doctor or nurse can bring to the suffering millions the peculiar kind of sympathy that manifested itself on the road to Calvary. In this very day, the ringing plea for a Catholic medical school in India comes from the pen of a missionary Sister who is also a doctor of medicine.

We in the United States must honestly confess that the stability of our faith, the sacrificial love of our Catholics, the piety and virtue of our youth are due in greatest measure to our devoted Sisters. To admit this influence on the domestic scene and deny its importance in the foreign missions is to forget that a Madonna in Nazareth teaching a child is not different from the Madonna who followed her Son outside the "city's gates" to the Mission Hill of the world's redemption.

The Gospel tells us, "Many women followed Jesus from Galilee to minister to Him." St. Paul in the same spirit wrote: "I call upon thee Evodia, and I call upon thee Syntiche, to make common cause in the Lord . . . they have worked for the Gospel at my side, as much as Clement and those other fellow-laborers of mine whose names are recorded in the book of life."

It is not new to call upon women for the missions; it only seems new, because we have forgotten the old. No one can take away from women the glory of being closest to the Cross on Good Friday and first to the tomb on Easter morn!

4. *Motherhood and the Missions*

"Meanwhile His mother, and His mother's sister, Mary the wife of Cleophas, and Mary Magdalen had taken their stand by the Cross of Jesus" (Jn 19:25).

These three women stand for the women who do not fail in any crisis of human history. They represent also the three types of vocations that are open to women and they all revolve around motherhood.

Motherhood is a much larger concept than is generally realized. Pius XII said: "Every woman is made to be a mother, either spiritually or physically." Motherhood is not just a biological factor; *motherhood is in the soul as well as in the body; it is in the little girl who plays with a doll as well as in a family;* motherhood is a gift of self. Self may be given in three ways: (1) to *God;* (2) to *man;* (3) to *society.*

Hence there are three types of motherhood:

1. Spiritual Motherhood — symbolized by Mary, our Mother, at the foot of the cross;

2. Physical Motherhood — symbolized by Mary the wife of Cleophas;

3. Social Motherhood — symbolized by Mary Magdalen.

Spiritual Motherhood or the Religious Vocation

The symbol of spiritual motherhood is the Blessed Mother who stands for all those who leave the lights and glamor of the world for the shade and the shadow of the cross where saints are made.

The religious life with its consecrated virginity is too often regarded

94

as something negative or something incomplete, or as mere physical intactness. But as pure water is more than the absence of impurities, as a pure diamond is more than the absence of carbon, and as pure food is more than the absence of poison, so purity is more than the absence of a man. When one defends a fortress against an enemy, it does not follow that the fortress itself contains no treasures.

The religious life is a *spiritual* motherhood for the same reasons that the Immaculate Virgin Mary is also a mother.

There is a superiority of spiritual motherhood over physical motherhood in the begetting of new life because of the greater freedom of the former. No physical mother can freely decide and determine the precise moment when a new life will be begotten in her, but a spiritual mother can. Not in some dark, unknown night of love, but in the greatest act of freedom in the world, Mary said to Christ: "Be it done to me according to Thy Word." Christ was *willed* in the body of Mary, the time deliberately chosen. She did not will to love a creature and then conceive a child. She willed to conceive a child the moment she identified herself with the Divine Will. Other mothers become conscious of motherhood through physical changes; Mary knew it through the message of an angel and the overshadowing of the Spirit.

So it is with the religious. The day she takes her veil, she renews the Annunciation and says to the Beloved: "I am Thine, O Lord"; the moment she takes her vows, "The Word is made flesh and dwells within her." The flesh cannot determine the moment a new life will come into a womb, but the religious can set the hour, the minute, the second when Christ will live in her soul. Physical mothers *accept* the child God sends them. Spiritual mothers will their Child — the Holy Child. All she has to do is to say *"Fiat,"* and Eternal Life throbs within her.

The number of children any physical motherhood can beget is limited; but there is no age limit or number limit to spiritual motherhood. Mary had one child by the flesh; by compassion at the cross she had children no man can number.

So it is with the religious. Her trials, her mortifications, her detachment, her daily routine, her summons to stand at the foot of the cross enable her to become the spiritual mother of converts and catechists on the missions, of returned sinners and lost sheep.

When we go before the judgment seat of God, He will ask us: "Where are your children?" Blessed will be the physical mothers who can point to little ones that equal in number either the Persons in the Trinity, or the Sacraments, or the Apostles. But more blessed will be the spiritual mothers who will point to their progeny as numerous as the stars of the heavens.

A mother in the world is fortunate if she can beget ten children, but take the foundresses of religious communities! Who shall count their daughters? Within their lifetime they have a progeny like that the Lord promised Jacob at Bethel! The religious mothers who pray for the missions and those who go on the missions are both opening wombs to a progeny in Africa and Asia as countless as the stars of the skies! Thanks to these spiritual mothers, Mary once more stands beneath the cross in Hong Kong, Leopoldville, Bangkok, and Delhi, and as they pick up the fatherless and motherless they breathe out anew the words of Christ: "I will not leave you orphans."

Physical Motherhood

Mary of Cleophas was the representative of physical motherhood at the foot of the cross, for she was the mother of two disciples of our blessed Lord. What now is physical motherhood from the Divine point of view? It has a threefold relation to the great mystery of the Trinity.

Physical motherhood is the prolongation of the eternal generation of the Son in the bosom of the Father. Generation is not an imitation of the beasts of the field but an imitation of the Eternal Generation of the Word of God. Human generation is not a push upward from the beasts, but rather a gift downward from the Trinity. God made the whole universe fecund. Through the prophet He asks: "Shall not I who make others bring forth children, Myself not bring forth?" It is man who makes; it is woman who begets. We make what is unlike us in nature, e.g., a carpenter makes a table; but we beget what is like us, e.g., a mother begets a child. All the science, architecture, and technology of man is a prolongation of God's creation.

Behind every desire to procreate is the hidden desire to participate in the Eternal. Husband and wife say to one another in the language of Tobias:

> We come of holy stock, you and I, and God has life waiting for us if we will but keep faith with him (Tb 2:18).

Or to put it in other language, as "the Word became flesh and dwelt amongst us," so every couple says to one another: "Let our love become flesh that it may dwell amongst us." Every birth is Bethlehem all over again.

Missionaries come from physical mothers; they are the generators of the heralds of Christ. Behind each priest, Brother, Sister, and lay worker in any part of the mission world is a mother who fed a natural eucharist to a child that one day would either give or teach the Divine Eucharist to the Gentiles. The breast and the tabernacle become related as antitype and fulfillment, for if she did not give the wheat and the grapes, our missionaries would not give the Body and Blood of Christ.

Social Motherhood

Here we touch on what is almost a new vocation. Too long has the unmarried woman, the schoolteacher, the secretary, the lay missionary, the social worker, the businesswoman been looked upon as either a "misfit" or a "leftover" from other kinds of motherhood.

Were there not three women at the cross according to St. John? Did not each have the name Mary? Did not all have a role to play in Redemption, and was not Magdalen as much a mother as the Blessed Mother and Mary of Cleophas? Did not our Lord say that He who did the will of His Father in heaven was his "mother"? After all, what is the essense of motherhood? As we said above, it is the *gift of self*. Hence, self is given to *society* through which one becomes a social mother; when the self is given to the missions one becomes a lay missionary.

Mary Magdalen stood at the foot of the cross in the name of social motherhood and the lay missionary. See what social motherhood involved in her case:

1. She put herself at the *service of the hierarchy* of the Church for, speaking of the Apostles, she spent her time "by ministering unto them and aiding them in their tasks."

2. The Lord knew the world needs compassion for the sick, the suffering, the abandoned, and the dying. Hence He gave a special vocation to Mary to fulfill these tasks. She was at the foot of the cross; she was there to aid when the body was taken down and wrapped; she was the one who brought spices with which to anoint Him on Easter.

3. She had those special qualities of soul which fitted her for the *regeneration* of society, for the Lord "showed himself first of all to Mary Magdalen" on Easter (Mk 16:9). When our Lord wished to give hope to sinners and to bring mercy to the fallen, He chose a social mother to announce the Resurrection.

4. But, above all, not only did she minister to the Apostles during the public life; on Easter she was the one who told the Church to get a "move on." "She went and gave the news to those who had been of his company" (Mk 16:10). Even when they refused to believe, she goaded Peter and John into action to visit the sepulcher — for Christ was truly risen.

Would to God the single woman would realize that she plays as important a role in society as the two other types of woman. In modern civilization her role is almost more important. Modern society has created problems which did not exist in other generations, calling for teachers in parochial schools; secretaries to Catholic charities, pontifical mission works, the hierarchy and chancery offices; care of the sick; child welfare; public assistance; social service; workers in politics, commerce, business, and law enforcement. Spiritual mothers cannot leave their cells; physical motherhood is absorbing and demands a concentration of energy in the home.

Who will bring Christ into these new areas and dimensions of our modern civilization and to the missions? Do not the beehive and the anthill have a special category of workers dedicated to the community? Shall not modern society have special women who, like Magdalen, will aid the hierarchy, will stand at the foot of the crosses of the world in sympathy, will bring the spices of hope to those who are dead in sin and will arouse others from lethargy when the joy of Easter ought to be in the air?

Social motherhood and lay missionaries have a *vocation*. Pius XII in an address of October 21, 1945, spoke of those women as having a "mysterious vocation. Their mission at the present day is revealed: a mission many-sided, militant, and calling for all of their energies, a mission such as they can more readily undertake than many of their sisters occupied as they are with family cares and the education of their children, or else subject to the restriction of the religious rule."

A vocation is doing the will of God. A nun obeys God's will; a wife obeys God's will in being subject to her husband, as the Church to Christ. A husband is not essential for happiness; what is essential is obedience to the will of God.

A social mother or a lay missionary obeys God's will for, as Scripture says of Mary — "The Master is here and bids thee come" (Jn 11:28). Social motherhood is not a remnant of life; it is a choice. It is never a motherhood without children, for though she may have none of her own, she has thousands, for she is the mother of innumerable children who fall out of their nests.

A second characteristic of this mother is that she generally has an exceptional amount of energy. This is partly because she is unmarried, and the powers and energies which would by instinct be spent in physical motherhood become orientated toward another goal. Everyone has a certain amount of energy. The energy that does not flow from the body often flows into the mind. Just as mental powers will sometimes develop more after a paralysis of lower limbs, so the energy that would have gone out biologically now goes out socially. It is not crushed energy; it is transformed energy, and the transformation is in favor of a much larger environment than a family. She may say "no" to physical generation, but she says "yes" to the ignorance of students, the hunger of pagans in missions, the distressed in homes. She is available to neighbors' needs, and the reason she is available is because she is detached and free.

The third characteristic of this vocation is that it is like the priesthood. It might be called the feminine side of the priesthood because such women are devoted to all families, yet belonging to none; they love everyone and are possessed by none; they have no children and yet are "mother" in the sense that a priest is "father."

St. Paul spoke of this kind of woman as he spoke of the priest. He said because a priest was not married he could care for all. So also he said:

> So a woman who is free of wedlock, or a virgin, is concerned with the Lord's claim, intent on holiness, bodily and spiritual; whereas the married woman is concerned with the world's claim, asking how she is to please her husband (1 Cor 7:34).

St. Paul says that the social mother and the spiritual mother are concerned with the Lord's claim, while the physical mother is concerned with the claim of her husband.

We may say of her with Isaias:

> Sing with praise, barren city that art childless still; echo thy praise, cry aloud, wife that wast never brought to bed; forsaken, she is to have more children now, the Lord says, than wife whose husband remains with her (Is 54:1).

These are the three women who do not fail. They serve the unity of the Church by being united at the foot of the cross: the spiritual mothers, like Mary of Nazareth, who have a first love that is a last love, namely, Christ the Son of the living God; physical mothers, like Mary of Cleophas, who raise up sons to lift white Hosts in adoration of the heavenly Father; and social mothers, like Mary Magdalen, who take the tangled skeins of a wretched and ruined life and weave out of them the beautiful tapestry of saintliness and holiness.

The two other mothers are known in the world: the religious and the physical mothers. But a new crown must be made for those who solve the new problems of our age, particularly in the missions. May they multiply that we may salute them not as the modern woman, "once our inferior, now our equal," but as the social mother — closest to the cross on the Good Fridays of the world and first at the tomb on its glorious Easters.

Part IV

The Church and the Missions

1. *Our Lord and the Missions*

Christ, the Son of God, came into the world to save all men, all nations and all peoples. Though this was His ultimate goal, His plan was to limit His Gospel at first to the Jews. Our problem is to discover how and when His mission was rendered universal, so as to embrace the whole world as well.

Home Mission Limitation

> These twelve Jesus sent out;
>> But first gave them their instructions;
> Do not go, he said, into the walks of the Gentiles,
>> Or enter any city of Samaria;
> Go rather to the lost sheep that belong to the house of Israel.
>> (Mt 10:5–6)

The first explicit direction to the Apostles was to avoid the Gentiles. Today they would be known as the foreign missions. Even the Samaritans were to be excluded for the time being, for they were a hybrid people, of both Jewish and Assyrian origin. This explicit instruction to the Apostles to confine themselves at first to the house of Israel was underlined by the fact that He chose twelve of them, who roughly corresponded to the twelve tribes of Israel. The lingering remembrance of this order made Peter hesitate when the time came to baptize Cornelius, the Roman centurion. For that act, he required an explicit declaration on the part of God Himself.

Despite this first mandate to the Apostles, our blessed Lord had several contacts with pagans; He even worked miracles on their behalf. Though these miracles do not give a complete answer to our question as to when our Lord began to make His mission universal, nevertheless they give us a clue to it.

The first of the three contacts which our Lord had with pagans, and, therefore, with the foreign missions, was with the Roman centurion; the second, with the daughter of the Syro-Phoenician woman; and the third, with the young man possessed of a devil in the land of the Gerasenes. There were many elements common to all three miracles, as we shall see shortly.

The first two miracles were performed at a distance. Probably the centurion was a member of the Roman garrison stationed at Capharnaum. By birth, therefore, he must have been a heathen. It is very likely that he, like the centurion, Cornelius, whom Peter baptized (cf. Acts 10:1), and like the eunuch in the court of the Queen of Ethiopia (cf. Acts 8:27), had become at least sentimentally attached to the worship of Jahve. This Roman official had been in the country long enough to know that there was a strong wall of partition between Jew and Gentile. This explains the fact that when his servant lay sick, even to the point of death, he did not directly approach our blessed Lord, but "sent some of the elders of the Jews to him, asking Him to come and heal his servant" (Lk 7:3 K). Our blessed Lord must have shown some reluctance to work this miracle, because Luke says that those who interceded "began to make earnest appeal to him" (Lk 7:4 K). While our Lord was on His way to the servant, the centurion sent word to Him through messengers not to trouble Himself:

> I am not worthy to receive Thee under my roof.
> (Lk 7:7)

St. Augustine was later to say of this: "Counting himself unworthy that Christ should enter into his doors, he was counted worthy that Christ should enter into his heart."

The pagan centurion compared our blessed Lord's power to his own authority over his soldiers. He himself was a sergeant with a hundred men under him who automatically did his bidding; but the Lord was the true Caesar or King, the Supreme Commander of the highest hierarchy, with angels to obey His orders. Surely, then, He would not have to enter the house to perform the miracle; the pagan suggested that He should give an order from where He was. The miracle was performed, as the centurion requested, at a distance. Reflecting on the faith of this pagan and anticipating the faith that would come from foreign missions, which He contrasted with the present home mission, our Blessed Lord said:

> Believe me, I have not found faith like this, even in Israel.
>
> (Lk 7:10)

This first pagan who received such praise from our divine Lord for his faith was one of "those children of God" scattered abroad in the world who were eventually to be brought into unity through the Redemption (cf. Jn 11:52 K).

The second miracle performed by our Lord on a pagan was the healing of the daughter of the Syro-Phoenician woman. This reluctance to work a miracle for the centurion had only been implied, but here He refused explicitly, perhaps to draw out the woman's faith. The miracle took place in "a neighborhood of Tyre and Sidon" (Mt 15:22). St. Chrysostom and other commentators have actually thought that our Lord left the borders of what was later on to be known as foreign-mission territory. The woman is described as coming from Canaan and being of Syro-Phoenician descent. She was, therefore, completely set apart from the Jews. When she asked a boon for her daughter, whom she described as "truly cruelly troubled by an evil spirit," our Lord

> gave her no word in answer; but His disciples came to Him
>
> and pleaded with Him. Rid us of her, they said,
>
> She is following us with her cries.
>
> (Mt 15:23)

The Apostles were not asking for a miracle to be worked for the woman's sake; they only wanted to be left alone, undisturbed, in selfish ease.

As she continued to plead and to worship Him, our blessed Lord proceeded to test her faith with a seemingly hard remark:

> It is not right to take the children's bread
>
> And throw it to the dogs.
>
> (Mt 15:26)

The children he was referring to were, of course, the Jews. The term "dogs" signified contempt, and it was not beyond the Jews to apply it often to the Gentiles.

As the Roman centurion endured a seeming delay, so this woman suffered a stunning rebuff. She however responded with a perfect act of faith. She said:

> Ah yes, Lord, the dogs feed on the crumbs that
> Fall from their master's table.
>
> (Mt 15:27)

In effect this woman from the foreign missions was saying to our Lord: "I accept this title and the dignity that goes with it: for even the dogs are fed by the Master; they may not be given the full feast which has been spread for the children of Israel, but they will get a portion; and it will still come from the Master's table." She was affirming that she belonged to the Master's household, even though her place in it was lower. According to the very name which the Lord had given her, therefore, she was not an alien. And by accepting this name, she could claim all that it included.

She had conquered by faith, and the Master said to her:

> Woman, for this great faith of thine,
> Let thy will be granted.
>
> (Mt 15:28)

Like Joseph of old, who showed severity to his brethren for but a brief time, the Savior did not maintain His apparent disdain for long; and He granted the healing of the daughter, again at a distance.

The third early contact of our blessed Lord with the pagans occurred when He entered the country of the Gerasenes. A man possessed of an unclean spirit came out of the tombs to meet Him. The actual scene was Decapolis, a predominantly Gentile city. Josephus asserts that Gerasa was itself a Greek city. The very fact that the people there were swineherds would seem to indicate that they were not Jews, but it is conceivable that they were Jews defying the Mosaic Law.

Considerable symbolism may be attached to the fact that in this pagan land our blessed Lord came face to face with discords and forces far worse than those which disturb the winds and waves and the bodies of men. Here there was something wilder and more fearful than the natural elements, which could bring confusion, anarchy, and ruin to the inner man. There had been a wholesome faith in the centurion and in the Syro-Phoenician woman. But there was nothing in this young man but the dominion of the devil. The other two pagans had spoken from their own hearts in tribute to our Savior. Here, however, it was an alien spirit, a fallen spirit, that made the young man affirm the Divinity:

> When he saw Jesus from far off, he ran up
> And fell at His feet, and cried with a loud voice,
> "Why dost Thou meddle with me, Jesus, Son of the
> Most High God?"
>
> (Mk 5:6, 7)

When the Savior released the young man from the evil spirit and permitted it to enter into the swine instead, the townspeople ordered our Lord to depart from their post. The spirit of capitalism, in its most evil form, made them feel that the restoring of a soul to the friendship of God was nothing compared to the loss of a few pigs. While the respectable Gerasenes bade Him depart, the Samaritans, who were sinners, wanted our Lord to stay with them.

These three incidents, involving foreign missions, were exceptions to the Divine plan that salvation must first come to the Jews, and that He must limit His teaching, for the time being, only to the lost sheep of Israel.

We do not yet have the complete answer concerning the world mandate of the Savior. These sporadic contacts with the foreign missions did not suffice to establish a principle of worldwide evangelization. On the other hand, it cannot be supposed that our blessed Lord turned to the Gentiles simply because His own people refused Him, as if the rest of humanity were only an afterthought in His life. He always knew that there would come a point when He would lose both the leaders and the masses of His own people. In fact, this came to pass after the miracle of the multiplication of the loaves. After that, our blessed Lord could count on neither an aristocratic nor a popular following among the Jews. Even so, He continued for the time being to concentrate on teaching His own people, to the exclusion of the foreign missions.

Our Savior did not use any of His three contacts with the pagans to tell His Apostles to take the Gospel beyond the confines of Israel. Nevertheless, there was clear and intrinsic connection between the Gentiles and the reason of His coming. He came into this world, not to live, but to die. His life was lived backward, and death was not an unwelcome interruption to His life or a stumbling block to His mission; it was the very goal and purpose of His coming. Noteworthy is the fact that in those moments where there was a very strong hint and suggestion of His death, and therefore of His Redemption, there was also some involvement of the Gentiles. Quite apart from the three miraculous contacts, there were three other moments when pagans were closely associated with Him. Each of these moments had some reference to His passion and to His death and glorification.

The first of these was at His birth. The shepherds represented the home mission; the Magi stood for the foreign missions. Jew and Gentile were both next to the crib, but the coming of the Gentiles coincided with the first attempt upon His life. Hardly was the Divine Ship launched than King Herod sought to sink It by ordering the massacre of all male children under the age of two. And it was the Gentiles whom Herod questioned concerning the prophecy about the star of Bethlehem. Already, the shadow of death had fallen across the Infant Jesus.

The second moment of the close association with Gentiles in His life was when the Greeks came seeking, through the intercession of Philip and Andrew, to see Him. On this occasion, our blessed Lord did not refer to a prophecy from the Jewish script (for that would have been unavailing to the Gentile); He appealed instead to a law of the natural order, the law of the seed.

> A grain of wheat must fall into the ground and die,
>> Or else it remains nothing more than a grain of wheat;
> But if it dies,
>> Then it yields rich fruit.

(Jn 12:24)

As the wise men from among the Gentiles discovered Wisdom at the crib, so the wise men from Gentile ranks now learned the law of sacrifice: that through death a new life would spring forth. The closer our Lord came to His cross (and here He was only a week away from it), the closer the pagans were to Him. They now began to appear for the first time in His entourage. And it was on the occasion of this visit of the heirs of Socrates, Aristotle, and Plato, that our blessed Lord began to speak of His glory:

> The hour has come now
> For the Son of Man to achieve his glory.
> (Jn 12:23)

The third moment when the Gentiles were closely associated with Him was during His Crucifixion. He was tried in a Roman court, and the wife of a Roman governor interceded for Him because she had been troubled in a dream. Simon of Cyrene, who was interested in watching this Man going to His death, was forced to help Him carry the cross. It is known that at least a hundred Roman soldiers were present at the scene of His Crucifixion, for a centurion commanded at least that number. Never before were there so many Gentiles and pagans around our Lord as at the moment of His death. Looking forward to that moment, after His miracles had failed to convince men of His Divinity, He had given the cross as the final argument. Now that the Son of Man was being lifted up, He began to draw all men to Himself. He made it clear that it was "all men" that He would draw, and not merely the people of Judea and Galilee. At the very moment when He spoke of giving His own life, He added:

> I have other sheep too,
> Which do not belong to this fold;
> I must bring them in too;
> They will listen to My voice.
> (Jn 10:16)

The Hour of Pagans Came After the Hour of the Crucifixion and Glory

The death of Christ was the realization of the Kingdom of God for the entire world. Up to the point of Calvary, men had been taught by preaching. After Calvary, they would be taught by His Resurrection and Ascension. The *principle* of universality became effective. It was the death of Christ that broke down the wall of partition between Jew and Gentile to reveal the universal mission of the Messiah, which had been dimly hinted at in the Old Testament. In other words, it took Golgotha to universalize the mission of Christ. The foreign missions are the fruit of the passion and death of our blessed Lord. What greater proof is there than this, that it was not until after His Resurrection and the moment of His Ascension that the missionary mandate was given:

> You, therefore, must go out
> Making disciples of all nations.
> (Mt 28:19)

Now the pagans would come into their own, not only those who had lived before His coming, but those who would live until His final glory. And there will come a day when:

> The men of Nineve will rise up
> With this generation at the day of judgment,
> And will leave it without excuse;
> For they did penance when Jonas preached to them.
> (Mt 12:41)

The Gentiles who lived in the days of Solomon, and in particular the Queen of Sheba, would point an accusing finger at Israel for not having been as responsive as the Gentiles to the death of Christ:

> The queen of the south will rise up
> With this generation at the day of judgment,
> And will leave it without excuse;
> For she came from the ends of the earth
> To hear the wisdom of Solomon.
> (Mt 12:42)

The coast of Tyre and Sidon that produced a woman of faith would receive a more tolerant judgment than Capharnaum, which had once cradled the Body of the Divine Fisherman:

> And I say this,
> That it shall go less hard with Tyre and Sidon
> At the day of judgment than with you.
> And thou, Capharnaum,

> Dost thou hope to be lifted up high as heaven?
> Thou shalt fall as low as hell.
>   (Mt 11:22)

Even Sodom, which had been synonymous with everything that was evil, would have more merciful judgment than Israel, to whom the revelation was first restricted:

> Sodom, itself, if the miracles done in thee had been done there,
>   Might have stood to this day.
> And I say this,
>   That it shall go less hard with the country of Sodom
>   At the day of judgment than with thee.
>   (Mt 11:23)

As for the future, all the Gentiles shall profit by His death and Resurrection:

> When the Son of Man comes in His glory.
>   And all the angels with Him,
> He will sit down upon the throne of his glory,
>   And all nations will be gathered in His presence.
>   (Mt 25:31–32)

Had our Lord been only a preacher or a teacher, there would never have been any foreign missions. The faith would never have been propagated all over the world. For the Gospel, which the missionaries bring, is not an epic that belongs to a particular people, but a redemption which is as wide as humanity itself.

The 200,000 missionaries in Asia, Afria, and Oceania, and other parts of the world have a mission to the world because of the universality of Redemption. Up until the death of Christ, what is now known as the missionary world had a prince ruling over it, a prince whose legion was manifested in the young man in the Land of the Gerasenes. It was when the Greeks came to Him, and our blessed Lord predicted His death, that He said:

> Sentence is now being passed on this world;
>   Now is the time
> When the prince of this world is to be cast out.
>   (Jn 12:31)

From the moment of Calvary, the missionary belonged to Christ and not to the prince of this world. Another King entered into rightful possession of the Gentiles. The principal distinction between the Old and the New Testaments was in regard to scope. The former had been restricted almost exclusively to a single nation, but the blood of the New Covenant shed on Calvary broke down that wall of partition between the Jews and other nations.

The sacrifice of Christ was universal in three ways: time, place, and power. As regards time, its efficacy was not limited to one generation or dispensation:

> Before the beginning of the world,
>   God has foreknown him,
> But it was only in these last days
>   That he was revealed for your sakes.
>   (1 Pt 1:20)

There is universality, too, in space, for the effectiveness of Christ's death was not confined to any single nation:

> Thou wast slain in sacrifice;
>   Out of every tribe, every language, every people, every nation
> Thou hast ransomed us with thy blood and given us to God.
>   (Ap 5:9)

Finally, there is universality in power, for there is no sin whatever that His Redemption cannot blot out:

> The blood of his Son Jesus Christ
>   Which washes us clean from all sin.
>   (Jn 1:7)

It was on the cross that Christ fulfilled His mission, and it follows that the closer missionaries live to the cross, the more quickly will they fulfill His mission to all nations.

2. *The Papacy and the Missions*

When all is said and done, the initiative for fulfilling the Lord's order: "Preach the Gospel to all nations," depends on the Vicar of Christ. Granted the courage of missionaries, who like Paul evangelized nations, granted the heroic and multiplied efforts of missionary societies, granted, too, the sacrifices of the faithful in response to appeals of mission-aid societies; they have the authority to do these things, but assignment of missionaries and the inspiration for evangelization ultimately derive from the Vicar of Christ. The aim of this chapter is to prove this point by citing papal influences at various periods of the Church's history.

St. Peter and the Apostolic Church

The Church came from the hands of Christ to the Apostles. The Savior poured out upon them a hidden power which associated them in an exceptional way with the prolongation of His Incarnation. They were the sole depositories of the revealed doctrine which, in turn, they were to manifest to the world. These powers were found in equal degree in each of the Apostles, but since they were granted only in view of the foundation of the Church which was to be governed by a single visible ruler, they tended to place the Apostles in dependence on the *transapostolic* power entrusted by Christ to Peter. The Apostles themselves were counted among those sheep of Christ having Peter for their visible Shepherd. The Apostles were equal as Apostles; but as the sheep of Christ, deprived here below of His visible presence, they were entrusted to the care of Peter, chief pastor. The thesis of Marsilius of Padua and John of Janduno that "the blessed apostle Peter had no greater authority than the other apostles and was not their head" was condemned by John XXII, on October 23, 1327.

The Savior made Peter not only the same promises He made to others but promises still more astonishing when He designated him the foundation stone of the Church and the key bearer of the Kingdom of God.

St. Thomas Aquinas writes, "Since Christ was about to withdraw His bodily presence from the Church, He needed to appoint one to take His place in governing the whole church. Wherefore, before His Ascension, He said to Peter, 'Feed my sheep'; and before His Passion, 'Thou being converted, confirm thy brethren,' and to him alone He made the promise, 'To thee will I give the keys of the Kingdom of Heaven'; whence it results that in order to safeguard the unity of the Church, the power of the keys was to descend from Peter to the others" (*4 Contra Gentes,* cap. 76).

Peter and the Gentiles

The Church was, at first, in appearance only a Jewish sect. The first great stride that it took carried it over into the borders of the Gentile world, thanks to a revelation to the first Pontiff. God laid His right hand on Peter and His left hand on Cornelius and drew them toward each other. The importance of this scene is the recognition of the Gentile Christians as an act of the whole community. The significance of the vision is plain enough, though Peter was much perplexed by it. The great sheet let down by its four corners onto the earth was a symbol of the universal humanity. The four corners corresponded to the four points of the compass, north, south, east, and west; the contents represented the swarming millions of men awaiting the Redemption of Christ. Cornelius was not a Jew, but a Roman officer or centurion, four of whom are mentioned in the New Testament and each of them left a most creditable record. One of these our Lord commended for his remarkable faith, another bore witness to the divinity of our Lord on the cross, another was of much comfort to Paul at the very lowest point of his fortune, and now Cornelius reveals how piety in military life can be like an alpine flower pushing up through the snow.

Peter is directed to convert Cornelius, an uncircumcized heathen. His conversion created more excitement than any single conversion on record, not because one more soul was added, but because of the new missionary principle it embodied, and the new policy it served to inaugurate. From this time on, the Gospel would act not on one people but on all nations. In Genesis, the world is unclean. In Exodus, one nation and a certain proportion of animals have been made clean. Now the Kingdom of God undertakes the task of cleansing the universe. When Peter visited Cornelius he said to him and to the company assembled, "You know well enough that a Jew is contaminated if he consorts with one of another race or visits him; but God has been showing me that we ought not to speak of any man as profane or unclean." After hearing this story of Cornelius, Peter adds, "I see clearly enough that God makes no distinction between man and man; he welcomes anybody, whatever his race, who appears and does what piety demands."

Jewish nationalism had unconsciously clouded in Peter's mind the truth that God was no respecter of persons. Peter had read the prophecies in the Old Testament about the calling of the Gentiles and had heard and received Christ's commission to teach all nations, and yet he had to have this added revelation to be convinced that as the Vicar of Christ he was also the Vicar of the missions of the world. Long before Israel was set apart, God declared they were to be the vehicle of blessing to other nations. Abraham in whom the special calling began was the very man to whom the Lord said that among his descendants there should be "a seed, a certain wonderful seed in whom all the nations of the earth would be blessed." Peter acknowledged this on Pentecost saying: "You are the heirs of the prophets, and of the covenant which God made with our fathers, when he said to Abraham, *Every race on earth shall receive a blessing through thy posterity.*"

Peter's action in regard to Cornelius precipitated a controversy which was bound to come if the Church was to be anything more than a Jewish sect. It brought to light the first tendency to form a party in the Church: "They of the circumcision." Peter threw open the doors of the first council of the Church, the Council of Jerusalem: "It is the Holy Spirit's pleasure and ours that no burden should be laid upon you, beyond these which cannot be avoided."

Peter in his first two discourses at Pentecost had already dimly felt the universal mission of the Church, but it took Cornelius to generalize it. At Pentecost, there were Parthians, Medes, and Elamites; those whose homes were in "Mesopotamia, or Judea, or Cappadocia; or Pontus or Asia, Phrygia or Pomphylia, Egypt or the parts of Libya round Cyrene; some visitors from Rome." A short time later, it is in the Gentile world of Antioch that the name "Christian" is used for the first time.

Missionary Adaptation Under Clement
During the First Few Centuries

The third successor of Peter, Clement, not only manifested an interest in the most distant missions, but even recommended bold strokes in adaptation. He saw all coming under the empire of Christ: "The ocean, impassable before to man, and the worlds beyond it, are regulated by the same enactments of the Lord." Recognizing but not despising the pagan use of oracles, Clement added, "Many kings and princes, in times of pestilence, when they had been instructed by an oracle, had given themselves up to death, in order that by their own blood they might deliver their fellow citizens from destruction." Here the Vicar of Christ makes use of pagan practices to point to the redemption of our Lord. Seeking to arouse the pagans to a belief in the Resurrection he points to their phoenix: "Let us consider that wonderful sign of resurrection which takes place in Eastern lands, that is, in Arabia, and the countries round about. . . . Do we then deem it any great and wonderful thing for the Maker of all things to raise up again those who served Him in the assurance of a good faith, when even by a bird He shows us the mightiness of His power to fulfill His promise?" Certainly, if a Vicar of Christ uses a fable or legend of the phoenix in the first century, then missionaries should not scruple to find something good in Indian hymns or Buddha in the twentieth century. Certainly no one people were excluded in the adaptation to diverse civilizations, for Clement ends his Epistle to the Corinthians with the words:

"The grace of Our Lord Jesus Christ be with you, and with all everywhere that are called by God."

The Evangelization of Nations and the Papacy

Since the relation between the Papacy and the missions has been so learnedly covered by that great missiologist, Andre V. Seumois, in his *La Papauté et les Missions au Cours des Six Premiers Siècles,* we hasten on to later periods. The few references we make to these periods are to reenforce the historical fact that the mandate to evangelize certain nations came from the Vicar of Christ.

Though there is much dispute concerning St. Patrick's birthplace there seems little doubt that in his dreams he kept seeing the children of Irish pagans extending their hands to him and asking for baptism. He seemed to hear their plaintive voices crying, "Come to us, come and save us." Despite this urgency, it was still necessary, if the missionary activity of Patrick was to be successful, that he be sent by the Vicar of Christ. This mandate was given to Patrick by Pope Celestine I. Patrick has been rightly called the Apostle of Ireland, but in the mind of that great soul there could be no Ireland without the Pope. Patrick went first to the Vicar of Christ, and from him received the name Patrick, "to signify that he would be Father of the citizens of heaven." The deep abiding faith which the Irish people have today in the Vicar of Christ derives from the utter dependence and fervent love Patrick himself bore to the one who made him a missionary.

As the Apostles were bound to Peter as their head, so the missionaries are bound to his successor as their head. This truth is particularly important when we consider the conversion of England. That country which broke with the Holy Father in the sixteenth century was nevertheless bound to the Papacy in its beginnings as closely as any other nation. The story of how Pope Gregory the Great became interested in the English people is known from the history of Venerable Bede.

Gregory saw some slave children of the English race in the Roman Forum. Struck with the beauty of the slave dealer's wares, with their blue eyes and golden hair, Gregory questioned the "owner" about them, understanding they were heathens. He said, "From what nation are they?"

"Angles," was the answer.

"Angels rather," said the saint.

To the further statements that they came from the province of *Deira* and that their king's name was Aella, he replied, "Of a truth they are *De Ira,* brought from wrath, and called to the mercy of Christ." Alluding to the king's name, Aella, he concluded, "Alleluia. The praises of God must be sung in those parts." The Pontiff then became interested in the conversion of the Angles. He commissioned the steward of the patrimony of the Church in Gaul to buy English slave boys, seventeen or eighteen years of age, to be trained for God as missionaries.

In the sixth year of his pontificate he made an attempt to convert the Angles of the North. In 596, he dispatched the prior of his monastery, Augustine, and a whole community of monks. He then wrote to Virgilius of Arles and to other bishops, exhorting them to do all they could to encourage the missionaries he was sending to the English. Augustine was consecrated bishop by Virgilius of Arles who was the Pope's vicar in Gaul. Gregory says of that Bishop, *"Data a me Licentia."* On June 1, 601, Gregory wrote to Augustine, the Bishop of the Angles, "O glory be to God in the highest who has caused the grain of wheat which has fallen to the ground to die and to bring forth fruit in abundance." Gregory then explained it was our Lord, "whose love sends us to seek even in the island of Britain for brothers whom we know not." Gregory also wrote letters of recommendation for his new missionaries to eleven bishops, three kings, and one queen of the Franks, so that they might everywhere on their journey meet with kindness and hospitality.

Gregory also gave one of the early principles of adaptation. In writing to England, he said, "The temples of God must not be destroyed; the idols must be destroyed but they themselves must be purified by the sprinkling of holy water and must have altars and relics placed in them." People will be more easily drawn to places to which they have become accustomed. Later on in his commentary on Job, Gregory thanks God for the faith of England: "Lo! the tongue of Britain which before could only utter barbarous sounds, has lately learned to make the Alleluia of the Hebrews resound in praise of God."

England was mindful for a long time afterward of the debt it owed to Gregory, and the century following his death it was decreed by the Council of Cliff in 747 that the feast "of our father Gregory should be kept as a holy day of obligation throughout England." This decree was renewed at the Council of Oxford in 1222.

Boniface and Gregory II

When a great missionary activity is launched, *"Cherchez le Pape."* This is true not only of Ireland and England, but also of Germany which was evangelized by St. Boniface, who was born Winifred in Devonshire, England, about 680. He came to Rome in the year 718. Gregory II and Boniface began having daily conferences on May 15, 719. Armed with the letters from Gregory II, Boniface was sent "to the wild nations of Germany to see whether the rude soil of their hearts, when tilled by the ploughshare of the gospel, would receive the seed of truth." In the letter of authorization to preach in Germany which Gregory addressed to Boniface, the Pope approved of his desire and wrote, "And so, in the Name of the undivided Trinity, and by the irrefragable authority of blessed Peter, the Prince of the Apostles, whose place we hold, go forth and preach to the nations in the bonds of error, the truth of both testaments."

In 722, Gregory II ordered Boniface back again to Rome and, on November 30, 722, consecrated him bishop. On December 4, 724, Gregory wrote a letter congratulating Boniface on his conversions. As Augustine of England had consulted with Gregory

I, so now Boniface in 726 conferred with Gregory II on various difficulties that had sprung up in the course of administering the young Church of Germany. In 739, Boniface received a letter from Gregory III dividing Bavaria into four provinces and bidding him in the Pope's name to hold a synod by the banks of the Danube.

Boniface continued his relations with the Papacy and in the year 742 wrote to Pope Zachary to congratulate him on his election. Then he asked Pope Zachary to confirm three bishoprics to the end that "present or future generations might not presume to interfere with these dioceses or violate the command of the Apostolic See." Boniface then had correspondence with the fourth of the Pontiffs, namely, Stephen II. In 755, he begged the Pontiff to excuse him for not writing sooner inasmuch as he had to restore thirty churches that had been burned by the pagans.

So often in writing mission history, an emphasis is so placed on the missionary that his credentials are forgotten. St. Paul gave as one of the tests of a preacher that he be *sent*. Even our Lord is called in the Old Testament "He who is sent." To the Apostles, He later says: "As my Father sent me, so also do I send you." Apostles of nations, missionaries must all be sent, and they can be adequately sent only by Him who is the Rock and the Key Bearer of the Kingdom of God.

As far as we know the truths of Christianity were first accepted, apart from the conversion of individual Slavs, by the Croats in Dalmatia. Their king, Porga, and his people were baptized by Pope John IV (640-642), himself a Dalmatian. But the conversion of what is today Eastern Europe was in large part due to SS. Cyril and Methodius. With the glorious names of Cyril and Methodius, Christianity in every Slavonic country from Russia and Poland to Dalmatia and the borders of Germany is connected either with authentic records of certain history or by means of a tradition. The two brothers, possibly themselves of Slavonic origin, were born at Salonica where there was a considerable Slav population. Cyril at one time had studied under Photius. Cyril had already gained fame as a missionary for he had labored among the Moslems, and later with his brother worked among the Khazars on the northern shores of the Black Sea. It remains to discover their relation to the Papacy.

In the year 867, Cyril was not a bishop and Methodius was not a priest. It was at this juncture that Pope Nicholas sent for them to come to Rome. The reason that they were asked to come to Rome was because they were introducing a liturgy into the Slavonic tongue which was very much out of the ordinary. This aroused the jealousy of the Germans.

When they came to Rome they brought the body of Pope Clement I, but Pope Nicholas died before they reached the Eternal City. There were in the West at this time a body of men known as the "trilinguists" who held that the only languages in which the liturgy of the Church could be conducted should be either Latin, Greek, or Hebrew. This senseless idea was carried so far that at the Council of Frankfort it was necessary to pronounce anathema against those who believed that God could be adored only in those languages. It was these theorists who opposed the Slavonic liturgy of Cyril. The brothers, however, pleaded their cause so well that the Pope not only approved of the new liturgy but placed a translation of the Gospels on the altar of St. Peter and took pleasure in assisting at Mass said in Slavonic.

Those who had falsely condemned Cyril and Methodius for not holding the true doctrine were answered by the Pope who declared, "They had recognized the rights of the Holy See and had done nothing against the Canons." The Pope continued: "He was resolved to consecrate Methodius bishop, knowing him to be of an upright mind and orthodox and send him back to the Slavs."

Hadrian II, when he heard of the trilinguists saying that God should be adored in only three languages because those were the languages that were written over the Cross, answered, "Let the Scriptures be fulfilled that all tongues shall praise the Lord and if anyone condemns the Slavonic writings let him be cut off from the Church." When Cyril died, February 14, 869, Methodius asked Hadrian II if he could take back his brother with him to be buried in the land where he was a missionary. When the people of Rome heard this request they asked the Holy Father that his remains be left in Rome. Moved by their words, Hadrian decided that the saint should be buried in St. Peter's in the very tomb that he had prepared for himself at the right of the high altar. When Methodius was consecrated archbishop by Hadrian, he returned to work among the Slavs and immediately did for the Slavs what Boniface did for the Germans, namely, establish a native clergy.

Because the German princes resented Methodius as an intruder, Methodius was imprisoned in the year 871 and cast into a dungeon, where he languished for two and a half years. Every effort was made to keep the Pope, to whom Methodius once appealed, in ignorance of what had passed. When, however, in the year 873 Pope John VIII learned the truth, he dispatched a legate to Bavaria. The German bishops were given to understand by John VIII that Methodius must be restored.

Benedict XII, in 1338, while at the Papal Court in Avignon received a special envoy from the Great Khan. He had come all the way from Khanbaliq in China, the capital of the Mongol empire. The Great Khan, in a letter addressed to the Holy Father, stated that he was sending an embassy, "for the purpose of opening the way for a frequent interchange of envoys between the Pope and us, and to remember us always in his holy prayers."

Father John of Pianoddi Carpine wrote that he "went to the Tartars and the other nations of the Orient by command of the Apostolic See."

It was March 12, 1245, that Father John received from the hands of Innocent IV a letter declaring that he, rather than a prince of the Church, had been selected as papal envoy to the courts of the Tartars. Despite the fact that he was then sixty-three years old, Father John and Father Benedict finally arrived at the Court of the Great Khan. Father John carried a letter from the Pope for the Great Khan who was now succeeded by Kuyuk Khan. The original letter of Kuyuk which Father John carried across Asian Europe still exists. It was rather a haughty letter which began with the words, "The Emperor of all men by the decree of heaven eternal sends this message to the great Pope that he may know and understand." Father John not only went at the bidding of

Innocent IV to Kuyuk Khan in 1245, but also returned to report to Innocent IV at Lyons in 1247.

About 1286, The Dominican Ricold of Montecorvino near Florence obtained a commission from Pope Honorius IV to preach to the Orientals. He traveled through Asia Minor, Mesopotamia, and India and was perhaps one of the most learned of all the travelers of his time.

The West was not to depend for long on vague rumors concerning the Tartars. With incredible speed they overran the countries of the central plain of Asia and then appeared in Europe. It was their belief like that of their conquering predecessors, the Huns of Attila, that they had been called "by oracle or vision to challenge dominion over the whole earth." In 1224, the Tartars rushed upon Russia and overran the country. Another invasion followed in the year 1236. In 1237, word reached Rome that they had slain no less than forty-two bishops in greater Armenia.

Another mission issuing from Innocent IV was given to the Franciscan, Lorenzo of Portugal, on March 5, 1245, recommending him and his companions to the Tartars. It is interesting that this letter was more doctrinal in character, as it explained the mission of our Lord and His constitution of a Vicar on earth of whom Innocent was now the representative.

On his return from the Tartars, Father John and his companions stopped in Russia at Kief on June 8, 1247, where the Russians declared themselves loyal to the Holy Father. Father John wrote of them, "They hold the Pope for their special Lord and Father and the Church of Rome for their lady and mistress . . . and for the same purpose they sent their ambassadors a letter by us unto our lord, the Pope."

Pope Innocent IV also sent Brother Andrew, a Dominican, and some of his companions to preach among the Tartars. On his return from the Tartars, Pope Innocent addressed the Dominicans on the necessity of sending the missionaries to the Tartars. So many offered themselves for the task that it came to be known as "the chapter of tears." Nor was it without good cause, for some wanted to be sent and begged the favor with tears while others grieved over the departure of the brethren whom they loved well. Such incredible hardships and martyrdoms — one group wept for joy on getting the coveted permission, the others bewailed their misfortune on being refused.

John of Montecorvino was not only the founder of the Vicariate of Peking, China; he was probably the first Catholic missionary in India from the West. As throughout history, the mandate for his mission came from Pope Nicholas III in 1278. Because of his success in East Tartary, Nicholas IV later appointed him papal legate and sent him back to the Orient with twenty-six letters and a large number of missionary recruits. Acting on information obtained from Franciscan and Dominican friars, such as Carpini, Rubruquis, and Andrew of Longumeau, the Popes now took in hand the organization of regular missionary expeditions to the most important sections of the huge Tartar Empire, to China, to Persia, to Southwestern Asia, and to different parts of Central Asia.

Friar John of Montecorvino established a Catholic mission in China which flourished under the Mongol rule and was certainly not blotted out until the Tartar dynasty came to an end.

After the missionary efforts of Innocent IV, the Popes kept in close touch with the Tartars. There was intercourse between them and Alexander IV, under whose pontificate they gave some satisfaction to Christendom. In his reign, too, there set out for the Far East the famous Venetian travelers, the brothers Maffeo and Nicolo Polo.

John of Montecorvino arrived in India in 1291, where he spent thirteen months, "wherein is the Church of St. Thomas the Apostle." After baptizing one hundred people in different regions, he set sail for China. Friar John arrived before the Great Khan in Peking in 1292 or 1293. John says, "I reached the great emperor of the Tartars who was called the Great Khan and by means of the letter of our Lord, the Pope Nicholas IV, invited him to adopt the Catholic Faith of Our Lord, Jesus Christ."

It was Pope Clement V who conferred upon Montecorvino the title of Archbishop of Khanvaliq and Patriarch of the entire Orient.

The same Pontiff ordered the minister general of the Friars Minor and his counsel to select seven learned and virtuous friars who would receive episcopal consecration and go to China as Montecorvino's consecrators and supplicants. When Clement V made him archbishop in 1307, he vested him with spiritual authority "over all souls dwelling in the entire empire of the Tartars." This was equivalent to saying that his province was equal to the Mongol empire. The first limitation of this empire came in 1318, when Pope John XXII erected the Archdiocese of Soltannia in Persia and placed a Dominican friar at its head. Eight years after the death of Montecorvino, some Catholic princes belonging to the Great Khan wrote to the Holy Father calling him "a capable and holy man."

Boniface VIII

Boniface VIII in the year 1299 wrote a letter to a number of Dominicans whom he called "our messengers to the land of the Saracens, pagans, and Greeks, to the lands of the Bulgarians, Cumans, Ethiopians, Syrians, Iberians, Alans, Gazari, Goths, Zicchi, Ruthenians, Jacobites, Nubians, Nestorians, Georgians, Armenians, Indians, Mosceliti, and Tartars, and to other eastern and northern nations." In sending them out, it was his hope "that these nations and these sons of subversion may by the antidote of illuminating preaching be converted to Him who is the true light."

Avignon

Not even in Avignon was there any decrease of the interest of the Holy See in the foreign missions. The migration to France and the creation of a preponderance of French cardinals and the consequent election of seven French Popes in succession did compromise the position of the Papacy in the eyes of the world in creating the suspicion that it had become the tool of France. The stress on the residence has thrown into the background the noble efforts of these much abused Pontiffs for the conversion of heathen nations. Their labors for the propagation of Christianity in India, China, Egypt, Nubia, Abyssinia, Barbary, and Morocco have not been fully appreciated. One treatise alone, among many, which indicates the interest of the Holy See in the missions, is to be found in the seven-volume work of P. Marcellino Da Civezza, entitled *Storia delle Missioni Francescane*. This work treats only of the Franciscan missions down to the sixteenth century. In the time of Clement VI, an effort was made to extend the sphere of the Church even to the farthest limits of Eastern Asia. The unwearied interest of the Avignon Popes in taking advantage of every favorable event in the East, from the Crimea to China, to promote the spread of Christianity by sending out missions and founding bishoprics is all the more admirable because of the great difficulties with which the Papacy at that time was beset.

The Papacy and the Missions in the Sixteenth and Seventeenth Centuries

On March 14, 1540, Ignatius, the founder of the Jesuits, said to Francis Xavier, "You know that by the order of His Holiness, two of us have to go to India." The Pope was Paul III.

The mission of the companions of Ignatius at the very beginning of the society was determined by the Pope. Rodriguez was sent to Siena, others were sent to Parma, another to Palestine. The Pope made St. Francis "Apostolic Nuncio to the islands of the Red Sea, the Persian Gulf, and the Indian Ocean, as well as the provinces and places of India this side of the Ganges and the promontory called the Cape of Good Hope, and beyond." The geography was bad, but what is important is the authority that was given by the Pope to St. Francis. Because many orders were beginning to take independent action and refusing to cooperate with one another, and because of the abuse of the right of patronage by Spain and Portugal, Pius V realized the necessity of creating a supreme central governing body in Rome. In order to free the missions from secular power, Pius V erected, in 1568, two congregations of cardinals for the Propagation of the Faith, one for the Protestant countries, the other for those overseas. The Congregation of the Propaganda which afterward developed activities of extraordinary usefulness may therefore be traced back to Pius V. It was Francis Borgia who, in an audience of May 20, 1568, suggested the Congregation for the conversion of the infidel.

In 1622, on Epiphany day, the most ancient festival which commemorates the call of the Gentiles to the faith, the work of the Congregation of the Propaganda was founded. This, too, was due to the act of the Pontiff, Gregory XV. For as the annals state, "Gregory XV, by divine providence, Pope, convinced the chief duty of his Pastoral office was the spread of the Christian Faith whereby men come to the Church in worship of the true God, created a congregation of thirteen Cardinals, two bishops, and a secretary to whom he entrusted and recommended the duty and responsibility of the Propagation of the Faith." Up to this time the missions had been chiefly manned by the religious orders which had received faculties to that effect from the Pope. It was now decided to turn not only to the generals of the orders but also to the nuncios.

The Congregation was given full powers to supervise all preaching and religious teachings in the missions, to appoint and dismiss missionaries, to deliberate on and take action in everything that concerned the spread of the Gospel to all parts of the globe.

The Sacred Congregation of Propaganda might truthfully be said to have rescued the missions from the stifling intervention of civil powers. Spain and Portugal, truly Catholic countries, were the great colonizing nations of the sixteenth century. The men, however, who executed the purposes of these nations in their colonizing efforts failed to recognize the full import of the mission of the Church and of the white man to the East. In their exploitation of the natives, they tended to refuse complete freedom of action of the missioners. The Padroados were established whereby the rulers of Spain and Portugal were given the privilege of designating the bishops for the mission sectors. The Popes saw the danger in this and declared all unexplored territory a vicariate of the Holy See, thus taking these rich fields away from the influence of the civil authorities. The government of this vast vicariate was given to the Sacred Congregation of Propaganda. In the future it was to be the task of this Congregation to map out the areas into separate fields of missionary effort called vicariates. From then until the present, it may be said that no missionaries have opened up any new fields of activity without the encouragement, permission, and guidance of the Holy See.

From this period on, the role of the Papacy in relation to the missions is better known. Who, for example, is ignorant of the impetus given to native clergy by Pius XI in naming cardinals from missionary lands? Pius XII made 116 dioceses out of vicariates apostolic while creating 47 vicars apostolic and 48 prefectures apostolic. John XXIII, the most missionary of modern Pontiffs, was once the national director of the Society for the Propagation of the Faith in Italy.

To be Catholic is to be missionary. But to be Catholic there must also be one governing head, as the many activities of the human body are directed by the head. The Papacy fulfills this role in the mission world. A negative confirmation is given that fact by the schism which denying its head ceased to be missionary, and by heresy which by losing its head permitted religion to degenerate into social work. It was to one man in the beginning that our Lord gave the commission to feed lambs and sheep; it is through one man since that new lambs and sheep are brought into the one fold, and that man is Peter — the Vicar of Christ.

3. Religious Societies, Dioceses, and the Missions

Biological life is catholic because the soul pervades every part of the body. If an arm were paralyzed or an eye blind, there would be "schism," "heresy," or "parochialism" in the organism. Ecclesiastical life is catholic because the Holy Spirit, the Soul of the Church, pervades all its members so that it acts as a unit.

> We too, all of us, have been baptized into a single body by the power of a single Spirit, Jews and Greeks, slaves and free men alike; we have all been given drink at a single source, the one Spirit (1 Cor 12:13).

The catholicity of the Church is inseparable from *extension*. This note has nothing to do with statistics. The Church was catholic on Pentecost, though it included only the Apostles and our Lady gathered in their midst. To be catholic means to be missionary, without any limitation or reservation.

The Kingdom of Heaven is like a leaven which a woman took and hid in three measures of meal until the whole was leavened. It does not seek a partial fermentation, but addresses itself to all humanity. It may not influence all mankind, but it is absolute in its potentiality to do so. Since the meal or the human lump has free will, there may not be a complete actualization of humanity, for in the last state of the world, our Lord warned: "Think ye when the Son of Man cometh that He shall find faith on earth?"

Financial Catholicity Toward Missionaries

At the very beginning of its history the Church ran up against a "financial heresy," namely, the refusal to allow the Holy Spirit to direct *all* the monies of the Church. There was an intent to keep some back as unhallowed, a resolve to limit the missionary activity of the Church through hoarding. The sin of Ananias was to lie against the Holy Spirit: "How is it that Satan has taken possession of thy heart, bidding thee defraud the Holy Spirit by *keeping back some of the money?*" (Acts 5:3.) It was not only the missionary activity of the Church which was hindered; it was the Holy Spirit who was *defrauded,* and the Holy Spirit was defrauded by Ananias lying to the Vicar of Christ.

Thus we see the catholicity of the Church receive its first rude shock in the Finance Department. Some of its money was to be unconsecrated, unhallowed, set aside, and untouched by the Holy Spirit. St. Peter here suggests that the devil, not "business prudence," was behind such a suggestion. Nor would inspired Scripture ever have painted this picture of "keeping back" money if it were not always to be a danger in the Church.

We can recall a meeting of all the directors of the Propagation of the Faith of the world in Rome when the list of allocations to all dioceses and missionary societies was prepared for the Holy Father. The General Secretary of the Propagation said: "The happiest day of our lives here at the Congregation for the Propagation of the Faith is when we have no money left in our treasury." Nothing the Catholics of the world give to the Holy Father is "kept back" for investment, for "sinking funds," for a "rainy day."

A suggestion was once made to the Congregation for the Propagation of the Faith that each year it invest $50,000. Then at the end of twenty years there would be a million-dollar investment, the interest of which could be given to its missionaries. Archbishop Sigismundi asked with pathos: "And what will happen to souls during those twenty years as we pile up the investment?"

This does not mean that there must be no security, no provision for future buildings, no reserves for unusual demands. All of these are essential in our complex modern world. But it does mean that all who are interested in the catholicity of the Church will scrupulously watch any undue "keeping back" from immediate needs of the Missions. *God forbid that there would ever come a day when our missionaries who struggle against famine, poverty, and persecution should ever live on the interest of investments placed by the Ananiases at home.* Interests or profits on investments have their place, but one exception must always be made: no missionary, whoever he be, must ever be compelled to live on the returns from stocks, bonds, or real estate. Others, yes, within a reasonable limit, but the heralds of the Gospel — No! What is spent on them should be *capital,* and what is capital but the sum the faithful have given to make Christ known and loved in the world?

If a missionary bishop in any territory under the Congregation of the Propagation of the Faith invested the allocation he received, his allocation would be cut down or eliminated the following year. Thus does the Church, in her official missionary capacity, frown upon a "keeping back" and bless the virtue of financial catholicity.

When the Jews gathered manna, they were allowed to gather only what was necessary for the day; if they hoarded more, it rotted. Investments to protect the equipment necessary for educating and training missionaries are good, but the same rule applied to the heralds of the Gospel is not good. Money hoarded at their expense is to be likened to excess manna; it will not prosper. The mission of the Church is *first.* Our missionaries in the field are our prime concern. No clipped bond coupons, no returns from stocks for them. They are in a special category. We at home are their servants. It may be easy for us to find a Sapphira who will agree that something should be "kept back" from the missionaries. But such a meeting of minds among financial advisers Scripture describes as follows: "What is this conspiracy between you to put the Spirit of the Lord to the test?" May our interest in missionaries always be so spiritual that they will never have to live on our "interest."

Financial Catholicity in Parishes

There was a rich man once that was clothed in purple and linen, and feasted sumptuously every day. And there was a beggar, called Lazarus, who lay at his gate . . . (Lk 16:19, 20).

Are there not poor mission churches at the doors of our American parishes? Are they not full of the sores of economic want and spiritual hunger? Does the gate or the door of the rich man mean a distance of one hundred feet, but not a distance of a thousand miles? Whatever is beyond the gate is "mission." Is there not a strict spiritual obligation on the builders of rectories, field houses, convents, and "wall to wall" carpeting in seminaries to be mindful that the Lazarus of Nigeria, the Lazarus of Korea, the Lazarus of Vietnam, and the Lazarus of New Guinea are knocking at our bronze gates? It is not just the rich landowners of Latin America who aggrandize wealth, who are pricked in conscience by the *Mater et Magistra,* but even ourselves.

May the Holy Spirit so guide us in the United States that we do not fall under the condemnation of the Angel of the Apocalypse who said to the Church of Laodicea: " 'I am rich,' thou sayest. . . . But in the eyes of the Lord, thou art a beggar, blind and naked; and my counsel to thee is to come and buy from me what thou needest; gold, proved in the fire, to make thee rich" (Ap 3:17, 18). If a parish is rich, it is entitled to a more beautiful church than a parish that is economically poor. But it is not entitled, in these days, to a luxurious church, when a financial retrenchment would give a taber-nacle in the Sudan to the Eucharistic Lord or a motorcycle to a priest in Australia for his parish of 125,000 square miles.

Catholicity is the secret of the inspiration for this sharing with the poor faithful. See how God made the organism in such a way that the body temperature is kept even in all parts. So with the Spirit in the Church. Our Body, if we live in a big city, is not only in the suburbs; it is in South Africa, it is in Burma, it is wherever there is need.

Catholicity, as regards finances, means that the materialities of the Church are to be held "in common" by the Church: "For neither was there anyone needy among them." Such sharing in the wealth by all members of the Church had grace as its cause: "Great grace was among them all" (Acts 4:33). Partaking of monies, like unto the partaking of bread, has its root in the deep Christlike spirituality which pervades the Church. There was no want or poverty in the early Church because of this grace. The equality typified in the daily collection of manna was literally fulfilled among them.

Bringing this spirit up to date, the encyclical of His Holiness Pope John XXIII, *Mater et Magistra,* emphasizes the necessity of economically rich nations coming to the support of impoverished nations. But if the nations without grace are bidden to do this, does it not, as the Holy Father states, more severely bind the faithful in the Church? Is a diocese in the United States justified, before the Spirit of Christ, in excessive spending on cathedrals, when a saving of just $10,000 would build a chapel in the mission lands where the missionaries average over a hundred converts per priest? When the African bishops turn away 50 percent of their applicants to the priesthood because they cannot afford to pay $150 a year tuition, is it lawful for us to spend millions for ecclesiastical structures without a retrenchment or a deduction of even 1 percent for the Lord who lives in huts in Africa? It is not the expenditure in millions that is to be censured. It is rather in not leaving the sheaf in the field as the Lord commanded in the Old Testament; it is the muzzling of the ox of the missionary that treads the corn in Asia that is to be unblessed.

Will the God of righteousness and justice bless the ecclesiastical economists who make such prodigal expenditures, when $100,000 would build a seminary in Asia? Is not a priest in the United States drinking of the common chalice and the faithful breaking the Bread of Life? This spirit of catholicity does not mean that the Church in the United States shall reduce itself to the conditions of Central Africa, or that a bishop shall sell his crozier to buy rings for African nuns who are taking perpetual vows. It only means that, as the God in the Old Testament said, the ox was not to be muzzled as he treaded the wheat, and the gleaners were to leave one sheaf in the field. So those of us who live in rich fields must leave something for the poor gleaners of the mission world. Under the New Covenant, St. Paul describes this as the Gospel of Christ: "that generosity which you show in sharing your goods with all men" (2 Cor 9:13).

Personnel Catholicity

Every cell in the body works; every member contributes to the well-being of the whole. So in the Mystical Body of Christ, though there be a differentiation of function, there is still the same Spirit. As there can be no hoarding of money in the Body of Christ, so also there may be *no hoarding of personnel*. As the "keeping back" of alms is contrary to the Spirit of Christ, so also is the "keeping back" of priests, Brothers, and Sisters from the mission of the Church. As the manna was to be consumed when given, so vocations are to be utilized when bestowed. The *Lord of the Harvest* asked: "How is it that you are standing here and have done nothing all the day?" (Mt 20:6.)

Some missionary societies give a beautiful example of the catholic spirit, setting a rule for themselves that not more than 10 percent of their total missionary society will be kept from mission fields. The African Mission Society which has set this goal for itself knows that when God gives a missionary vocation it is precious and is not to be wasted.

When the missionary activities of St. Paul had closed and he was locked in a Roman dungeon, his mind went out to the missions of the Church as he wrote: "Here, then, is one who wears chains in the Lord's service, pleading with you to live as befits men called to such vocations as yours." Fidelity to the summons is an absolute Divine requirement. If God calls a man to the missions, to the missions he should go. If Christ were to walk through our rectories and religious houses today and find anyone who was not being utilized for the work to which he was called, would He accept the excuse, "Nobody has hired us"? Or would He say, as He actually did say: *"Away with you to the vineyard like the rest"* (Mt 20:7)? The Lord apparently accepts no excuses for failure to tend the vineyard of the Church.

But this note of catholicity refers not only to the religious who might very well make greater sacrifices of personnel for the sake of the Church; it refers also to the general problem of vocations. One wonders why there is a dearth of vocations in the Church. Many reasons can be given, but one in particular is worthy of consideration. *Could it not be that there is a decrease of vocations because those that are given to us are not utilized as they should be?*

In order to be on solid ground in a question of this kind, one must remain close to Scripture. The Acts of the Apostles seem to indicate that with the growth of the Church there came a murmuring about material things, for enlargement often brings with it either sloth or worldliness. Some vocations were ruined because of a love of money — those of Judas, Ananias, and Sapphira. Then there came a complaint by Greek-speaking disciples against those who spoke Hebrew, which brought on a crisis concerning vocations. Were their widows to be told that they ought to be concerned only with eternal life, thus leaving grievances unredressed? Or was it not the duty of the Apostles to diminish their spiritual labors and give up their time and strength to the organization of catholic charities and the distribution of daily needs? The answer of the Apostles was: "It is too much that we should have to forego preaching God's Word and bestow our care upon tables" (Acts 6:2).

In verse four "the ministry of preaching" is opposed to administration or "the care of tables." The passage gives necessary warning to the ministers of God's Word not to spend too much time and strength upon secular work, even though it be a needful work. Laity were to be chosen, "while we devote ourselves to prayer, and the ministry of preaching" (Acts 6:4). By prayer the priest draws from the Fountain of Truth and Divine Strength; in preaching he gives forth that which he has received. Without the inner communion with God, there would be no power to prevail over the hearts of men.

The administration was then given over "to seven men who are well spoken of, full of the Holy Spirit and of wisdom" (Acts 6:3). Administration and philanthropy were to be committed to seven who were chosen from among the faithful by the bishops.

After this decision had been taken, the Acts note the effect upon the Church, namely, its *growth*. "By now the word of God was gaining influence, and the number of disciples in Jerusalem was greatly increasing; many of the priests had given their allegiance to the Faith" (Acts 6:7). In other words, there was an *increase in conversions,* an *increase in vocations*. There is also every indication that the men who were chosen were better able to serve the counting table than the Apostles.

It should be seriously considered how far the growth of the Church, conversions, and the increase of vocations had been weakened because of worldly cares. Since Scripture states that the transferring of considerable administration from the bishops and priests resulted in conversions and an increase of priestly vocations, may one not reverse the inspiration of Scripture and ask if a decline of conversions and vocations is not due in part to excessive administration which deprives the clergy of prayer and preaching the Word of God? Is there not today in the Church a tendency to waste the sacredness of the priesthood on tasks which could very well be done by men chosen from the faithful in the Church? If the early Church scrupled at supplying the needs of widows and surrendered that work to others, should there not be a query in the modern Church as to whether a priest should be used for the direction of insurance, architecture, finances, radio and television, real estate, etc.?

As the Lord of the Harvest looks down on us, may He not well inquire: "Why all this waste?" St. Paul said to Timothy: "Has God not called us to a vocation of holiness?" (2 Tm 1:9.) If we have not been faithful in using the few vocations that are given to us, how can the Lord of the Harvest entrust us with more?

One bishop of the Western World, when he came into his diocese, told the assembled priests that he had had only six vocations the previous year. He then asked any priest in the diocese who was willing to lead a life of sacrifice on the missions and who had the spiritual and physical capacities to present himself, and he would be allowed to serve the Church in other lands. Because he could ill afford to give any clergy, he had to take some from administrative posts that could better be filled by the laity. Due to this trust, the following year the Lord gave the diocese sixty vocations.

A decree of the Sacred Congregation of the Consistory (November 18, 1910) spoke of "many institutions which have been founded in the Catholic world with the object of assisting the faithful in their temporal needs, notably banks, credit unions, rural banks, savings banks." Though the Congregation approves these and "shows favor to these various undertakings," nevertheless it legislates: "It is not right that they should divert clerics from the duties of their state and office, involve them in material affairs and even expose them to the cares, anxieties and dangers which are inseparable from these occupations."

Administrative tasks are absolutely essential, but it is the doctrine of the Church that they be complemented by the spiritual, "It may be that several among you are daily engaged in the difficult struggle to avoid being overcome by administrative duties, and to find the means and the time required for the true care of souls. Now, though organizations and administration are also undoubtedly invaluable aids in carrying out the apostolate, still they must be relegated to their proper place and subordinated to the spiritual ministry and to those duties that are truly, properly and actively pastoral" (Discourse of Pius XII to the Preachers of Rome, February 6. 1940). "We mean to put you on your guard against an excessive bureaucracy" (Pius XII, *A.A.S.,* Vol. 43, 1951, p. 112).

4. *Being Mission-Minded*

In days of prosperity, the Church has administrators; in days of adversity, shepherds. America is the richest country in the world; it is, therefore, very natural for those engaged in missionary work to think of it in terms of procures, diocesan missionary offices, money-gatherers, publicists, printers, and investors. Pragmatism, which is the philosophy of the useful, could grow and did grow in the soil of America.

But those who are summoned to be missionaries have the obligation to resist this current: "Be not conformed to the world; travail until Christ be formed in the hearts of men unto the obedience of the Holy Spirit."

Just as there comes a time in the life of priests and religious when they must make retreats and get back again to their spiritual beginnings, so there comes a time in the missionary activities of any nation when it must reexamine its soul.

The True Mission Spirit Is Based on the Love of God

Knowledge and love are not the same. One can *know* the missions and not *love* them; one can *publicize* them and not *serve* them; one can promote missions and not *propagate* them. This distinction is so fundamental that our Lord thanked His Father that He had hidden the truth of His mission from the university professors and the self-wise and given it to those who know because they love. The Church of Laodicea, which boasted of its works and finances, received from the Spirit the message: "I counsel thee to buy of Me gold tried by fire." The Church had knowledge, but no love. Our Lord was *not in it.* He was at the door *knocking* — on the outside. As St. Paul said, there can be a philanthropy that is not charity, a faith which is useless without spiritual profit; so working for the missions is not the same as being mission-minded.

No one can bring new life into being without fire, enthusiasm, passion. Virgin though she was, Mary conceived not through human fire, but by the Fire of the Spirit. Even the Church was begotten in Fire on Pentecost.

Therefore, the missions will spread, vocations to foreign areas will increase, the Church in Asia and Africa will grow, if there is a love, passion, and dedication to the missions which surpasses all conferences, all pamphleteering, and the use of rock and roll singers to gather crowds to our missionary fund-raising meetings.

Would Matthew ever have left his income tax office and been martyred as a missionary if the Spirit had not moved him to be un-American about money? Would the planting of Paul and the watering of Apollo, or the turning of Lydia's house over to the conversion of Europe ever have been, without the operation of the Spirit? Would the Lord ever have said that a Magdalene's reform and self-abnegation in pouring precious perfume over His feet would be known until the end of time, had it not been for the Spirit of Love?

Suffering and Trial Go With Mission-Mindedness

The test of how much love we put into the missions depends on how much it incorporates us to "the fellowship of the Cross." These trials can come from the devil, from God, from within the Church and from without. If we are serious about pushing back the frontiers of Satan in pagan lands, the devil will not leave us alone. The more beachheads we establish against polygamy, animism, polytheism, the more armor and steel hell will send against us. The devil will leave us alone if we do nothing. Archbishop Sigismundi of the Congregation of the Propagation of the Faith said at an annual meeting, "There is no one at this meeting who is devoted to the missions who does not have a heavy cross." Cardinal Stritch told the writer after His Eminence had lost his arm, "Now I know that suffering goes with the Propagation of the Faith in pagan lands."

The mission procurator, the mission superior, the director of the Propagation of the Faith who loves the Church of the future, knows very well that God will trim the sails of his egotism and self-complacency to make him more devoted still. The Crucified prunes, purges, uses false brethren, and the most unexpected means from the most unexpected quarters to tear down the wall of partition between Him and us that we may love more His missions on the earth.

Actually there is a very intimate relationship between the Mission of the Divine Persons in our soul and the relations of our soul to the missions of the Church. In both cases, the greater the purity, the closer the ties; in both, a purification ends in greater consecration; in both, the greater the separation from the material, the richer the spiritual harvest; in both, God is absent with His consolations, but makes His power more present.

The Mission-Minded Are Catholic

The more the soul is possessed with *"Jesu, voluptas cordium,"* the more catholic it becomes; the less it serves particular causes or groups, the more it thinks in terms of the whole Mystical Body, rather than of its arm or a leg. What a beautiful example of this is provided in a certain bishop in Africa who asked to be made auxiliary of his diocese, in order that he might serve a native African bishop whom he hoped would be named in his place. The Spirit of Love will also dictate that our alms be not directed exclusively to missionaries from the United States. Some favoritism there must be, for we must protect and prosper the culture in which we live. But missionaries from the United States are only 2 percent of the total number of missionaries. Only 1 percent of the missionaries in Africa are from the United States; only 1 percent of the missionaries in Asia are from the United States. He who loves the missions will love them as *catholic,* that is, all of them, wherever they be. Nationalism almost ruined the missions in the nineteenth century; it must not endanger them in the twentieth. Where would the Church in the United States be today if 100 years ago Austria helped only Austrian missionaries, and Germany helped only German missionaries, and France helped only French missionaries? The Council of Baltimore said that next to the aid of Providence, The Society for the Propagation of the Faith of France was the principal cause of the growth of the Church in the United States. As God loves all, as the Mystical Body is made up of all nations, so in addition to helping our own, we will not forget those who are serving the cross of Christ though they were not born under our flag.

Missionaries Are an Inspiration to Be Mission-Minded

The mission societies at home do not make the mission spirit of the missionaries in the field; it is the missionaries who create the mission spirit. What an inspiration they give us! Poverty like unto the Master in many instances, tonsures stained with blood, cassocks tugged at by the hungry, nuns in the wildest part of the Amazon in a few years recruiting 100 native vocations, Brothers and catechists opening church doors at 3 a.m. to instruct the faithful.

The spirit of martyrdom enkindles the zeal of our missionaries, not just the physical shedding of blood, but the spending of themselves for the love of the *Sitio* on the Cross. In a later chapter it will be observed that today we have not only "wet martyrs" who shed their blood, but "dry martyrs" who die a thousand deaths without shedding blood. Some day we will have to have a new definition of martyrdom to fit the new witnessing to Christ in our age. There are two instances of dry martyrdom at least that are mentioned in the Breviary; one speaks of a martyrdom of love, and the other is the martyrdom attributed to St. Martinus whose feast is celebrated on November 11.

> O sanctissima anima, quam etsi gladius persecutoris
> non abstulit, palma tamen martyrii non amisit.

In each country where the spirit of Calvary has been canalized into its missionaries, there has been an increase of conversions. In one area of Kenya, where there were persecutions and martyrs, the conversions per year jumped from 5 per priest to 100 per priest; in Korea and Vietnam, where there has been persecution under the Communists, conversions per priest in some areas have jumped to as high as 106 a year.

Dr. Thomas A. Dooley was led to sacrifice himself for the suffering of Asia because he looked at the people, not through American eyes, but rather through Christlike eyes. One day on a plane, he took out a paper on which he had written thoughts some time before; after spending months with the poor, he realized how much more true were the words now than ever:

> Most people in Asia will go to bed hungry tonight.
> Most people in Asia live in grinding poverty.
> Most people in Asia have never seen a doctor.
> Most people in Asia believe anything different would be better than what they have and are determined to get it.
> Most people in Asia have never known civil liberties.
> Most people in Asia believe that the freedom of enterprise means the right of the Western colonial powers to exploit them.
> Most people in Asia distrust people with white skins.
> Most people in Asia are determined never again to be ruled by foreigners.

Mission-mindedness is developed in one of two ways: either by going on the missions or by deep spirituality. It would seem at first that it would be necessary to be a missionary in order to be mission-minded; it is not to be forgotten that Pauline Jaricot was never on the missions, nor was the Little Flower, who was made the Patroness of the Missions, ever farther from her home in France than Rome. The more intense the development of the Spirit of Christ in the soul, the greater the anxiety and the impatience to establish the regnancy of Christ in human hearts.

The other way is to spend oneself and be spent on the missions. It is interesting to note how often army, navy, and air force chaplains become absorbed in the Propagation of the Faith work after they have served a round of duty in the mission lands.

Application of the Mission Spirit

    1. To Meetings of Mission Sending Societies and Meetings of Directors of The Society for the Propagation of the Faith

    2. To Vocations

   1. In our missionary gatherings, it is necessary to give some

limited time to such subjects as magazines, public relations, "methods of the marketplace," "investments," promotion, and publicity. But these may never be a substitute for the purpose of the gathering: to save souls in mission lands. Granted the need of imitating some worldly methods; even these can become harmful when the acquired habit of naturally good works is made a substitute for the supernatural virtue of charity.

What an example we find in the missionary gathering at Antioch, mentioned in the Acts and attended by Simon Niger (was it he who carried the Cross?), Lucius of Cyrene (was it he who is mentioned in Rom 16:21?) Manahan, Saul, and others (Acts 13:2). After fasting and prayer, there was a *sending forth* of missionaries, two of whom became notable: Barnabas and Saul. Future meetings of mission sending societies could repeat this departure ceremony and reaffirm before the world that we exist first and foremost for the evangelization of the world.

A forthcoming gathering of mission sending societies might consider problems that are *more missionary* such as the following:

Should not all religious societies and communities impose on themselves a tax of at least 10 percent of their personnel for assignment to mission lands?

Should Brothers in mission lands be given the power of deacons, and thus assigned to baptizing and distributing Holy Communion?

Should not seminaries for missionaries from the United States be opened in mission lands, in order that youths be less accustomed to the luxuries of American life, more habituated to the rigors of missionary life, and through the food they eat, the fields and the people they see, the language they speak, become identified with those in the missions whom they are to serve?

Should not the Eastern Rite be introduced into China when Communism perishes, because it gives the people a greater participation in the liturgy, and is better adapted to the gestures, the language, and the psychology of the people? Should Latin priest missionaries not be made bi-ritual for this purpose?

Should it not be recommended through the hierarchy that the Church enact legislation that only priests, Brothers, and Sisters who have served on the missions should be eligible for any disciplinary or administrative office in a strictly missionary society?

Should not graduates of colleges of both men and women be invited to spend two years in mission work under the direction of the bishop in a mission land?

Should not a new apologetics be written for the millions of Buddhists, Confucianists, Hindus, and Moslems in which these religions are used not as an object of attack, but as a natural base of operations to introduce the supernatural order? The East has the same right to use Confucius, for example, as a starting point for the faith as we to use Aristotle or Plato.

Is not the time ripe to open a general seminary in the United States for Negro missionaries to Africa?

Should not the philosophy courses in missionary seminaries stress the Oriental thinkers more than Kant, Hume, and Locke, in order that the future missionary will understand the thought of the Eastern World?

2. *To Vocations.* The United States has over 8000 missionaries outside its borders, which represents less than 2 percent of the total number of missionaries. How to increase this number is a major concern of all dioceses and missionary institutes. As one studies vocation literature, one finds some appeals unworthy of members of the Mystical Body of Christ. To appeal for vocations in the name of the "upbeat"; to photograph in a glamorous fashion the more beautiful novices, as if the Divine Bridegroom chooses souls as Hollywood chooses bodies; to appeal to the young by showing pictures of novices on tennis courts, instead of appealing to their desire for sacrifice and union with the Crucified; to make it appear through falsified statistical studies that 73.6 percent of the missionary vocations are due to promotional material mailed from a central office; to resort to "spiritual cheesecake" to romanticize the missions, is to forget that vocations to the missions have their origin in God's call when we were born. As St. Paul told the Galatians:

He who had set me apart from the *day of my birth,* saw fit to make his Son known in me, so that I could preach his Gospel among the Gentiles.

St. Paul did not say that God called him at the martyrdom of Stephen or on the road to Damascus, but when he was born. What we do, therefore, in vocation work is merely to develop, unfold, ripen, and fructify a vine that already exists, and one which for want of watering may not entwine itself in the divine vineyard. Taking young people on picnics may win them to their benefactor, but it will not win them to Christ.

Youth today has a potential for sacrifice that has not been tapped. The appeal of Nazism, Fascism, and Communism was to youth and on the basis of dedication, consecration, and sacrifice to a race, a state, or a party. It would almost seem as if dictators had snatched the crucifix from our hands, torn the Christ from it, held it aloft, and said to youth: "Take up your cross daily and follow the dictator." Too often, we have, on the contrary, taken the Christ without His cross, a Redeemer without His means of Redemption, a Teacher to be equated with Buddha, Confucius, Tao.

When the fig trees of youth which have the potency to bear fruit do not do so, it is well to remember that our Lord did not say to the barren fig tree: "Put perfume on it," but, "Dung it, prune it, cut it." To use worldly appeals for a vocation is to spoil the seed the Lord has planted and to drown out His voice with "sounding brass and tinkling cymbals." And, if there be a high mortality rate in seminaries, could it not be due in part to the fact that they find less picnics, less glamor, less handsome companions, less flattery than they were promised in the vocation appeals? But if the appeal to become a missionary is spiritual, then the seminarian will be filled with that Divine impatience to drink the cup the Father gives — a cup filled with "the wine that germinates virgins."

Furthermore, the responsibility of missionary societies to their young members is frightening. The young joined in order to "preach among the heathens." Suppose the president of a medical school had the same authority over graduates that the superior of a mission society has over Sisters, Brothers, or priests. Suppose 50 percent or 20 or even 10 percent of them were never allowed to practice medicine. Suppose they were made bookkeepers, accountants, letter-openers, map-makers, public-relations officials, or convention attenders? Would they not explode into frustrated, mixed-up neurotics and psychotics? During World War II many doctors who were assigned to other duties than those for which they were prepared had mental breakdowns.

If then a youth joins a missionary society with the express purpose of becoming a missionary, does he not have the same right to become a missionary as a student has to become a dentist after finishing dental school? Is there not a breaking of a trust, a failing in justice, a miscarriage of duty in keeping him caged in Jerusalem when he is summoned to "Samaria and the ends of the earth"? This does not mean that he should never be assigned to other tasks, such as a teacher or treasurer, but these should be subsequent to the fulfillment of his vocation for at least a time. It is different with those societies whose purpose is not wholly missionary, and where there is no volunteering for the missions. The Society of African Missions makes it a matter of conscience to keep the bare minimum of priests at home and the maximum on the missions. Their very commendable ratio is one priest at home for ten priests on the missions. Contrast this with some other missionary groups that have over three priests at home for every ten on the missions.

The call to youth to follow Christ the King is inseparable from His cross, for all four evangelists point out that His Kingship was the cause of His death. For that reason, the inscription "King" was nailed to that tree thrown into the bitter waters of the world's sin. The vocation to be a missionary, like any other vocation, is an appeal from the cross to carry the cross. Any ginger bread appeal to youth on the grounds of adventure is to forget that on Mt. Tabor our Lord did not speak to His seminarian-apostles on either the splendor of His body or the joys of His mind, but on nails, thorns, scourges, and a crucifixion in Jerusalem.

Our missionaries will increase as we understand the mystery of the unworldliness of a vocation.

> Let us fix our eyes on Jesus, the origin and the crown
> of all faith, who, to win his prize of blessedness,
> endured the Cross and made light of its shame, Jesus,
> Who now sits on the right of God's throne.
>
> (Heb 12:2, 3)

Conclusion

As missionaries, and as aides to missionaries, we are to "go into the world." But by its nature, this implies a sacrifice. The words which Scripture attributes to our Lord coming into the world are "Sacrifice and oblation thou wouldst not, but a *body* thou hast fitted to me" (Heb 10:5). In place of the sheep, goats, and bullocks of the Passover sacrifice, there would be the sacrifice through a body given to Him by His Mother. He became a Victim, not merely at Calvary, but at Bethlehem as well. Pilate gave Him a cross at his palace gate, but Mary gave Him one at the crib. The Woman opened to Him the door of miseries; the executioners on Golgotha closed it. The cross of Mary was flesh and blood; the cross of Calvary was wood and steel.

Missionary activity does not begin in Bolivia, Kenya, Borneo; it begins at home, at the birth of a vocation, at the Nazareth of a novitiate. Seminarians are not to be told they must be prepared to sacrifice themselves when they receive "obedience"; in the mission field, they should exchange one form of oblation for another. Maybe the Nativity was harder on Mary than Calvary; there was no record of her being troubled at Calvary; but she was troubled at the thought of making God possible; for unless she gave Him a body He would not be a Victim-Priest.

A practical application of this would be for superiors to give "obediences" early in the seminary training, due allowances being understood for changed missionary conditions or new demands. If a young man or woman in the novitiate were told that his cross would be Kenya, or Laos, or Japan, he could immediately begin studying the language, geography, and psychology of the people; he could pray daily for his future mission and learn to love it as the Lord loved the world before He looked out on it with human eyes.

There is a dramatic feeling of authority and power in a religious superior who assigns the "obedience" after the ordination or novitiate. But the surrender of pride would have its compensations in the exaltation of missionaries prepared for their tasks. If Calvary began at Bethlehem then let the "obedience" begin in the novitiate.

Another application of the mission spirit is to spend as many resources as we can on the missions. Missionary societies with the spirit of the Lord Jesus will never hoard up any reserves of personnel and investments beyond the point of that which is prudently necessary. It is easy for those in charge of funds to be individually poor, but to be corporately selfish; to practice the vow of poverty personally, but as the custodian of corporate finances to have an avaricious spirit. Nothing functions well if the superior has the spirit of Christ in the chapel and the spirit of Wall Street in the office.

What a tragedy it would be for the missions if a day ever came when a mission society had, say, several million dollars invested in Wall Street, or owned the major interest in a luxury hotel. *Quod Deus avertat!*

Why would it be serious? Because our Lord said: "Where your treasure is, there is your heart also." If the heart is not in the missions, what does it profit us to have investments?

The luxury of investments is no less harmful than the luxury of personnel, or the sentencing through holy obedience of young women who enter the religious life to serve the missions to the routine task of opening letters, or the assigning of potential missionaries to promotion work beyond the Christlike minimum which a true missionary-consciousness dictates. If we appeal to the people to give their superfluities then we must spurn our own.

The Holy See is an example of the true prodigality for the missions. Each year the Holy Father and his Congregation for the Propagation of the Faith spend all the money given to him by the faithful. Nothing is hoarded; nothing is kept. Investment is in souls, not in stocks.

And here the plea ends to be mission-minded. Our vocation as mission procures, promoters, and directors of the pontifical mission works is noble; it becomes profane as we allow it to freeze either in knowledge or in administration that is divorced from the daily crucifixion of the missionaries. We handle money, but we are not money changers; we read our missionary press releases, but our ears hear the groans of the poor and the sighs of the lepers. The madness of the Gospel alone will make us sane; the deep sense of being untiring coadjutors of God alone makes us worthy of serving His heralds in Asia and Africa; our priests, Brothers, Sisters, and faithful in Chinese labor camps, Vietnamese prisons, and Korean cellars are witnessing to Christ. That same Christ is calling to us in the wine of His Truth, the fire of His love, the Blood of His Redemption to be worthy of those whom it is our joy to serve.

5. *America Was Once a Foreign Mission*

When an adult is shown a cradle in which he was rocked for two years of his infancy, he finds it difficult to reconcile his present independence with his past dependence. It is still more difficult for America to realize that, within the lifetime of many of its bishops and priests and faithful, America was once a mission country.

1. America was once a missionary country or a "foreign mission." The United States was under the Propaganda and, therefore, was regarded by the Holy See as a "foreign mission" until 1908.

2. While the United States was a "foreign mission," the bishops of America begged, pleaded, implored, and pressed The Society for the Propagation of the Faith to come to their relief to build churches, seminaries, convents in exactly the same way the bishops of the "foreign missions" of Vietnam, Japan, India, Africa, Marshall Islands, Burma, Pakistan, etc., implore the bishops of the United States today, through The Society for the Propagation of the Faith, to come to their aid.

3. The Society for the Propagation of the Faith continued to give large sums of money to the bishops of the foreign mission of the United States, for which they expressed their gratitude, saying that the Church would not have prospered in the United States without the Society for the Propagation of the Faith.

4. The bishops of the United States promised during those days that if aid were forthcoming then, that some day, thanks to the blessings of Providence, they would aid other "foreign missions" even more bounteously than they themselves were aided.

5. The bishops of the United States have kept their promise. Like

150

the faith of the Romans, their generosity is now spoken of throughout the world.

1. The United States Was a "Foreign Mission."

In the year 1822, there were only twenty-four states in the Union. The Church then had one archdiocese and only eight dioceses. The Catholics numbered about 200,000.

In that same year, May 3, the feast of the Finding of the Holy Cross, at the Hotel de la Poste at Lyons, France, two priests and ten laymen met to found The Society for the Propagation of the Faith. The first donations of The Society for the Propagation of the Faith amounted to $4,583.

The Society for the Propagation of the Faith regarded America as the principal foreign mission of the world, because two thirds of that amount was divided between Louisiana and Kentucky, the amount they divided being $3,722. The other one third was given to aid Asia.

2. The Bishops of the United States Implored Aid From The Society for the Propagation of the Faith in the Same Terms the Bishops of Africa, Asia, Oceania, etc., Beg Today From the Bishops of the United States Through The Society for the Propagation of the Faith.

For example, Bishop England of Charleston wrote to The Society for the Propagation of the Faith: "The foreign contributions are applied to the following purposes: (1) For the foundation and upkeep of seminaries to educate a native clergy. (2) For the education and support of the convents that have charge of the education of girls. (3) For the establishment of colleges and schools to secure the religious and scientific training of boys (in some places these colleges have already become such a source of income that they help to support the seminaries). (4) For the building of churches, or assisting in this, in poor and needy parishes. (5) For sending missionaries to the dispersed Catholics to give them an opportunity to receive the Sacraments."

On February 23, 1828, The Society for the Propagation of the

Faith received a letter from Bishop John DuBois of New York, stating what he called the most urgent need of the foreign mission of America at the time, namely, paying the debt of $28,000 on the Cathedral of New York. *"Quid vero dicam de gravi aere alieno, quo cathedralis ecclesia ipsa opprimitur, videlicet 28,000 nummis argenteis Americanis circiter 147,000 gallicana pecunia."*

Bishop McCloskey of Albany wrote to The Society for the Propagation of the Faith, stating: "My diocese is now exactly in that position when its future prospects may be said very much to depend upon the degree of aid and encouragement it receives from The Society for the Propagation of the Faith."

The Fifth Council of Baltimore in 1841 wrote to The Society for the Propagation of the faith, begging: "It is to your charitable solicitude that we recommend our infant churches; you will aid us to lay these foundations (six new dioceses will soon be added to the sixteen which now represent our Province) which are the ramparts of truth."

The First Plenary Council of the Bishops of the United States of May 20, 1852, wrote the following letter to The Society for the Propagation of the Faith: "We pray you not to forget in the object of your fruit and charity, the multiplied needs which are necessarily borne in America . . . there is not here a single diocese, the organization of which is complete and which is capable of responding to the demands of the faithful. New Sees cannot exist but by your charity, and among them we recommend in a particular manner that of Oregon."

3. The Bishops of the United States Express Gratitude for The Society for the Propagation of the Faith to Which They Attribute Principally the Growth of the Church in the United States.

The expression of gratitude was well deserved, for from 1822 to 1833, The Society for the Propagation of the Faith sent to the bishops of the foreign mission of the United States 42 percent of its total allocations and increased it in the decades to follow. No nation since has ever received as large a percentage as the United States.

From 1832 to 1841, The Society for the Propagation of the Faith sent to the bishops of the foreign mission of the United States $543,591.80.

From 1842 to 1851, The Society for the Propagation of the Faith sent to the bishops of the foreign mission of the United States $1,023,861.

From 1852 to 1861, The Society for the Propagation of the Faith sent to the bishops of the foreign mission of the United States $1,222,475.

In all, the bishops of the foreign mission of the United States received from The Society for the Propagation of the Faith $7,020,-974. This represents in present-day values more than $70,000,000. As a proof of it, recall that in 1854 the Bishop of Milwaukee, thanks to The Society for the Propagation of the Faith, built a three-story seminary, 160 feet long, with a chapel 70 feet long, at a cost of $15,000.

So grateful were the bishops of the United States, who assembled in their First Provincial Council in Baltimore in 1829, that they wrote to The Society for the Propagation of the Faith in Paris, stating their hope that the Society "will place us in a position to be able in our turn to form churches which they will not delay to be established from the banks of the Missouri as far as the Pacific Ocean. . . . Bishops and clergy of the United States make it a duty never to offer the sacrifice of our altars without thinking of all the members of the venerable association of the Propagation of the Faith."

The First Plenary Council of the Bishops of the United States, assembled in Baltimore on May 20, 1852, addressed this letter to the clergy and the laity of the United States: "From the time of its first establishment, The Society for the Propagation of the Faith has contributed generously and uninterruptedly to the support of our missions. If our churches have so rapidly multiplied; if our religious and educational establishments are now comparatively numerous; if new missions and new dioceses, amidst most appalling discourage-ments, still continue to be founded — we must, in truth and justice, acknowledge, that in all this, The Society for the Propagation of the Faith has afforded the most generous and enlightened co-operation."

On February 24, 1860, the bishops of the Province of New Orleans wrote to The Society for the Propagation of the Faith stating: "We maintain and proclaim it that, after God, it is to the grand Society for the Propagation of the Faith that is, for the most part, due the very fruitful benedictions which have not ceased to descend upon our people."

The bishops, united at Baltimore in Provincial Council on May 2, 1869, wrote: "If the Church has received rapid and marvelous development, we owe it in large part to the cooperation of your admirable Society."

It was thanks to the munificence of The Society for the Propagation of the Faith that Pittsburgh, Hartford, Milwaukee, Chicago, and Little Rock were erected as dioceses in the year 1843. In twenty-five years, Pittsburgh alone received $85,600 from the Society. Chicago, within twenty years, received $100,000. Milwaukee received, in the same period, $56,432. Little Rock, over a longer period of time, received $105,000. Hartford, within a little over twenty years, received $51,000. Louisiana received from The Society for the Propagation of the Faith alone $124,160. Bishop Deneckere said: "Establishments already founded in Louisiana would have perished without the help of this great organization which proved itself for many years the bulwark of the distracted bishops of Louisiana."

When bishops of Chile and India and Africa are at times dissatisfied with the allocations of the Society, it is well to remember that Bishop Deneckere also complained that allocations were too meager.

The Diocese of Bardstown received $160,000 from The Society for the Propagation of the Faith up to the time of the Civil War. New York received, up to the year 1866 alone, $112,160 from the Society. The Diocese of Mobile received $110,000; Charleston received $200,360; Richmond, $128,125; St. Augustine, $118,347; Indianapolis, $237,978; Detroit, $113,453.

In addition to what was given to the dioceses, the following sums were given to religious societies for use in the United States: Jesuits, $263,089; Lazarists, $158,000; Oblates, $45,657; Congregation of the Holy Cross, $18,657; Redemptorists, $11,088; Fathers of Mercy,

$7,980; Benedictines, $6,000; Dominicans, $5,320. These allocations totaled $516,595.

4. The Bishops of the Foreign Mission of the United States Promised to Pay Back The Society for the Propagation of the Faith for Its Kindness.

The Fathers of the Fifth Council of Baltimore on May 20, 1843, sent the following letter to The Society for the Propagation of the Faith: "It is your Society to which, we, in large part, owe these marvels (of increase). . . . We will endeavor to respond to the appeal of your zeal, and to extend the name and influence of this precious Society before God and man."

The bishops of the United States, gathered in Plenary Council at Baltimore in 1866, wrote to The Society for the Propagation of the Faith: "We openly acknowledge that your offerings have had a considerable share in the development of our Church. Henceforth, the Church of the United States will endeavor to occupy in your reports a place more worthy of the rank assigned to it by the extent of its territory, the abundance of its resources, and the wonderful increase given to it by the Almighty."

On December 6, 1884, Cardinal Gibbons wrote in the name of the Third Council of Baltimore to the Society: "We dare give you this hope that if Divine Providence blesses our efforts, the gifts of our faith will become, at the same time, a powerful means of aiding you to extend charity, and as a restitution of the benefits which your solicitude has showered upon us."

5. The American Bishops Have Kept Their Promise.

It was a daring thing for the bishops of the United States at the close of the Civil War, when much of the country was desolate, when a depression was weighing upon bodies and minds, and when needs were so great, to promise The Society for the Propagation of the Faith that one day they would hold a place "more worthy of the rank assigned by the extent of its territory, the abundance of its resources, and the wonderful increase given to it by the Almighty."

One hundred years ago, France contributed 60 percent of the total amount received by The Society for the Propagation of the Faith for the foreign missions of the world. Today, the United States contributes over 60 percent of the total received by The Society for the Propagation of the Faith for the foreign missions of the world.

The Church in America is now established, with its own native clergy and over 165,000 nuns teaching in religious schools. All this is made possible because our per capita income today is $2,600 a year, whereas the rest of the world has little. One third of the population of the world earns less than one dollar a week. In Italy, for example, the per capita income is only $393 and the average wage is 29 cents an hour. Because God has blessed us, the American bishops recognize that we are trustees of His wealth.

Our prosperity is not an heirloom, but something which involves responsibilities to the other peoples of the world. America can give more because it has more, but it does not give more because it has more. Abundance does not necessarily create generosity. As one of the early Fathers of the Church said: "Regardless of how many hairs there are in one's head, one hates to have one pulled out." The generosity of the American Church is due to the fact that we are conscious of our Christian responsibilities. Our outpouring has its origin in the Trinity where there is an eternal generation of self-giving; the Father in one ageless and continuous act gives and reproduces within Himself the Image which is His divine Son. Our inspiration is also in the kenosis by which the Son of God did not regard His Divinity as something to be clung to, but emptied Himself. The inspiration of the bishops is that goodness which is diffusive of itself and tends to expand itself.

This chapter on what the Church in the United States has given to The Society for the Propagation of the Faith does not tell the whole story of aid to foreign missions or home missions. Each religious society that is engaged in missionary work has also received its bounties from the American people. There is no way of knowing how much each society has received, but the very prosperity of their houses and the increase of vocations bear witness to the fact that they, too, have dipped deep with large cups into the fountains of American generosity.

But what has been given directly to The Society for the Propagation of the Faith for the general fund of foreign missions has done much to intensify the bond that exists between the Catholics of America and the Vicar of Christ. By sending the money to His Holiness and allowing him, in his superior wisdom as the Shepherd of all the missions of the world, to make the allocations, the Church strengthens its faith in him as successor of Peter. Perhaps never in the history of the world have there ever been so many Catholics in one country who have been more united to the Holy See than the Catholics of the United States.

6. *The Burden Is on the Believers*

In bringing souls to the faith is the burden on the believer or on the unbeliever? The position generally taken is that the burden of coming to the truth is on the unbeliever. It is claimed that he has to overcome his ignorance, heresy, schism, hate, and bigotry. The position taken here is just the contrary; the burden is on the believer. He who has a well in a season of dryness has the burden of giving water to the thirsty; the burden of aiding the poor falls on those who are wealthy, for the superfluities of the rich are the necessities of the poor; politically, in a democracy, the burden is on the majority, for the majority is the custodian of minority rights. In like manner, in religion the burden of charity and understanding toward the unbeliever falls on the believer, on those who have the fullness of faith, and not upon those who have fragments of it.

The burden is on the believer, not in the realm of principle, but in the realm of charity. Coexistence has nothing to do with compromise of the truth, but rather charity toward unbelievers. Truth is not of our making, but God's. We have no rights over it. About truth there must be intolerance; about persons who do not possess truth, there must be tolerance, coexistence — aye more, the infusion of love where we do not find it. Right is right even if nobody is right; wrong is wrong if everybody is wrong. As Chesterton put it: "What the world needs is a Church that is right not when the world is right, but when the world is wrong."

Loving one another is not the test of truth, but the consequence of it. When a butcher adds twenty and twenty to make one hundred and four, we are very intolerant about the truth being forty, but we do not cut off the butcher's head. The Church will always accept the erring back into the treasury of her souls, but never the error into the treasury of her wisdom; she will eat with sinners and publicans at the banquet of life, but never with the sin in the banquet of her theology.

Open Mind, Open Heart

If we mean by the "open mind" one that can never come to a conclusion about truth, then our attitude must not be the open mind, but rather the open heart. An open mind is not always an intelligent mind; a wise mind every now and then closes on something because it is sacred and worth dying for if need be. An open perfume bottle loses its scent; an open mind often becomes a vacant mind. There really is a great value in corks.

The open heart is loving toward unbelievers for three reasons:

1. The open heart is an understanding heart, even to those who appear prejudiced against the faith. Every believer knows that if he had been told the same untruths about the Church as others, and had been fed upon the same prejudices, with his own temperament he might hate the Church ten times more than they do. Not even the bigots hate the Church; they only hate what they mistakenly believe to be the Church.

2. The open heart also humbly recognizes that he can see the Divinity of the Church, not because he is more brilliant than the unbeliever, but because God has given him the fullness of the light of faith. He will not think the unbeliever is stupid because he does not see what he sees, any more than the man with vision thinks the blind man lacks an intellect. Our faith comes to us from above and through no merit on our own part. As our Lord told Peter: "It is not flesh and blood, it is My Father in heaven that has revealed this to thee."

3. The open heart confesses that every religion under the sun has a segment of the circle of truth. Some natural religions may have only an arc of ten degrees; Christian sects may have an arc of over one hundred and eighty degrees. The open heart in approaching the unbeliever will not look at the incomplete segment and

point out the error; it will rather look at the truth that it already possesses, and strive to complete the circle of truth in the plenitude of Christ. When the believer attacks the erroneous position of an unbeliever, the latter's mind will come to the defense of his error as the arm comes to the defense of his body when a blow is struck. St. Paul at Athens did not deliver a diatribe against the pagan deities he found on the streets; rather he took the one good thing he could find in Athens — a statue to the Unknown God — and then raised the Athenians to the knowledge of the true God.

The Burden of Believers Toward Communists and Protestants

We speak not of Communism, for that is an intrinsically evil philosophy based upon the materialism of a Feuerbach and the idealism of a Hegel which affirms that a person has no rights, no liberties, no conscience apart from the party.

As regards Communists, we must love the Communists and hate Communism, as the Church hates sin and loves sinners.

Communists may be persecutors of the Church, as they presently are behind the Iron and Bamboo Curtains. We should love them even as persecutors the way Stephen loved those who stoned him. The history of the Church reveals that God can do more with persecutors than He can with the indifferent whom He vomits from His mouth since they are neither hot nor cold. Think how many Christians in the early Church, when they heard of Paul's persecutions, must have prayed that God would send him a coronary thrombosis. From tens of thousands of mouths there came the plea to God — "Give us someone to answer Saul." God heard their prayers; He gave them a Paul to answer a Saul! Within the past few years a Chinese priest who went to his death at the hands of Communists said that among those who stoned him would be future apostles of China. It is not militant atheism which gives the Communists their energy to persecute; for, if God were only a myth, whence come the sacrifices they make to destroy the sacrifice of Calvary memorialized on our altars? Men cannot be violent against myths. It is only the reality of Christ whom they hate that saves them from being fools fighting like Don Quixote the windmills of their imaginations.

The Communist persecutors do not deny God; they fight against Him. They seek to destroy all who would dare serve Him, like a man who, unable to love a good woman, seeks to shoot her lover. In our own personal dealings with Communists, we have never had to prove the existence of God. We have merely had to change their hatred of God into love of God; for what is hatred but love upside down? The editor of the Communist *Daily Worker,* a lawyer for the Communist party, and a spy of the Soviets — all these were received into the Church not so much by proving the existence of God through order in the universe as by their need of God through the disorder in their own souls.

The open heart will be kind to the Communists because the zeal of the faithful has grown cold and we need their converted fires to make us apostles again. The believers have the truth but little zeal; the Communists have the zeal but no truth. Fire has both these qualities: light which is truth, and heat which is zeal. How often we who have the truth will say a prayer for the conversion of the Communists and then sit alongside a fellow traveler in a bus or at a dinner table and talk about the weather or politics, while the Communists, on flame with unpentecostal fires, speak to us of their frigid ideology. The Communists sin against the light; we too often sin against love. Their present disobedience does not mean they will not one day be obedient sons of the Church.

The son in the parable of our Lord, who was at first unwilling to go and then went afterward, merited the praise of our Lord. If we hate the Communists we multiply hate. That is why our Blessed Lord bade us turn the other cheek. If ten men are in a row and the first strikes the second, and the second the third, there is only one way to arrest the onslaught of hate; that is by one man turning the other cheek to absorb it. The Church is absorbing that hate behind the Iron Curtain and the Bamboo Curtain by returning love for persecution. As one old Chinese Catholic said to a Communist who beat him with the butt of his gun: "It is your duty as a Communist to kill me; it is my duty as a Catholic to love and forgive you."

The believer is not to look for the holes in the unbeliever's doughnuts, but rather for that portion of Divine Truth which he loves so well. If we had not lived the way we did in the fourteenth and fifteenth centuries, we might not today have separated brethren.

The Catholic should always look upon the existence of Protestantism as, to some extent, a judgment on himself. The Lord punished us for failing Him in the way we lived, but He punished the twigs more that fell from the trunk of the Tree of Life. Those among the Protestants who have held to the more Divine elements in Christianity have produced a profound interpretation of Scripture, enriched the literature on the divinity of Christ, and aroused souls to the offense of sin and need for redemption.

Experience with thousands of them who have been received into the Church affords an added proof of the reality of God's grace. Some of them have never committed a mortal sin in their lives, have been inflamed with a spirit of self-denial and visible sanctification which would make blush the hearts of those who have a richer blessing. Though the Protestants are separated from the rock upon which the Church was built, they are not separated from Him who laid that rock.

The Burden of Believers Toward the Missions

The burden is on the believer toward the unbelievers in the world. If they filed by a given point one per second, night and day, it would take them well over thirty years to pass. Many of them have a natural religion with a high ethic which has served them for centuries. But almost all of their religions are based upon the principle that man can lift himself up to God by submission to his will, by self-denial, by the sublimation of desire, and by contemplation. One quickly reaches the limit of this ascent as man cannot lift himself by the lobes of his own ears. The believer is to bring to them the historical truth that it is not man who goes to God; it is God who first comes to man, remitting his sin and endowing him with His Spirit; then man is prepared for his ascension to God.

The burden of charity toward the mission lands is on the believer because of the crises that are presently affecting the world. It is not the whole truth to say that Communism is the whole cause of the crises. The real cause is the passing of political, economic, social power from the West to the East. This tremendous dislocation is like a great tidal wave sweeping from the West to the East. Communism is the surfboard that rides that wave. It did not cause it, but it takes advantage of it. God fixes the limits of nations, and the West has reached its limits. The rise and fall of kingdoms is a kind of Way of the Cross by which the salvation of the Gentiles is achieved. More important still, as Pius XI said: "The sun shines on different continents at different moments of the day. So does the Son of grace shine on different continents at various periods of history. At this moment the Son of grace shines on Africa."

The burden on the believers is to aid these countries by alms and prayers and vocations. Last year the wealthiest country in the world gave to the Holy Father for all of his missionaries a per capita donation of 28 cents for the entire year, or the equivalent of the price of a package of cigarettes. No other nation of the Western World gave as much. Only by the outpouring of sacrifices to his Pontifical Society for the Propagation of the Faith will the Bark of Peter be the first to arrive at the Eastern shores.

If the first man to help carry the cross of Christ was a man from Africa, then it may well be that Christ will return to Africa to help carry the cross of many Simons. Then a day will come when black hands will lift up white hosts in adoration of a heavenly Father; when a Japan that made a man a god will accept a God that became Man and thus come to understand the real meaning of the Rising Son; when an India that goes through a succession of reincarnations without achieving a peace will have one rebirth which will do away with endless wombs in the birth to the eternal Christ; when the Moslems who boast of being the sons of Ishmael will recognize that Ishmael's half-brother Isaac is the heir to the law which issues in the love which is Christ.

7. *Why Only Individual Conversions?*

In former times, the Church converted nations and tribes; today, her converts are mostly individuals. Two hundred and fifty years after Peter and Paul were martyred, the Roman Empire became Christian. Before the beginning of the Middle Ages, whole peoples and communities were converted, such as the Goths, Visigoths, Scandinavians, Poles, Slavs, Saxons, and Irish.

About the only place in the modern world where such conversions are taking place on a large scale is in Africa. One other very small example is to be found in Brazil. There are more Japanese Catholics in Brazil than there are in all of Japan. These Japanese Catholics were converted in Brazil within the last fifty years, while not nearly as many conversions have taken place in Japan during 400 years.

Works of the Whole Church

Why is it that vast communities were converted in the early days and very few are converted today? It is not because there was greater zeal in those days than now, nor because the missionaries were more sacrificial in the past than at present. The difference is that in those days the work of conversion was that of the whole *Church,* that is, priests and laity. Today, the work of apostolate in the Missions is the work principally of the clergy and religious. The laity, except as catechists, play a lesser role.

This omission of the laity is very serious even from a theological point of view. It was customary in the early Middle Ages, particularly at the time of Charlemagne, to speak of the two swords, namely, the sword of the Church and the sword of the State. This analogy is no longer used. A modernization of it would be that there is a double power in Christ which furthers the Kingdom of God: one is the power of Christ the Priest; the other is the power of *Christ the King*.

Christ as Priest is continued in the hierarchy and in the priest-hood which is destined primarily for the sanctification of souls, though the laity in an extended way share the "royal priesthood." Christ as King continues through the hierarchy, but in our modern times, through the laity. Thanks to Confirmation, the laity's work is not the sanctification of souls but the sanctification of the world or what Pius XII called *consecratio mundi*. Holy Orders and Con-firmation are two distinct Sacraments, yet they are both related to the royal priesthood and a nation of priests and kings.

Ever since the religious revolution of the sixteenth century, the laity have been little used by the Church. It may be that the relatively ineffective missionary apostolate of the last few hundred years has been due to the fact that we have been using only one-half of the spiritual power of the Church. Because souls are sancti-fied individually, conversions have been on this basis. Because the sanctification of the social and economic order is made effective through the laity, the Church has had little effect in missionary lands other than the purely spiritual.

Society Is to Be Saved

It is not only souls that have to be saved; it is society. It is not only souls that have to be sanctified; it is bodies as well, for as St. Thomas says, the soul is not a person. A person is a composite of body and soul. Society is a composite of the Redemption pro-longed in the Mystical Body of Christ and the lump or mass of the world which, to some extent, feels the spiritual repercussions of that gift of Redemption.

Ever since the French Revolution, the Church has been pushed more and more out of education, national life, legislation, the arts, etc. The Church was told that she was to work for souls and souls alone. Now some queer psychological theories would steal even the soul away from the Church, by reducing psychology to physiology. The total apologetic effort of the Church for the last few centuries, therefore, has been on the defensive. Because it was generally assumed that the Church worked only on souls, the whole burden of caring for them was thrust upon the priesthood, to the total neglect of the kingly power of the laity and their spiritualization of the temporal order.

Both the clergy and the laity have powers of "consecration," but they exercise themselves in totally different areas. The power of consecration of the priest belongs in the Mass, by which the bread becomes the Body and the wine becomes the Blood of Christ. The laity receiving this Eucharist have another power of "consecration," which brings the influence of Christ's Truth, Purity, Goodness, Honesty, and Justice into everything that belongs to time.

No Catholic may take the attitude of working to save his own soul but letting the world go to hell. He is responsible for the world in which he lives. He prays in the context of "Our Father"; he asks for "our daily bread" and the forgiveness of "our trespasses." The Missions, the work of apostolate, the preservation of the peace of the world — all these are communal efforts of Melchisedech, who was both priest and king. Without Holy Orders the lay apostles would have neither sanctification nor a mandate to exercise kingly powers. Without the laity, the Church would work only in sanctuaries and sacristies.

TWO CONCRETE SUGGESTIONS

Board of Strategy

The mission world represents the great mass of the world, and this includes not only the unevangelized but also the hungry. There are many ecclesiastical jurisdictions under the Congregation of the Propaganda. Each of the bishops and vicars apostolic in each area has to be appointed by the Vicar of Christ, but the mission problems in these missionary jurisdictions are not just the same as the problems of areas where the Church is established. Even where the Church is established, there are now national conventions or unions or meetings of the hierarchy in order to discuss those problems which affect not only the spiritual but the temporal well-being of the Church.

It should be so in the Missions. Missionary problems overflow jurisdictions. The problems of the Missions in North Africa are quite distinct from the problems of the Missions in Southeast Asia. A missionary problem in South Africa is totally different from that of Indonesia. In addition, there are great movements which touch mission areas, such as aggrandizement of wealth in Latin America, Communism, Moslemism, bigotry, etc.

Because missionary problems overflow dioceses, should there not be established by the Church a board of strategy, in which a group of missionary experts would work out a strategy for various large areas of the world? This board should not be composed of theoretical missionaries or missiologists alone but principally of missionaries who have served twenty or thirty years in those areas, shared the sufferings of the people and understand their psychology and their difficulties.

The great nations of the world have a board of military strategy. They are prepared to meet an attack upon one area of the country, and to use an entirely different approach if an attack should come upon another part of the country. The missionary board of strategy would do the same; it would develop a kind of spiritual logistics under the Commander-in-Chief of the spiritual army of Christ, namely, the Holy Father. We are always at war against the forces of Satan; the Church should, when great crises arise in certain countries, call upon groups of priests and religious to go into these areas to bring peace of soul and healing of body. For example, in moments of deep spiritual need fifteen or twenty per cent of certain religious societies could be impounded or drafted by the Church. Bishops could also be taxed a certain percentage of their clergy to educate seminarians, staff colleges and universities in mission lands.

The Role of the Laity

But where does the laity come into such a board of strategy? One of the first important problems facing such a board would be to have the clergy and the laity work together. Teams would be formed for certain specific purposes. There would be a revival of the spirit of the early discoverers. How, for example, was Mexico converted? It was converted not only by the priests, but also by the laity who went as masons, engineers, farmers and architects. In other words, it was not just the truth of the Gospel that was preached; it was a new society that was formed. Eternal truths were integrated into every form of social life of the people. Priests could work on the great eternal ends of man, and the laity could work on the more immediate and concrete ends of civilization.

The heart of the matter is touched when it is realized that the great problem today is not "Is Christianity *True?*" but "Is Christianity *Workable?*" In a civilization which is largely concerned with acquiring daily bread and sometimes just keeping from starvation, even an eternal truth can have but little lasting appeal. St. James warned against mere speculation on the truth while at the same time ignoring it in the practical order. It is the role of the missionary to preach the truth; it is the role of the laity to make that truth workable.

We have done much talking about the necessity of adapting ourselves to the culture of a people. This has all been on the basis of theological and philosophical adaptation. The real problem is far deeper. The adaptation of Christian truth to the culture of any people is to be done by the laity. In the beginning, it was done by the laity outside and as quickly as possible by the laity of that culture.

A calloused finger does not do as much harm to health as a decayed kidney; what happens to individual cells of the body is of less importance than that which happens to organs. Applying this to the mission of Christ to the world: Though the conversion of individual souls will always remain an important condition of the advance of the Kingdom of God, nevertheless society will not be transformed until its organs, such as labor unions, the legal profession, medicine, education, manufacturing associations, industries, all become suffused in some way with the Spirit of Christ.

8. *"Little Flock"*

Throughout Scripture many names are given to the flock of Christ, such as "a purchased flock," "a flock washed in the Blood of Jesus," "a chosen flock," "a marked flock," "a flock patient under sufferings," but the title which is most important in our world today is "little flock." By it our Lord may have meant either small at its beginning or small compared with the great bulk of mankind. Our Lord prefaced His words describing the "little flock" by saying: "Do not be afraid, you, My little flock. Your Father has determined to give you His Kingdom." Despite the fact that there would be many wants and disadvantages and sufferings, they were not to fear because God would be to them as a father.

They were called a "flock" to show the particular regard which the Divine Shepherd had for them; they were called "little" as compared with the multitude of the ungodly. The flock will perhaps always be little because admission into the flock is contrary to the baser movements of the human heart, because membership in the flock demands self-denial, and because of the constant attrition that it will meet from enemies.

One finds this idea of "little" developed in Jeremias.

> Wandering hearts, the Lord bids you come back to Him, and renew your troth; by ones and twos, from this city and that, from this clan or that, He will claim you for His own and bring you back to Sion; and you shall have shepherds of His own choice to guide you well and prudently (Jer 3:14, 15).

Smallness in a Growing World

Although there is much talk of a population explosion, it cannot equally be said that there is a religious explosion. Religion is being reduced more and more as an influence in social life. One out of every four persons in the world is Chinese, and China is completely Communist. One out of every three persons in the world is under Communist control, though not one in every three is Communist. One out of every six persons in the world is Moslem. Excluding the Philippines, there are 14 million Catholics in the mainland of Asia, which has one half the population of the earth. There are more pagans born in one year in Asia than we have members in the Mystical Body — this, over 1900 years after the unfurling of the Cross of Salvation.

The only continent in which there has been a notable increase of the Catholic population over the general population is Africa. The population increase was 2.6 percent; the Catholic population increase was 12.5 percent. In the United States last year the total population increase was 1.8 percent; the Christian population increase (both Catholic and Protestant) was 1.9 percent.

In the face of this growing population and the decreasing quantity of the flock of Christ, what attitudes are to be taken?

Some Non-Catholic Attitudes

One solution would be to enlarge the concept of Christianity by a union of churches in which social fellowship would be emphasized and doctrinal integrity to a large extent ignored. This movement would unite the various Christian sects loosely, so that the 8 percent of the world's population which is Protestant would be added to the 17 percent which is Catholic and the 5 percent which is Orthodox and ancient Eastern, constituting a total of 30 percent. Some Protestant scholars are emphatic about this unity of all religions, because they state that if the present rates of growth in world population in the Christian community continue, the proportion by the year A.D. 2000 would be 20 percent Christian in the loose sense while Protestants may be only 5 percent of the globe.

Protestants in certain categories argue that the "Christian Church," in the loose sense of the word, would be larger through a merging. For example, the Protestant population of the British Guianas is 24 percent; Bermuda, 38 percent; Bahamas, 33 percent; Jamaica,

33 percent; British Honduras, 25 percent; Basutoland, 29 percent; Southwest Africa, 30 percent; United South Africa, 50 percent; Canada, 42 percent; United States, 35 percent; Finland, 99 percent; Netherlands, 38 percent; Norway, 92 percent; Sweden, 96 percent; Switzerland, 54 percent. The "Church" would not be so small to these thinkers if the "Church" meant a broad unity of believers in contrary and contradictory doctrines.

Solution of World Religions

A second solution to the "little flock" is not the uniting of Christian sects, but the uniting of all religions, Christian and non-Christian, in order to make the "religious" flock larger. As Professor Wilfred Cantrell Smith writes, "The Christian community is at the moment theologically unequipped for living in the twentieth century with its pluralistic mankind." A religious syncretism of the East and the West is suggested as a means of giving greater numerical superiority to religion. Protestant theologians who support this syncretism base their ideas on Harnack, who regrets the freezing of the primitive Gospel into a theology, and on Tillich, who bemoans the use of conceptual tools to express religion. Tillich believes that the hope for religion is a return to the prephilosophical or mythological period of history. Religion must be emptied of the Logos concept, according to Tillich, because it is unknown in any system of thought, except the Greek. Just as soon, therefore, as theologians get away from the Greek mind-structure, a way will be opened to a unity of all religions on a broader basis, and the Gospel of Christ will be in a less competitive milieu.

W. E. Hocking, first in his book, *Living Religions and World Faith,* written in 1940, and then in an article of 1955, recommends rethinking "religious experiences and motives, wherever found, within or outside the original scope of the founder's essence." By doing so, all sources could be drawn into the sphere of religion, allowing each culture to be identified with a religion that took roots in its soil. Identity, therefore, means an identity with a milieu, not an identity with the Mind of God. He would have religion draw its essence from its environment, Europe remaining Christian and Asia remaining

Buddhist in what would be nothing else but a sociological eclecticism.

D. W. Ferm claims that Christianity must give up its idea of uniqueness and bury the carcass in favor of a "vital universalism." The view of Christ as the Logos or the Word made Flesh will have to be abandoned, because the rest of the world does not accept the Greek structure of the Logos. Bultmann, continuing this antirational point of view, argues: "It is clear that the early Christian doctrine of man is diametrically opposed to that which prevailed in the Greek tradition. Man is not regarded as an instance of universal human being, which in turn is seen to be an instance of being a cosmic being in general . . . man's essential being is not logos or reason or spirit. If we ask primitive Christianity where the essential being of man resides, there can be only one answer, in the will."

Hendrik Kraemer, in the same spirit, holds that conceptual language is inadequate to convey the deep meanings of the Christian faith. Aulen insists that "the acclamations of faith are without exception of a symbolic character." If the Bible is to be used, it is because one will make a distinction between the Greek apprehension of it and what Kraemer calls the "existential grasp." Other currents toward universalism, which emphasize the will and the emotions and neglect truth, receive some emphasis from C. G. Jung, who finds something deeper than religion in the mysterious collective consciousness of mankind, revealed in the spontaneous modern sensitivity to primitive art and jazz and dance. To him these are a return to elemental patterns with enslavement toward none in which there is "a fusion of opposites in an all-embracing unified form."

Arnold Toynbee, in his turn, finds an innate intolerance and arrogance in Christianity in its emphasis on a unique revelation. Religion to him is seen in the Hindu perspective of a kind of a pantheon of gods and beliefs.

W. T. Stace in his book, *Time and Eternity,* prefers the Eastern point of view, because it enables one to combine all experiences and forms of religion, thus making conceptual differences irrelevant. From this point of view, all thinking about God is merely an elaboration of an experience and, therefore, symbolic. F. S. C. Northrop's *The Meeting of the East and the West* stresses that world understanding is conditioned upon a fusion of the beliefs of the East and West, between democracy and Communism, between Latin and Anglo-Saxon values. He would bring the West under the denominator of what he calls the "theoretical component" and the East under that of the "aesthetical component"; the first is scientific, rational, and discursive and the second is intuitive, emotional, and total.

The general tendency is to consider religion not as a matter of truth, for this is presumed to be the business of philosophy, but as a discipline for attaining a goal by oneself, without any direction from God.

Catholic Reflections

The learned and distinguished Dominican theologian, Yves Congar, in his book, *The Wide World, My Parish,* plunges into the question of the small church in a large world. He gives two explanations of the difficulties, both from Scripture. The first is that sometimes God punishes a mere emphasis on numbers, as He punished David for enumerating his kingdom to emphasize his own power rather than God's.

The second explanation is that in Scripture the few represent the many. The New Testament is concerned with totalities or wholes which are represented by individuals or parts of those wholes. St. Paul wrote to the Colossians: "the Gospel which has reached you, which now bears fruit and thrives in you, as it does, *all the world over.*" Abraham was already the people that would make up the company of believers, and the promises given to him were given for the elect. There is a minority in the service of a majority. Congar writes: "For us, Israel is now the Church, and it is to Christians that we have to apply the idea of being the dynamic representative minority that is spiritually responsible for the final destiny of all."

Answer to the Syncretists

While it is true that the flock is small and that a little leaven fills the whole mass, may it not be that there is another way of presenting this problem? An analogy may help. The solution offered by many secularist thinkers, as we have seen, is that there is no such thing as truth; since man expresses his emotions in various ways, it is possible to form some kind of syncretism of all religions which will make it a major force in the world.

This proposal is very much like one that a first-grade teacher might give her students. Some pupils say that two plus two equals four; others, two plus two equals six; others, two plus two equals twenty; and others, two plus two equals eight. The teacher, in the face of these varied solutions, might syncretize and synthesize them all and say that two plus two equals nine and one-half. Can we not relate this to the idea of a union of churches and a religion made up of the East and the West?

Another solution, which resigns itself to the belief that we will always be a small church in a large world, is to argue that only one pupil knows the truth that two and two make four and there is little hope for the others unless they grasp it. This solution reposes in the fewness and uniqueness of those that come to the knowledge of the truth.

Another solution, which is not altogether contrary to this but is an enlargement of it, is the following: Although there is only one pupil that knows that two and two make four, nevertheless, the pupils that say two and two make six or twenty or eight, or any other sum but four, are striving for mathematical certitude. Inasmuch as they have good will and are using the knowledge that is available, they are still kept in the class, though they have not yet come to absolute certitude concerning two and two. This solution is one that places the emphasis upon the relationship of unbelievers to the Church.

If one places himself at the point of view that all men are looking for the truth, then instead of sacrificing the truth one finds that the Church is not as small as it would seem. There are two classes of people in the world: those who have found Christ and His Church and those who are looking for it. If there be a third class, it would be those who suspect its truth but fight against it because of an unwillingness to surrender either their pride or their lust or their avarice. There may be many more in the world who belong to the

Church *in voto* than are generally suspected; and certainly not all of those who are presently nominal members of the Church will be saved. There is always a danger that we may underestimate the striving and the yearning for truth in many of those who are not yet actual members of the Church. Did not Elias himself boast that he was the only one who was loyal to God:

> I am all jealousy, said he, for the honor of the Lord God of hosts; see how the sons of Israel have forsaken thy covenant, thrown down Thy altars, and put Thy prophets to the sword! Of these, I only am left (3 Kings 19:14).

But God spoke to him and said:

> Yet I mean to leave Myself seven thousand men out of all Israel; knees that have never bowed to Baal, lips that have never kissed hand to do him worship (3 Kings 19:18).

Portion of a Circle

Even in the worst of times God always has a remnant that is striving toward Him. It could very well be that men who at this very moment are immersed in wickedness of every kind may have the eye of God fixed on them for good and be made "willing people in the day of God's power." If there ever was a man who seemed to be beyond the reach of Divine grace, it was Manasses, "who defied the Lord's Will by courting the false gods of those nations which the Lord destroyed. . . . He raised altars to the gods of the countryside . . . he carved an image too, and cast a sheath for it, and set it up in the Lord's house." Yet, despite all of this, in time of distress, "he turned to the God of his fathers and made humble amends and sought His favor with earnest prayer. That prayer the Lord answered." Manasses was an enemy of the Lord, but still he became a friend.

Dante in his *Paradiso* says: "And you, mortals, refrain from judgment; for we who see God, do not yet know all the elect." As Pius IX put it: "We must certainly believe that no one may be saved outside of the Apostolic Roman Church, for this is the only ark of salvation, and those who do not enter it will perish in the flood;

but at the same time, we must hold for certain that those who are ignorant of the true religion have thereby no fault in the eyes of God, if that ignorance is invincible."

Pius XI, following up that idea, said: "Who will ever be able to measure the limits of good faith? And the greater the ignorance the less the responsibility: Jesus Himself seemed almost to find extreme consolation in this ignorance, when from the Cross He said to His Father, 'Forgive them, for they know not what they do.'" And again Pius XI said, "The distinction between excusability and inexcusability is among the most difficult for even the greatest minds to apprehend. God alone who is Truth, the whole Truth who calls all creatures to a knowledge of the Truth, and gives them the means of finding it, God alone surely sees these distinctions, even if the Apostle Paul spoke of inexcusability. . . . God alone knows the limits of excusability and good faith among men, and we must leave it to Him to decide, and to judge."

Bringing this into the missionary field, missionaries must not approach the non-Christians as if they had no truth. The fullness of truth is a 360-degree circle; every religion in the world has a segment of this truth. Natural religions may have 15, 30, 50 percent; Christian religions may have 120, 180, or 200 percent. Missionaries are not to stress the part of the circle which is missing, but rather the part of the circle which they already possess. Unbelievers are not being brought wholly from infernal darkness to light, but from candle-light to the sun! Missionaries must complete the segment of truth which is already possessed. Their stress is upon the fullness of truth rather than error.

The truth remains: "Outside of the Church there is no salvation." But the formula does not refer to *Who* but to *What*. If it referred to *Who,* the Church would be making a personal judgment about the salvation of a soul, which it has never done and never will do. The *What* refers to the Divinely commissioned means of salvation, namely, the one Ark, the one Body of Christ, the one Lord, the one Baptism, the one Church, outside of which, either by fact or desire, salvation is impossible.

The Church is not as small as it seems. If it is understood as those who accept the fullness of revelation and all that the fellowship in Eucharistic worship implies, then it is bounded by meager statistics. But if the Church means not only those who are united to it in fact, but even in desire, then it would seem to be exerting more and more influence in the world.

Persecution

Start with the purely negative point of view, namely persecution. There is little or no persecution of Buddhism, Moslemism, or Holy Rollerism. These are not sufficiently Divine to evoke the prejudice and hatred of the forces of Satan. The world does not show fears of losing its values except in the face of the Church. With the decrease of doctrine in Christian sects, there is little or no readiness for any member to die a martyr for a belief which is merged with a contrary belief in some vague fellowship of sects. The very antagonism against the Church is a proof of its Divinity; a church that is merely tolerated by evil forces lacks something. The Cross by its nature unites not only friends of Christ but also His enemies. That is why, as the world draws to its end, the zone of indifference to Christ, His Body, will narrow; the good will become better, the evil will become worse, and polarization for Christ and anti-Christ will set in.

The Church is known much more than is generally believed. There is not a member of the Communist party who does not know it and fear it. A Communist leader in China asked a missionary: "What is the most powerful weapon the Western World possesses against Communism?" The missionary answered: "The atomic bomb." The Communist gave the right answer: "No, you are — you missionaries."

It may be objected that Communist persecutors by no stretch of the imagination may be included even in the churchyard of the Mystical Body. True, not in their actual hatred and rejection of grace. But may not the *initium fidei* be in them even in their persecution, as it was in Paul? Is not the Church exercising an influence on the Polish Communists who refuse to allow holy pictures to be sent into Poland, or to allow anyone to teach catechism to children? Is not this a fear, not of a phantom but of the greatest Reality? A fellow prisoner of a Communist in France wrote a book about the

Communist, saying that he really yearned for God. The Communist protested in writing: "From what word of mine, what sign, what misleading action, what stammering utterance, what slip, by what method of interpretation whatever, can it be supposed that there is in me a love of God?" The Communist did not deny; he merely queried: How did you know? His expressed psychological attitudes were all against God, but there was some deep, hidden yearning which he did not permit to be conscious. Someone we know, who has had experience in bringing leading Communists into the Church, has never given them a proof of the existence of God: he always starts with the tension, the dialectic, the cross-purposes inside their minds and hearts.

If the Church were as small as it is statistically, it would not loom so large in the persecution and politics of the Communists. The instinct of the devil is infallible: he knows his Enemy. So do the minions of Satan. But even among the persecutors there is hope. It may very well be that a renewed Pentecost will take place in the Church with the conversion of persecutors. Those who hate have a capacity for love; the energy expended in one direction equals the energy expended in another. The Apostles were fearful of Saul the persecutor and sent Barnabas to investigate, but in the end Paul was able to say that he had labored more abundantly than they.

Fellow Travelers

Another category of moral influence of the Church is in that group who says: "If I ever took up religion, I would be a Catholic." The implication is: I am intellectually convinced of the truth, but it makes moral demands on me which I am not able to undertake. I find no difficulty with the Creed, but I stumble at the Commandments. One never hears this about a worldly religion, and few are they who find divorce and remarriage any obstacle to membership in a Christian sect. No one knows how long the sinful woman struggled with this problem before she entered into Simon's house and into Christ's Heart. St. Augustine had the same hesitation: "I want to be good, dear Lord, not now, a little later on." God is in the heart of many of these people by *black grace*. Black grace is a sense of the absence of God, as *white grace* is the sense of the presence of God through sanctifying grace. God, by stirring hearts to uneasiness and satiety, is already leading souls to the threshold of the Church. They may be like the son in the Gospel who said he would not go into the field and later on went. In the end, he was found more praiseworthy than the son who said he would go and did not. At any rate, these people are sinning by excess of love, not by excess of hate. Not all the virgins got into the wedding of the Bridegroom. How often, too, when there is a sin against chastity in another, there is often a greater sin against charity in the critic.

The Church is not small when it attracts millions who want the pearl but will not presently pay the price. Maybe the transition from carnal love to divine love fails because those who have the faith have not accepted their first trivial movements of love in the poured-out ointment of their broken hearts. Anyone who has had much practical experience in dealing with sinners of this kind has a deeper consciousness of being Christ and having His Spirit, when he extends patience and hope to these poor souls who "have loved much" and yet have loved so little, who were "fearful lest having Him they must have naught beside."

"I would become a Catholic" is not a mile away from "I will, by the grace of God, to be a Catholic." As Pius XII said: "An act of love for God can suffice for an adult to obtain sanctifying grace and supply for lack of baptism."

Latin America

The one instance, probably, where there is an exaggeration of Catholic membership is in Latin America. There are not nearly as many *theological* Catholics as the figures would claim, but there are that many *psychological* Catholics. In many areas where there has not been a pastor for forty to eighty years, such Catholics were baptized, a few received First Communion, and fewer were confirmed. Few of them, perhaps, have ever pledged their religious affiliation to anything else except the Body of Christ whose Head is Christ. The devotion with which they respond to priests who share their poverty and their woes and to bishops who live like shepherds never above the level of the sheep, indicates how much their wills are committed to the mystery of God revealed in the Church. The one sheep that was lost in the Gospel belonged to the sheepfold; he was not an alien. The Catholics of Latin America are like that one sheep, for whom shepherds in the United States and particularly Spain must leave their well-fed flocks to rejoice the angels of heaven.

Lovers of Fellow Man

Whence comes the dedication of our age to integration, aid for the downtrodden, the underprivileged, and the social wrecks of humanity, if it be not that the leaven of the Church is working in the world? Slavery disappeared to the quiet influence of Christ in His Body affecting the world. This does not mean that social action today is supernatural in intent, but that there is nothing done supernaturally that does not look to Christ prolonging His Incarnation. Is there not vaguely and implicitly a love of God in a love of neighbor, as there is a want of a love of God in an absence of love of neighbor? Our Lord commended the dishonest steward because he was wiser in his generation than members of the Church who did not make friends with the poor against the Day of Judgment. That dread day will not be the kind we expect: judgment will be based on the good we did or did not do; how we helped the missions; how we aided lepers; how we improved the homes, the farms, and the rice fields of Asia; how we sent doctors to Africa and Vietnam and nurses to India. St. Peter described the Master as "He went about doing good" — and is not this what many are doing in our modern world? But whence comes this goodness, this neighborliness, if it be not to the radiating power of Christ in His Church?

A priest in Paris in the past century was asked to give hospitality to a priest from Italy; the stranger was put in the attic. When Don Bosco was later canonized, the pastor, then an old man, said: "If I had known he was a saint, I would have given him a better bedroom." Browning tells of one who turned a beggar from his door and then asked himself: "What if that man be Christ?"

Communism builds no hospitals for the sick in other lands because people are sick; it heals no cataracts simply because the victims are blind. All is related to propaganda, the party, the world revolutions. But these Simons of Cyrene who help carry the world's cross know not as yet whose cross they are carrying. They are carrying a nobler cross than they know! A nobler cross than they deserve! Many who are keeping the Second Commandment do not fully realize that they are striving to keep the First. Those who have the faith lack something when the keeping of the First Commandment does not inspire them to the utmost in fulfilling the Second. Those who *know* the Creed in its entirety will not be judged in their theology, but by their compassion or the practice of their theology. The Apostles would have turned away both hungry pilgrims on a mountainside and mothers with babes in arms, but our Lord fed the one and blessed the others. The neighbor is a "mystery" and those who aid him today are fulfilling the Spirit of Christ, though they know it not. The Church numerically may be a "little flock," but there are many sheep who are not yet of the fold, who are looking longingly and lovingly to the Shepherd and His Vicar on earth.

The Unconscious Catholics

The mission world is made up of at least a billion unconscious Catholics who are at a lower stage than potential Catholics, such as catechumens. The latter belong to the Church intentionally, though not sacramentally. A witch doctor recognizes the need of healing and the reality of health, though the means he chooses are not adequate to the end. In like manner, the so-called pagans, whatever be the religion they profess, recognize the need of Divine help, though the means they use to secure it are not wholly adequate for salvation. Cornelius, before his conversion, was doing good in his Roman pagan way; he was then unconsciously the first Gentile member of the Church. The Roman centurion who built the synagogue may have been a proselyte, but more likely was just a generous pagan. The Syro-Phoenician woman who picked up pagan crumbs that fell from the table of Jewish Revelation was unconsciously stumbling toward the light, as millions of Hindus and Buddhists are doing today. If one, like the modern man, rebels against the Church, it is not because he hates the Church, but rather that he hates a person or persons in the Church, or what he *mistakenly* believes to be the Church.

Among those not yet evangelized in mission lands, the desire for the fullness of Christ need not always be explicit as it is in the case of catechumens. As the Church has said: "When someone is in invincible ignorance, God accepts an implicit desire, which is so called because it is contained in the good spiritual disposition by which a person desires to conform his will to God's will." As souls before Christ were saved because of an implicit desire for Him who was to come, so there is present in many souls in mission lands an implicit desire for Christ who lives in His Body the Church.

Looked at in this way, the Church is not as small in its radiating influence as it is in numbers. But it is this unconscious and implicit and potential yearning for Christ and His Church which points up the need of truly Christlike missionaries. The number of missionaries is important; but what is more important is that each priest, Brother, Sister, and layman who confronts a pagan should appear as our Lord did to the woman at the well: "It is I, the Christ, who speaks to you." If it is an American or a Frenchman or a Dutchman who speaks, the waterpots of paganism will not be left behind. They are Christ or they are nobody. And happily they are Christ!

The implicit desire in unbelievers must lead to a formal incorporation through missionaries. Otherwise unconscious Catholics will be like the hungry with four ounces of rice a day instead of the Banquet of the Eucharist; their blood will be sickly and anemic unless transfused with the "Wine that germinates virgins"; their minds will lie fallow unless brought to that "Truth by which the Son of God makes us free." Missionaries are absolutely necessary. Otherwise, there will be so many souls in the world of whom we must say, "They never have lived," because Christ alone is life.

The "little flock" is a leaven, not a stone. A leaven ferments the mass; a stone does not. If the "little flock" is becoming proportionately smaller, it is a challenge to our zeal, a goad to add apostolate to our administration, and a summons to make our laity catechists and disciples. The "little flock" is not to be made larger by making truth unimportant, but by making charity more important. A union of Churches through the uniting of those who believe in the divinity of Christ and those who do not is impossible. A union of churchmen through charity, brotherly love, and the attribution of good will to one another is possible.

Neither is the "little flock" to be made larger by a marriage of "Western Logos" and "Eastern mysticism," but by Christ and His Church "informing" (in the Scholastic sense) the culture and "matter" of all the peoples of the world. We have to be so apostolic as to be sick at heart if anyone is left out of the ark of salvation. A blind boy at Lourdes was cured during the Way of the Cross as his father asked God to restore his son's sight. The first word of the boy as he saw his father and other persons was: "Fine! Everybody's here." That will be the missionary's cry at judgment when he sees his flock and is overwhelmed by the goodness of God. "Fine. Everybody is here."

Part V

Spirituality and the
Missions

1. *The Mission of Holiness*

The Gospel has been preached to practically the entire world; Asia has heard of it for centuries, even Tibet. Russia has had the Church preached to it. The few peoples who have not heard of the Crucifix and its meaning do not alter the historical fact that generally the world has heard many words about the Word.

Many peoples today can say to the missionaries: "We know about Christ already; we have heard of Him; we know His teachings about the Church. It is an old story to us and we do not want to hear it again." When St. Paul preached to the Athenians, when St. Thomas preached to the people of India, when Ricci held up a crucifix before the leaders of China — the Gospel was the "Good News." Today, it is no longer "News" in the modern sense of the word. The Gospel therefore cannot be *announced:* it *has* been announced. It must be *reannounced.*

The Difference Between Announcing and Reannouncing the Gospel

The Gospel is announced as a doctrine, as a creed, as a truth, or as something worthy of faith; the Gospel is reannounced by the missionaries showing forth the *charity,* the *love,* the *Christlikeness* such Divine truth creates in their souls. We announce through our knowing; we reannounce through our sanctity; we tell others about the Gospel through knowledge; we reannounce the Gospel through the love of Christ. We announce through the preaching of the Creed; we reannounce through living it out in radiant holiness; we announce by telling about what happened on the Cross; we reannounce by showing what the Cross has done to us; we announce through loudspeakers;

we reannounce through the soft whisper of a holy life: "I have given you an example."

Holiness of the Missionary Is the New Missionary Technique of the Twentieth Century

Pius XII said "the Church today needs witnesses more than it needs apologists." A witness is a martyr, and a martyr is not just someone who sheds his blood; he is also one who sheds his love. As we read in the Breviary of confessors who were not blood martyrs: "*Martyres sunt, sed amoris.*" When our Lord left this earth, His last message to His Apostles was to be "witnesses . . . to the ends of the earth." And to witness in Greek means to be a martyr. The apologist gives reasons which appeal to the head; the witness gives motivations which stir the heart. The Communists in China are more afraid of those who suffer and die for the faith than of those who preach it. Hence they allow priests to function and to preach in the "Patriotic Church." They tell the faithful priests in prison: "We are not going to make martyrs out of you." Have they read Tertullian, that the "blood of martyrs is the seed of Christians"? Did they hear an echo from the Fortress of Antonia: "His Blood be upon us and our children"? Did they hear the clamor that just Abel's blood raised to high heaven? In any case, it is "love unto the end" — holiness — that they dread, for they know that every increase of the reign of Christ in human hearts spells the end of the kingdom of Satan.

The Oriental mind is less influenced immediately by truth than by holiness. Not by truth, because the Oriental believes in the relativity of truth, but not in the relativity of holiness. To him, holiness is an absolute. Not reared in Aristotelian logic, he is less impressed by the absoluteness of truth, than he is by the elevation of a soul and its immediate contact with Divinity.

Oriental philosophies have this in common: happiness is to be achieved through a series of negations, detachments, purgations, and extinction of desires. The more unworldly the missionary, the more they seek to imitate him. If his detachment from the world is accompanied by a greater attachment to the Divine, they want to know the secret of his inner peace.

When the pagan hears our Gospel, and often our preaching, he, too, often interprets it as a moral or a code of ethics. This puts Christianity in the same category to him as Buddhism, Taoism, etc. Nothing perhaps so much sets back the Oriental in his growth of the knowledge and love of Christ as ethical and moral talks in which the believer is told "what not to do." He immediately begins to compare Christian morals with his own philosophy of morals, thus losing all sense of the transcendence of Christianity.

What is true of the Oriental is true in a different way of the African. The African has what might be called *imprevoyance* — he is heedless about tomorrow, which is a beautiful preparation for trust in God. Just as the Irish had a natural background for the faith when Patrick preached to them, so the Africans have a natural background for confidence in Providence as the missionary preaches to them. The more the missionary appears to them with this deep sense of trust and faith, the greater is the appeal.

The more the Oriental or the African can "use" what the missionaries give him, the less apt he is to commit himself entirely to God. Rice can be "used"; social services can be "used"; education can be "used." One of the large universities of the East, which is educating native men and women, records that only 2 percent of their students who have spent from four to six years absorbing Catholic doctrine ever come into the Church. Education is "used." In the world a woman may love a man because of his gifts; the Church can be "loved" for exactly the same reason.

Furthermore, the Oriental or the African is apt to see that education and other services are our techniques for winning them; therefore, they withhold themselves from being won over. Why is it that social workers, our Sisters who are doctors and nurses, have much more influence on the pagans than educators? It is because of the *sacrifices they make for* the leper, the sick, the hungry. They are not just using a technique — they are offering themselves. This kind of service constitutes a challenge to those who make use of it as they ask: "What is this love which makes them burn for me?" They do not always say that about the teachers and the truth he communicates. Self-surrender cannot be "used." In the legend, the Grail which satisfies all hunger in virtue of the Eucharist will be given to the first comer who asks its guardian, a king three quarters paralyzed by the most painful wound, "What are you going through?" In the East, where suffering is so great, no social worker who sees in a hungry woman a specimen from a social category marked "unfortunate" will ever win the soul. Not pity, not impulsiveness, not a warm heart, but a capacity to bring Christ's wounds to their human wounds alone will win such souls.

The inhabitants in the missions to whom we are sent are unregenerate in the scriptural sense of the term; they are once-born, not twice-born; they are in the flesh, not in the Spirit. Even unregenerate men admire holiness more than anything else. That is the one thing that is different. A missionary is thought to be of Western civilization when he teaches, opens soup kitchens, and when he builds a hospital. But even in doing these things he ceases to be Western in their eyes when he is saintly. The mission countries do not associate holiness with Western civilization; that is why holiness in the missionary blots out the geographical division and destroys any hatred of the West. The more holy the missionary, the more he is presumed to be Eastern.

The people in mission lands are feeling the impact of Western civilization, its physics, its economics, its science, and its communications. In a word, they are suddenly confronted with the basic ideas of Western material civilization: "This-worldliness." Suddenly the spirit world and traditional customs which were predicated on another world have become antiquated superstition.

To meet this vacuum, the missionary seeks to restore other-worldliness. The Oriental and the African has to become once more a citizen of two worlds; though the preaching of a Christian social doctrine will edify, it will not necessarily convert. To woo people away from the importance of a consumptive society, that is, one that consumes things and then advertises to create artificial needs, nothing is as appealing as the renouncement of worldly goods, for by that very fact he restores a balance, not by what he says, but by the way he lives. The eternal order is far from irrelevant. Holiness is the best restorative of a two-dimensional world and a realm of mystery. But with holiness in the missionary, the African and the Oriental without their myths and taboos are apt to say in the language of Israel Zangwill:

> The nymphs are gone, the fairies flown,
> The ancient gods forever fled;
> The stars are silent overhead;
> The music of the spheres is still;
> The night is dark, the wind is chill,
>   And man is left alone with man.

Let it not be thought that this plea for sanctification as an apologetic method frowns on truth or the communication of knowledge, or that it is a disparagement of education or social service. Rather, it is based upon the historical fact that the Old Testament was the announcement of the Word of God; the New Testament is its reannouncement: "The Word became flesh." Truth became personal, Holiness was seen to walk on earth. Truth was not in a book; It was so bound up with flesh and blood, eyes and ears, touches, kisses, lepers, sores, hems of garments, and straw mats and biers, that people crowded and thronged around Truth Incarnate; they pushed Him literally into the sea, so that He had to take refuge in Peter's bark. He could not be hid from the people, for they found Him out. On one errand He was interrupted and had to go on another; the Apostles even said the people crowded Him on all sides; mothers stormed Him with their children. Holiness and sanctification were passing out through the hem of His garments, His lips, His feet. Truth was not something just to be believed; it was something to be so lived that, if it were a germ, it would devastate society.

Communism and Holiness

A negative reason for this new kind of reannouncement comes from Communism. Communism has its own degree of "holiness," for if the devil quotes Scripture, he also knows how to win souls. Communism is also on a mission saying: "We have nothing; we are like you; we share your ills. You are burdened economically; we bear your scourges; they are laid on our backs, when they are laid on yours. Our Marx and Lenin have brought the Gospel of salvation to Moscow, and we will bring it from there to the ends of the earth. We are on fire with our cause; we not only give you an idea; but we say to ourselves, 'Woe unto us if we do not Marxize.' "

This is the devil's holiness, an identification with the people, living out with zeal the ideology in which they believe. And while they start economic fires, we with Divine Truth tell people, light your little candle. Our Lord never said light a candle; He came to "cast fire upon the earth." His relatives thought Him to be "beside Himself" . . . and indeed He was, with zeal for the Father's house.

Whence comes the greatest progress in the missions? What made conversions in Kenya rise from four per priest per year to a hundred? Martyrs under the Mau Maus. What makes conversions in Formosa grow by leaps and bounds among the same people who would not be converted on the mainland of China? Detachment from tribal customs and social inhibitions — unworldliness. What inspires twenty-seven villages in Southern Vietnam to seek instructions? Persecution by the Communists. What is making Korea turn to the faith? Communist persecution and the zeal of the priests and religious under trial. The closer the missions come to the fellowship of the Cross, the closer they come to multiplying "Thy Kingdom come" on the lips of the believers. As Zachary said when he got back his voice, "He has raised up a scepter of salvation for us . . . which He made by the lips of *holy men* that have been His prophets from the beginning."

Holy men have always been the method of giving salvation — men full of the Spirit. As bad music is nothing else but disorganized emptiness of time, so materialistic thinking is nothing else than the organized emptiness of the soul. The Communist "saints" preach bastard brotherhood without the fatherhood of God, and sacrifice themselves on picket lines for the sake of economic ideals. They have secularized the Beatitudes; at every step they say that the low shall become the high; the last shall be first; the overlooked shall be the preferred; the poor shall be rich; the scorned shall be reverenced; that old truth shall be the error, and man shall be reborn. They have perverted truth and the Gospel; they have turned the announcement into their reannouncement; they have taken the Pentecostal fires and made them burn downward instead of upward; they have made *this world* all-important. Will a proof for immortality in the face of this perverted "holiness" convince the Oriental and the African and the man from Oceania that he ought to believe in a future life? There is only one way to make this world unimportant and that is by unworldliness. To the Communists and the Sadducees of his day our Lord sent His missionaries saying: "I have taken you out of the world."

When we are tolerated, we are holding our own; when we are the victims of intolerance, we are winning the masses. Our Lord spoke to Pilate; He announced His Divinity; but when Pilate refused to accept that truth and live by its declaration, our Lord reannounced it. He went to His cross. He would "draw all men to Himself." When the announcing failed, the reannouncement would prevail. We live in the age of the reannouncement of the Gospel, not its announcement. Men have heard the Gospel of Christ; now they have to *see* the cross above the placards on the crossroads of the civilizations. Even the lighthearted of the world are affected by the sanctity inspired by the cross. Livingstone, who did so much for Africa, was found dead on his knees. Later he was buried in Westminster Abbey. The comic magazine pictured Mr. Punch doffing his jester's cap in reverence at the grave saying:

> Let marble crumble.
> This is Livingstone.

Holiness affects even the comic and the scoffer. There is a fascination about the holy, an eternal, unrelenting, restless fascination, because God is *Sanctus, Sanctus, Sanctus!*

2. *The Apologetics of Sanctity*

The Second Vatican Council is for a new world; missionaries are for a new world. For four hundred years we have been living under the discipline, the legislation, and the spirit of the Council of Trent. For four hundred years, the major concern of the Church has been with the errors of Protestantism. Most of the textbooks in seminaries, as well as the developments of dogma, have revolved around such errors as justification by faith without works, Calvinistic predetermination, the Protestant denial of a visible hierarchical Church, and the Mass as the prolongation of Calvary.

Since all error has a tendency to proliferate, to evaporate, or to split up into tiny fractions, there are very few Protestants today who maintain belief in the Protestant doctrines of the sixteenth century. On the other hand, the spirit of the world has completely changed. The Council of Trent principally envisaged Western Christian civilization, though without ever minimizing the necessity of preaching the Gospel to all nations. The world is different now from what it was in the sixteenth century. Today there is very little or practically no formal heresy.

There has arisen an entirely new "mystical" body of the anti-Christ. The major problems of the world today are social; they center around the problem of economic sufficiency. Internationalism, or the attempt to achieve one world, at least socially, if not politically and economically, has become the very air we breathe.

Perhaps no single force in the world today may be as important for the betterment of the future as the good that will come from the Second Council of the Vatican.

The Major Concern of Councils: The Body of Christ

There is no one way of describing this Council in relation to all of the other Councils; but, in a most general and sweeping way, it will have some relationship to what might be called the Body of Christ. Almost all the Councils of the Church during the first centuries were directed to the *physical* Body of Christ. The Church had to defend herself against errors which distorted either the intellect of Christ, or the will of Christ, or the nature of Christ, or the person of Christ. In each instance it was the Christ who became Man who was the center of reference.

The next major defense of the Church at the time of the Reformation was the *Eucharistic* Body of Christ, for Protestantism was essentially an attack on the Body of Christ that lives sacramentally on the altar, and in the Sacrifice of the Mass.

Our new age, and one which demands a new Council, is the conflict between two bodies, the *Mystical Body of Christ* and the "mystical" body of the anti-Christ. Nor was evil as corporate in the past as it is now; materialism existed before in the minds of individuals or groups, but never as an imperialistic political system. The brackish waters of all the previous heresies of centuries have now become a planned floodtide inundating one third of the world. Arianism, which denied the Divinity of Christ, has come to its logical conclusion in the militant denial of God.

This is the new world that the Second Council of the Vatican confronts. The day of heresy and the day of schism are past. It is not the truths of the Church which are attacked from within; it is the world itself which is in danger of dissolution. Other Councils have built dams and levees and ramparts to hold back the assault of theological error; out of this Council will come torches lighted by the fire of Christ's charity to enlighten the world seated in the darkness of the "mystical" body of the anti-Christ.

Application to the Missionary World

If this is a new kind of a world in which we live, with new problems to be met, with new avenues to be opened up, does it not follow that the spirit of the Second Vatican Council will demand a rethinking of our missionary concepts? There are five characteristics of the modern age which demand a rethinking of the missions and the missionary spirit:

1. *The Church is becoming more and more a numerical minority in the world.* There are about 14 million Catholics in Asia, but each year the population of Asia increases by 24 million. This means that in one year there are 10 million more born than we have evangelized in a Christian lifetime. The population of Brazil is increasing by 1,400,000 a year, though the number of priests who can care for this increase is becoming proportionately less.

2. *The new world is one of decreasing colonialism and increasing imperialism.* Since 1939 the Western nations, which for centuries developed colonies, have given independence to 735 million people. Since that same year the new imperialism of Communism has subjugated 835 million people.

3. *The older world never thought of history as working out any definite purpose; the new world believes that history is necessarily determined to work out an economically Communist civilization.* Because of Khruschev's belief in the deterministic evolution of the historical process, he warns that our grandchildren in the United States will live under Communists. The old world believed that we were making history; the new world believes that history makes us.

4. *The new world is tending toward polarization and away from indifference.* The eighteenth and nineteenth centuries were characterized by a religious indifference; today that area is narrowing: the good are seeking the better, and the bad are becoming worse. This process of polarization, which always takes place in a grave historical crisis, such as in famines (as described by Thucydides), is now becoming a normal development. There will be fewer Peter Pans and more leaning either toward Peter or toward Pan, toward the Mystical Body of Christ or the "mystical body" of the anti-Christ.

5. *The nationalism of Western Christian civilization is becoming the nationalism of non-Christian civilizations.* Nationalism is right when it means piety, or love of *patria;* but it can become an evil when it forgets solidarity of all peoples both in nature and grace.

Nationalism is still the major force in the revolution that is stirring the missionary continents of Asia and Africa. In some instances, this nationalism takes either the form of refusing the entry of Christian missionaries, or else a revival of the old religions. By a peculiar paradox the West that brought new enlightenment to the East in humanist democracy now finds the East growing up and spanking its nurse.

New Missionary Spirit

Though the Church has the same specific unity at all times which comes from the Holy Spirit and from its visible Head, the Vicar of Christ, nevertheless, the application of its Divine truths varies from time to time. In one age, the Church is united with Western Christian civilization; in another age it is materially a tiny little state, which serves as a fulcrum which can move the world. The leaven is the same, but it affects a different mass; the city is the same, but it grows on different hills; the light is the same, but it is placed on different candelabras. As St. Thomas Aquinas put it: *"Est alius status ecclesiae nunc et hunc, non tamen est alia ecclesia"* (Quod. XII question 13, a. 19, a. 2). In the light of the above, there must be new thinking, new approaches, and a new spirit in the mission world.

Sacramentalize What Is Good

The aim of the missionary in the twentieth century should be not to concentrate on the errors of other peoples, but rather to complete and perfect the truth which they already possess. It might even be well, instead of speaking of adaptation of Christian truth, to speak of *sacramentalizing* the truths the non-Christian world already believes. A sacrament, in the broad sense of the term, is a material thing that is used as a channel for spiritual communication. In the Divine order it is the spirit, or the invisible element, or the form, which divinizes matter. The Church takes salt and breathes a prayer into it. Christ takes water and makes it the matter of Baptism; bread, and makes it the matter of the Eucharist; oil, and makes it the matter of other sacraments. So too, there are many elements in the world religions of Africa and Asia, which have the raw material, not of the sacraments in every instance, but of the sacramentalizing process, namely, the infusion of the Spirit of Christ into their customs, feasts, religious practices, aspirations, sacrifices, and ceremonies.

Adaptation looks to the Divine truth making its adjustments and applications to the converted world. The *sacramental concept* looks rather to the good that is already in nature and in peoples, but doing to it what the Church did to the stones of pagan temples when they were converted into the Churches of Rome. The important point is the recognition of natural goodness and natural truths that are already in pagan religions, as well as the supernatural good and truths that already exist, in part, in all Christian sects.

The world will be brought to Christ not by telling hungry souls to avoid eating poisoned bread, not so much by proving that there are vitamins in bread, but rather by giving the hungry the nourishment of Divine Life through the "breaking of bread" in charity. It is well to remember that many of the feasts that are now Christian feasts were once pagan feasts, the Church having sacramentalized them. The Church, too, has taken over all major feasts of the Jews except one, and that one exception is because the final gathering in of the nations will not be until the end of time.

"You Will Be Witnesses"

Christ has sent us into the world to be witnesses, not successes. We are not so much to bring the world to Christ, as we are to bring Christ to the world. When our blessed Lord ascended into heaven, He told His Apostles that they would be "witnesses" and the word "witness" means martyr. He also said that they were to preach the Gospel to every creature. Two things are to be noted here. First of all, He merely said that it was to be preached, not that everyone would be converted. Second, it is to be preached to every creature, not necessarily to every man. In other words, matter has to be sacramentalized, as well as the soul divinized.

Our Lord pictured us going out as sheep among wolves, as being led before magistrates and kings; it is only in that hour of the the Passion that we have the gift of the Holy Spirit. *In Illa Hora* always refers to the Passion and the suffering, not to the pulpit without preparation. Our blessed Lord also said that there were certain cities that would not receive, and one of them was to be cast to the very depths of hell; just as there was a Bethsaida, a Corozain, and a Capharnaum in the preaching of Christ, so too, there will be nations equally impervious to the Gospel. From the point of view of our material investments and numbers in China, the Church there seems to be a failure; but there has been a witnessing to Christ which, when the eternal scrolls are unfolded, may prove to be one of the glorious pages of the Church's history. As Pius XII said: "In this day we need witnesses more than apologists."

Success is very much an American slogan, because pragmatism is part of the national business philosophy of the nation. But success is not necessarily a concomitant of even the best of missionary activity. When John in the vision of the Apocalypse saw the book that was sealed, he shed tears. In that book was recorded all of the resistance to the missionary effort of the Church throughout the centuries, its suffering, its persecutions, its exiles, and its martyrdoms. That book will remain a sealed mystery until the Lamb opens it on the day of the heavenly nuptials. Then we will see clearly what we now see only in a dark manner, that a missionary is sent to be a witness, not to be a success. If Christ wept over a Jerusalem that did not know the time of its visitation, we are not to be surprised that He should weep over a Shanghai.

Reconciling the World to Christ

The aim of missionary activity is not so much to implant the Church in pagan lands, as it is to reconcile the world to God. The phrase "planting the Church" has very often been identified with the establishment of a native clergy and hierarchy. The liturgical description of planting the Church, which is found in the first response of the third nocturn on the feast of the Apostles, has a different meaning: "They planted the Church with their blood. They drank

the chalice of the Lord, and they became the friends of God." This
planting implies that supreme act of charity which is quite beyond
the first sense of the phrase.

Furthermore, those who used that expression, "planting the
Church," did it to indicate that it was not precisely the salvation
of souls that was the aim of the missionary. As the one who popu-
larized this phrase wrote, "The missionary is *not charged to save
souls,* but to install where it did not exist before, the visible Church."
In the new world of the missions, it might be well to perfect the
notion of planting the Church in this sense, first because it emphasizes mostly the structural life of the Church instead of the primacy
to charity. Charity in the sense of *Agape,* or grace, is, as St. Thomas
says, "the form of all the other virtues, every other activity being
directed toward charity." It was this supernatural love, or *Agape,*
the night of the Last Supper that our blessed Lord said was the
foundation of the unity of Him and His Apostles. After the Resurrection, He made it the condition that Peter should exercise authority
as the visible Head of the Church: "Simon, son of John, lovest thou
Me more than these?" St. Paul in writing to the Corinthians made
everything else insignificant or passing compared to charity.

Planting the Church is *a work* of the Church, making it more
cultural, more social, and more indigenous in missionary lands; but
it is not the objective of the Church. The end of the Church is that
charity of Christ by which the world is reconciled to God. Once
more "planting" keeps the infidel in mind, and sets the Church in
contrast with its environment. Charity stresses more that foretaste
of heaven in which we all are Christ's. The aim of a great American
corporation in Africa or Asia might be to plant a new industry
there, but its formal aim is to make money. Now what money is to
economic planting, that charity is to Church planting, namely, reconciliation of the world to Christ.

Starting then with the basic concept of charity which is poured
in our hearts through the Holy Spirit in virtue of the Redemption
of Christ, the new missionaries will be bent more on reconciling
the world to Christ than in planting the Church. This is the way St.
Paul spoke of it:

It was God's good pleasure to let all completeness dwell in him, and through Him to win back all things, whether on earth or in heaven, into union with himself, making peace with them through His blood, shed on the cross (Col 1:19, 20).

Enemies of God, we were reconciled to Him through His Son's death; reconciled to Him, we are surer than ever of finding salvation in His Son's life (Rom 5:10).

This, as always, is God's doing; it is he who, through Christ, has reconciled us to himself, and allowed us to minister this reconciliation of his to others. Yes, God was in Christ, reconciling the world to Himself, establishing in our hearts His message of reconciliation, instead of holding men to account for their sins (2 Cor 5:18, 19).

It is only through the Redemption of Christ and the sending of the Holy Spirit, or, in general, the reconciliation of the world to God that we have a hierarchy to plant. Furthermore, the planting of the Church emphasizes its visible structure; but the idea of the reconciling of the world to Christ emphasizes the invisible grace which informs that which is visible. When finally, through this charity, missionaries do reconcile a certain area of the world to Christ, what is it? It is the *Church*. St. Augustine in one of his sermons (Sermon 96) gave this simple, beautiful definition of the Church: *"Mundus reconciliatus, ecclesia."*

"The Fields Are Ripe for the Harvest"

Missionaries are sent, not so much to pagans, as to potential members of the Mystical Body of Christ. The more we know of people in non-Christian lands, the more we become convinced that they were never without religion. It is possible that even the Oriental religions have brought natural contemplation to a higher degree and to more universal practice than Christianity has brought supernatural contemplation. It is to be noted that though Benedict XV in his encyclical *Maximum Illud* used the term *infideles,* Pius XI in *Rerum Ecclesia* substituted for it the word *ethnici* which, unfortunately, many translated as *pagans.*

It would be well if that supernatural charity, for which we have been pleading, was applied not only to the use of the word "pagans," but also to the use of the words "heretics" and "schismatics." Indeed, there are material heretics and material schismatics in Christian civilization, but in the eyes of God how many of them are formal heretics and formal schismatics? Just as we can exclude people from other lands from the benefit of the Church by approaching them as irreligious pagans, so too, we make it difficult for Christians of goodwill and for the Orthodox to enter the Church by hanging the formal label of heresy and schism around their necks. With how much greater grace did Pius XI call them "our separated brothers"!

The amount of spiritual progress that we meet in bringing souls to Christ depends to a great extent upon the goodwill we attribute to their consciences. There is some common denominator with every type of unbeliever and even every immoral person. Our blessed Lord found a common love of a drink of cold water as the bond between Himself and the woman with five husbands. St. Paul used the inscription on an Athenian monument as a text for his discourse to the senators on the hill of the Aereopagus. In like manner, our missionaries would receive a far greater welcome in the missions if they began with the assumption that many of these souls belong invisibly to the visible Church; or if they took the attitude that there are only *two* classes of people in the world *those who have found God or those who are looking for Him.*

There are three ways of belonging to the Mystical Body of Christ:

1. Members who belong visibly, such as the faithful in the state of sin who nevertheless retain faith and hope, but lack charity or grace;

2. Members who belong visibly and spiritually or invisibly: the faithful who are in the state of grace;

3. Members who have only the simple spiritual membership or votum: the just who are "without" and whose desire has not yet been actualized or even intellectualized.

There can be a supernatural life outside of the visible Church, for there is extra-sacramental grace in baptism of desire; but there is no supernatural life or extra-sacramental grace outside of the Church that does not look to the Church itself. It must be recalled that the 29th proposition of Quesnel, condemned by Pope Clement XI, read: "No grace is to be had outside the Church: *extra ecclesiam nulla conceditur gratia"* (Denzinger 1379). There are many people in missionary lands who have a certain desire and an unconscious yearning to be saved, and these are, in some way, ordered to the Mystical Body of Christ even though they are deprived of the favors which only the Church can give.

The whole spirit of the Church has been one of great charity toward those who are outside of it. The Council of Orange in 529 absolutely excluded the possibility of God predestining anyone to evil, thus implicitly asserting that all men receive from God sufficient means for salvation if they would but do their part. Innocent X condemned as heresy the proposition that Christ suffered only for those who were saved. Alexander VIII refuted the assertion that Christ had sacrificed Himself only for the faithful. Leo XIII consecrated all mankind to the Sacred Heart considering it as the Refuge of all souls indiscriminately. Pius X ordered this consecration to be repeated annually. Pius XI established as a universal feast one that is most significant and opportune for the whole mission world, the feast of Christ the King. Pius XII in a supremely tragic hour consecrated the *whole human race* to the Immaculate Heart of Mary. Here the concern is, as always, the reconciliation of the world and mankind to God through the merits of Christ in His Mystical Body. The missionary who goes to the missionary world and looks upon the faithful as dry sticks fit for the flames of Christ, rather than as wet sticks, has a deeper understanding of the tremendous potential there is for the Mystical Body of Christ in the missionary world.

"Pray the Lord of the Harvest"

Increase vocations. There is no need for reemphasizing the necessity of the native clergy on which the papal encyclicals on the missions have insisted so much. Negatively, the strongest argument for native clergy is the underdeveloped Church in those areas where missionaries from colonial countries failed to develop a native clergy. There is even some warrant for the truth of the statement that the great social work done in Paraguay, a few centuries ago, would not have failed so completely if there had been left behind priests from the Guaranis.

Because we are coming to the point of the importance of vocations in missionary lands, it is well here to emphasize that *no country in the world was ever converted solely by missionaries from other lands.* The Lord has refused to bless those who have not fulfilled what was written about the priest in the Epistle to the Hebrews, namely, that he is *assumptus ex hominibus,* that is to say, from the race, the culture, the environment, the immediacy of flesh and blood. Too long in the Church have foreign missionaries multiplied *sacerdotal pots* instead of planting *sacerdotal trees.* The flower that is kept in the pot, namely, the foreign missionary, has not the fecundity of the tree that is planted in native soil. Multiply the number of foreign missionaries in any land and you enlarge the hothouse; develop native clergy and you create a forest.

Foreign missionaries are less on a *crusade* than they are on a *mission.* Those on a crusade are very much like the crusaders when they have left their own land to establish a nationalist outpost; those who are on a mission, on the contrary, seek to build up the native clergy.

God, in His wisdom, has given to the Church two social sacraments: one, marriage; the other, Holy Orders. St. Thomas Aquinas, in his always brilliant way of thinking, says that the Sacrament of Holy Orders "is directed against the dissolution of the multitude; matrimony is directed against the decay of the multitude through death." Marriage begets persons while Holy Orders takes those persons to establish Divine rule into the multitude. May it be, therefore, that missionary activity in the new age will stress more and more vocations in native lands.

Does a missionary do more eventual good for the Church by making 10,000 converts or, within the same period of time, by preparing 100 native indigenous clergy for the people?

The two are not exclusive. But suppose our priests, Sisters, and bishops in mission lands made this a program, namely, to raise up priests of Jesus Christ. Would there not be more converts as a result of this concentration on the priesthood of Christ? Suppose a missionary did not like a foreign country but was told by his superior that he could return to his native land as soon as he built five mission chapels. How quickly he would undertake that architecture! Now, suppose that his ideal was not just to return home, but to create a native clergy — to make himself spiritually unnecessary in that area and to deliver the Church over to native priests. How quickly he would find vocations!

Communism does not start first on the masses; it starts with revolutionary leaders well trained in the philosophy of hate who act as the inspiration of the masses. Have they not stolen the idea of the leaven and the city on the hill and the light on the candlestick? Perhaps our concentration on the masses has made us forget that the native priesthood, native Brotherhood, and native Sisterhood are the leaven by which the entire mass of a country will be transformed and regenerated in Christ. When Communism sought to destroy the Church in China, Russia, Poland, and other countries behind the Iron Curtain, it struck first at the priests. The instinct of heresy and every diabolical corporation is unmistakable, just as Judas knew where to find our Lord after dark. If it is the priests and the religious that are first attacked in the destruction of the social structure of the Church, then it shall be the native clergy and religious that must first be built up in order to perfect the structure.

The Church in the United States Is Not an "Ecclesia Pagans"

Too long have the missionaries of the world looked to the United States as the *Ecclesia pagans,* which is a bad Latin way of saying "the paying Church" or "the Church which foots the bills." Whenever money is needed, or a new hospital, or a new jeep, it is always to the Church of the United States that the missionaries look. There is something right and meet and just about this, for the Lord has blessed the United States as no other country in the world has been blessed. The superfluities of the United States are the necessities of the poor. One of the greatest joys of the National Director of The Society for the Propagation of the Faith in the United States has been to scrape together every single cent possible in order to lay it at the door of the Vicar of Christ for the needs of the world.

But we do not want the rest of the world to think of us only as an

Ecclesia pagans, otherwise, the word *pagans* may be translated into English as a kind of a pun. We would like the Church in the United States and the Catholics in the United States to be thought of as the *Ecclesia vocans* — calling the world to new techniques, new methods, new spirit, new zeal, new kinds of apologetics, new missionary concepts, and a new outpouring of the Spirit of Christ. The Church in the United States must be thought of as having something else besides money, namely, zeal and ideas. With the prophet Osee this is our ideal: "Those who are no people of mine, I will call my people; she who was unpitied and unloved will be loved and pitied. In places where they used to be told, you are no people of mine, they will be called now, sons of the Living God."

The New Apologetics: Sanctity

The missionaries of the new era will rely more than ever on the apologetics of sanctity. This is a new dimension to the apologetics of presenting Christian truth; it relies not on the preaching of truth, but the truth fortified and vivified by example, and particularly holiness. In the Trinity, the Logos and the Holy Spirit are one in the Divine Nature. On this earth, truth was not meant to be separated from holiness. Human wisdom and the Spirit of Christ are not the same; it is the difference between a Bossuet and a Francis Xavier. In the hearers, it is the difference between "How interesting!" and "How I would like to be like him!"

It may be objected that there is nothing new in this "apologetics of sanctity." From one point of view there is none; but sanctity is not the same in all ages of the Church, because the infinite holiness of God needs so many facets to reflect it. There is also a variety of virtualities in man, new milieus, new challenges, and new needs among different people. How different is an Aquinas from a John of the Cross; the gentleman St. Francis de Sales from the impoverished Vincent de Paul; the little St. Thérèse who could not pray according to method from St. Teresa the Great who opened the doors to seven castles; a Thomas More, the Lord Chancellor, from a Benedict Labré, who cared so little for worldly decorum; Perpetua and Felicita from the Martyrs of Uganda, though both were of

Africa! The Stylites are out of saintly fashion, but now the "apologetics of sanctity" is in fashion.

What is it? The answer is to be found in the words of Pius XI, who asked whether we should take the extended hand of Communists. His answer was, "Take their hand only to lead them to the Divine Teaching of Christ. But how lead them to this doctrine? By expounding it to them? *No!* But in *living it!* The preaching of truth has not made many conquests to Christ. *It is by charity that we win souls.* Look to the missionaries. How do they convert unbelievers? By the benefits which they multiply and confer on people because of charity. You will convert those who are seduced by Communists in the measure which you show that the faith and the love of Christ are the inspiration of your devotion and your kindness, and that nowhere else can one find a comparable source of charity. Put the accent on this point. I know you have done much already, but you must go to the point of sacrifice. You have not forgotten that St. Ambrose asked that the sacred vessels be sold to come to the aid of human misery."

Here is the new missionary appeal of the twentieth century. Holiness is the one apologetic the modern world has not yet generally used. Almost everywhere in the world where we preach the Gospel there are those who say: "We have heard that before."

It is not only what is *heard* but what is *seen* that constitutes the new apologetics. Caiphas and his court after the Resurrection recognized that Peter "had been with Jesus." "Follow *Me,*" said our Lord. The ear hears the preaching, the eyes see the new hospitals, churches, and schools, but the soul sees Christ in the holy missionary. People will love the Church if they love Christ; and how can they love Christ except by seeing in the missionary an exclusive, passionate attachment to His Person?

In one area of the missionary world, there are two religious groups of women. Both have been in the same area for ten years. One group has had one vocation in ten years, the other 36 vocations in one year. Why the difference? The first group conducted a school for rich girls, the second for the poorest of the poor girls. And the young instinctively knew where Christ was to be found. They found Him in the Sisters who shared His poverty.

A priest, a refugee from behind the Iron Curtain in a missionary country, approached the writer to find him a bishop in a large city diocese in the United States because his parents were refugees there and he wanted to be in the United States with them.

When all soft, evasive answers failed to dampen his ardor to be in the United States, the writer said to him: "We have hundreds and hundreds of priests from the United States in this missionary land. None of them left to escape the cruelty of Communism; they left freely because they saw the need of priests in this land. What is more, they left their parents behind them, committing a kind of social martyrdom for the sake of the Gospel. Now, if they left their parents to be missionaries, why cannot you forego being with your parents to be a missionary in the same land as they?"

His answer was: "You expect from me a degree of sanctity which I have not." The response to that was. "But, if you lack that degree of sanctity, I could not recommend you to any diocese in the United States."

The time of "preaching" religion is over, that is, as preaching only. The world hears too many conflicting opinions, points of view, philosophies. The battle of "words" is over. From now on there is solely the Word — the Word made flesh in saints, who make unbelievers ask: "Why is he different from me? Why is he not downcast with failure as I am?" That inquiry in the face of a saint opens the door to the Church.

We are living in a radically religionless world. God is being pushed back out of the hearts of men; the increasing minority of the members of the Mystical Body is making new techniques necessary. Hospitals, schools, dispensaries, social works along with preaching are more important than ever. The bodies and minds of the pagans will be bettered by these services just as well as if they were done by infidels. But what of the influence on souls? Ah! that depends on the Spirit of Christ radiated by our doctors, nurses, teachers, and religious. The "apologetics of sanctity" is the only argument that is new to the modern world. It converted the world in the first century; it can reconvert it in the twentieth.

3. *The Lord Does It*

A Catholic information center attributed 45 converts to a pamphlet entitled: "Stop, Look, Listen." Another religious group plans on publishing records in which the Epistles and Gospels are read, not by priests, but by actors.

This brings up the question of the secular and the Divine. When our blessed Lord said: "Without Me you can do nothing," He did not mean that as missionaries we could not collect money, solicit vocations, and develop annuity funds, for all these belong to the natural order. "Do not the heathens do this?" Our Lord meant that we can do nothing supernaturally good, unless we are rooted in Him. An instrumental cause must not think itself the Primary Cause. "Does the axe boast against the hand that lifteth it?" A forgotten truth that needs to be revived is that all of us who work for the Church, all missionaries in particular, as well as all directors of The Society for the Propagation of the Faith and procures, are but instruments of Christ — continuing His theandric action among men.

The model for all apostolates is the Acts of the Apostles. From this history of the Church, two lessons are learned:

1. That it is Christ who does all things.

2. That those who are engaged in materialities such as missionaries, superiors, procures, and directors of The Society for the Propagation of the Faith are to be not the most material-minded but the most spiritual of men.

Christ Does All Things

Because our blessed Lord has ascended into heaven, He does not cease to operate through His Mystical Body. St. Luke begins his Acts of the Apostles with these words:

> The first book which I wrote, Theophilus, was concerned with all that Jesus set out to do and teach, until the day came when He was taken into Heaven (Acts 1:1).

The natural inference is that the Acts of the Apostles will tell what Jesus *continued* "to do and to teach" after He was taken up. The Gospel of Luke is the story of our Lord during His physical life; the Acts of the Apostles is the story of our blessed Lord in His Mystical Life, the Church. Run through every form of missionary activity and it will be discovered that all was referred to Christ Jesus Himself.

First, take the naming of a successor to Judas which applies to the naming of missionaries, the appointment of procures and directors of The Society for the Propagation of the Faith. Notice that the Apostles asked our Lord to show them who was to be sent, whether it would be Joseph or Matthias, as they offered this prayer: "Lord, who knowest the hearts of all men, show us which of these two *Thou hast chosen* to take his place in this work of apostleship." The bishop and the superior do not choose; it is the Lord who chooses through them.

The influence of the Risen and Glorified Christ on the missionary Church is evidenced again when St. Peter is called upon to explain the gift of tongues at Pentecost: "And now, exalted at God's right hand, He has claimed from His Father His promise to bestow the Holy Spirit; and *He has poured out that Spirit,* as you can see and hear for yourselves."

Miracles did not finish simply because our Blessed Lord left this earth. Peter and John went into the Temple to heal the lame man. Peter spoke to him thus: "Here is a man you know by sight, who has put his faith in that Name, and that Name has brought him strength; it is the Faith which comes through *Jesus which has restored him to full health* in the sight of you all." It could very well be that the power of healing has diminished in the Church because of our overemphasis on the human factors. Few are willing to make the repudiation of their own activity as did Peter, when he said: "Why do you fasten your eyes on us, *as if we* had enabled him to walk through some power or virtue of our own?"

When one thinks of the praise that is bestowed on bishops and priests, national directors, and procures for the building of schools and the in-gathering of money, one wonders if there is not a forgetfulness of the fact that Peter disavowed his power and his own holiness. Divine Truth would make us a disclaimer of men's admiration for our works. Our foolish hearts must guard against taking credit from Jesus who can work with such very poor tools as ourselves.

Turning to the subject of converts on the missions and at home, we are often wont to attribute this work to ourselves. The head of an information center will boast of the number of converts that he has made. Missionaries will sometimes, though not too often, attribute the conversion of villages to their superior organization. The Holy Spirit in Scripture would remind us that we do not make any converts; that if the Church is making any increase whatever, it is due solely and uniquely to the Risen Christ who is operating through His Church. The Acts of the Apostles gives us the true perspective:

> And each day the *Lord added* to their fellowship others that were to be saved.

It was the Lord who did it. It was not the bishop; it was not the missionary; it was not the director of the information center; it was the living ascended Christ who works in the community of believing souls. It is He who sent the Spirit down on Pentecost. It is He whom the dying martyr sees standing at the right hand of God ready to help. It is He who opens hearts for the reception of His message; it is He who stands by the apostle in a vision and bids him to be of good cheer.

At every crisis of the history of the Church, it is Christ Himself who is working in the Church. Ascended, He is the ever present Guide, Counselor, Inspirer, Protector, and Rewarder of those who trust in Him. *He adds to the Church,* not we, nor our preaching, nor our eloquence, nor our fervor, nor our efforts. These are weapons in His hands; the hand that wields the weapons gives them all their power to wound and to heal. The Church is expanding in Formosa and in Kenya; villages are being converted in Rwanda and the Congo. It is the Lord who does it. If His missionary orders are receiving vocations it is not because of their magazines, not because of their literature, not because of their promotional efforts. It is the Lord Himself who does it. If the directors of The Society for the Propagation of the Faith and the National Director are making America conscious of the fact that the Holy Father is the patron of all the missions and that he is to be first and principally aided, it is the Lord who does it.

When there is suffering in the Church, it is the Lord Himself who complains that He is being struck: "Saul, Saul, why persecutest thou Me?" Someone steps on our foot, our head complains. If Saul strikes the Church of Damascus as Stalin struck the Church of Warsaw, who but Christ protests? When the first convert is made in Europe, and incidentally she was a woman, it is not Paul who makes the convert, it is the Lord: "One of those who was listening was a woman called Lydia, a purple-seller, from the city of Thyatira, and a worshiper of the true God; and the *Lord opened her heart,* so that she was attentive to Paul's preaching." The implication is that Paul's words would have fallen on deaf ears, if it had not been that the Lord had applied His finger to her ear saying: "Ephpheta!" Peter goes to Lydia and there finds Aeneas, "who had not left his bed for eight years, being palsied." Peter worked a miracle, but he completely disclaimed the power to do so as he said to the palsied man: "Aeneas, *Jesus Christ sends thee healing;* rise up and make thy bed; whereupon he rose up at once."

The work of our blessed Lord was not ended when He went up to heaven. He is still working the miracles, He is still preaching. He builds the churches, He builds the schools, He gives the increase. When Peter is released from prison, it is the Lord who releases him; it is not the Chinese Communists, it is not a legal process, it is not any human force. It is the Lord Himself who does it. Peter did not make the mistake of attributing it to any other power than the Divine: "Now I can tell for certain, that the *Lord hath sent His Angel to deliver me* out of Herod's hands." When Peter finally got

into the house of John Mark, after much knocking, and after the
confusion of poor Rhoda (whom I believe to be the same woman
who was in Caiphas' court the night our Lord was denied by Peter),
Peter reminded them that they were not to praise him: "Calling for
silence by a gesture of his hand, he told them how the Lord had
delivered him from prison."

It could very well be that our decrease in conversions and in
vocations and in our apostolic labors is due to the fact that the
Ordinary gets the credit instead of the Lord, that the directors of
The Society for the Propagation of the Faith are praised instead
of the Risen Christ, or because the procures have utilized rov-
ing solicitors instead of the Spirit to bring increase to their
coffers. What Christ did for us a long time ago in Galilee is
not past; it is He who reigns "to do and to teach" according
to our necessity. It is not *we* who have to fight against the evil of
Communism; at best we are but the sword which Christ wields and
all the power is in the Hand that wields it. If we have anything,
whether it be money for the missionaries or new buildings for the
novitiate or new vocations, it is because we got it from Him. The
boast is His, not ours. Jesus Christ is the *only Worker;* we are but
reeds through which His breath makes music. It is wanting in
spirituality to get actors to read the Gospels to show priests how to
read the Gospels, who should be inspired by His Spirit rather than
by the superficial glow of thespians.

Gamaliel was right when he judged whether work was built on
sand or on rock. His advice to those who would persecute the
Church was: "Have nothing to do with these men, let them be. For
if this is man's design, or man's undertaking, it will be overthrown;
if *it is God's, you will have no power to overthrow it.* You would
not willingly be found fighting against God." This is the supreme
alternative. Either we are humanists believing that we make the
converts, gather the alms, or else we work as instruments of God.
Madison Avenue of New York may write the vocation pamphlets,
but because the work is of man, it will perish. God alone gives the
increase. Because He ascended into heaven, we are apt to believe
that the work of the Church is ours, forgetful that He operates now

through His Mystical Body as He did through His physical body. It is only to the extent that we approach nothingness that we get close to Him, for it was from nothingness that we came.

The Spirituality of Those Who Deal With the Material

Those who have to deal with money are in one of the greatest occasions of sin. The shortest distance in all the world is the distance between the pocket and the heart. Avarice is one of the "clean" sins, in the sense that it seems to suggest organization, power, talent, and leadership. It can be particularly insidious in those who are consecrated to God, and even in those who have the vow of poverty, for they may be individually poor but corporately selfish. The individual vow of poverty does not in any way prevent the spirit of aggrandizement for the good of a society. The pastor who talks about money every Sunday may be personally poor, but his sermons certainly give primacy to Mammon over God, if Mammon is the subject of most of his sermons.

The Acts of the Apostles has much to say about those who are at the receipt of custom or the collecting of alms. Acts tells us that the Apostles were very much concerned with the problem of relief, or what has since been called Catholic charity. They called together the disciples and said: "It is too much that we should have to forego preaching God's Word, and bestow our care upon tables." The tables were counting tables, or administrative tables, or the places where money was gathered and dispersed. They, therefore, sought out seven directors or procures who they said were to "be put in charge of this business, while we devote ourselves to prayer and to the ministry of preaching." The seven procures, or diocesan directors, or national directors, as you wish, were Stephen, Philip, Prochorus, Nicanor, Timon, Parmenas, and Nicolas. It is particularly to be noticed that they were not chosen because they were good financiers. Three other requirements are mentioned in the Acts:

1. They had a good reputation or "were well spoken of."
2. They were "full of the Holy Spirit."
3. They were "full of wisdom."

One wonders how many procures, diocesan directors, chancellors,

and financial experts of dioceses are chosen today on the same grounds
as the early Church chose its first financial section of the chancery.
The Apostles admitted that it was a very important business to
look after the widows and to dispense the modest charity of the
half-pauper Jerusalem Church, but what is paramount is this: *A
purely secular thing was to be done by men who were full of the
Holy Spirit and wisdom.* The Holy Spirit had to find men who were
like unto Christ before they could pass out loaves and increase the
general fund for the Propagation of the Faith of the early Church.
The first martyr of the Church was a procure, or a director for the
Propagation of the Faith, because he was full of the Holy Spirit.

After the martyrdom of Stephen, and incidentally it was through
his martyrdom that Paul was converted, we next hear of the second
procure or director for the Propagation of the Faith, namely, Philip.
While he is engaged in secular activities in the Church, Philip nevertheless becomes a convert-maker. It is evident that God intended
that those who deal with materialities should escape the temptation
to avarice by apostolate. Philip is directed by the Spirit to an
Ethiopian on the lonely road to Gaza. This man, who left Jerusalem
after the death of Stephen, was the first preacher of the Gospel in
Samaria, and now he becomes the instrument to carry the Word of
God to one of the first heathens ever gathered into the Church.

Here, then, is revealed the sublime lesson of those who deal with
the materialities of the Church. Two men who were chosen for
secular work, Stephen and Philip, had more to do with the events
in the expansion of the Church than many of the Apostles. It was
Stephen who brought in Paul, and it was Philip who went beyond
the charmed circle of Judaism to preach the Gospel. He was an alms
gatherer who actually went on the missions. This same Philip, who
suddenly became an instrument of the Spirit, kept plodding on for
about twenty years in Caesarea. It was very likely that he was in
Caesarea at the time of Cornelius, but Cornelius was not bidden to
apply to Philip who was at his elbow, but to send to Joppa for the
Apostle Peter. Sometimes procures, diocesan directors, can be passed
over even when they do the fullness of their work, but there is to be
no sulking. One who came after Philip, Saul, was preferred before

him. Though he dealt with the secular, he was the one who said with the Baptist: "He must increase, but I must decrease." Years later Philip welcomed Paul in his house in Caesarea and rejoiced that one sows and another reaps. There is consolation in the Acts for those who are summoned to administer at the desks of diocesan directors or procures for it emphasizes that they are full of the Holy Spirit. No one can ever take away from those who deal with the materialities of life the glorious honor that the first of all the martyrs was one who was chosen to gather alms for the sake of the Holy Father whose name was Peter.

4. *Witnesses to Christ*

The one word that does not exist in Christian language is "despair." Its name is written over the gates of hell, but even in the midst of catastrophic defeats like Calvary, no Christian mind thinks it, no Christian lip breathes it. Despair is a consciousness of nothingness. It is alarming how important the idea of "nothingness" has become in the modern world. Christianity puts "nothingness" at the beginning of human life, in the sense that man was created from nothing. Modern philosophers, such as Sartre, put nothingness at the end, saying that man is destined for nothingness. Their reasoning is this: Since everything that negates my ego is nothing, and everything except my ego negates my ego, then everything is nothingness.

The Christian, hearing of the destruction of the Church visible in China and Northern Vietnam, is tempted to permit the foul breath of "nothingness" to blow across his face. To prevent this disenchantment, which is the vestibule to despair, it behooves the Christian to realize that the Holy Spirit sent out the apostolic missionaries to the ends of the earth to be "witnesses" to Christ. A "witness" is a martyr, and a martyr is one who gives testimony to Christ and to the invisible things of the world by contempt of the visible things, even life itself. "Though our outward man is corrupted, yet the inward man is renewed day by day. For that which is at present momentary and light of our tribulation, worketh for us above measure exceedingly an eternal weight of glory. While we look not at the things which are seen, but at the things which are not seen. For the things which are seen are temporal; but the things which are not seen are eternal" (2 Cor 4:16–18).

The kingdoms of earth must keep their towers, their parapets, and their institutions, for such is the mark of progress. The loss of the material is the loss of power. But it is otherwise with the spirit. God is not only no respecter of personalities; He is also no respecter of materialities.

Judging by the standards of the world, it would seem that the cataclysmic destruction in the mission fields is a sign of retrogression. Influenced by the philosophy of progress, we are inclined to feel that there should be a continuous development. That which is planted should not be uprooted, and what is built should not be torn down. But with the Church, this is not so. There is never a crown without a cross, or a feast without a fast. The Chinese are close to it in their *Yin Yan* philosophy, which was born of seeing the light on one side of the mountain and the shade on the other. The Yin and Yan is not repetitive and cyclical action, but rather a response to a great challenge pulling one up to a higher level. It is what Toynbee calls a *Withdrawal* and a *Return,* a moment of detachment which prepares for a higher attachment, bringing an elevation of character and an ennoblement of functions.

As Solomon said, there is a time for laughter and a time for weeping. So in the missions, there is a time for progress and a time for witnessing. China and other countries of Asia are now entering into that second era, which fits no less into the Divine plan than the moment of building and relative peace. There was a time for teaching with words; now has come the time for witnessing with blood and suffering.

This moment of spiritual Yin Yan, or more properly "witnessing," is less an occasion for despair and defeatism than for patience and for hope. Tribulation begets hope, and witnessing requires patience. Like Peter, the missionaries looking on their charred ruins can say that they "labored all the night and took nothing." But it was only when Peter made such a confession of absolute frustration, that he found his miraculous draft of fishes. The log sings in the fire, but not in the contentment of the forest. The only recorded time our Lord ever sang was the night He went out to His death.

The Spirit of the Church demands witnesses at this moment; Mindszentys in Hungary, Stepinacs in Yugoslavia, and missionaries in China. She wants them to stay there in this dark hour never in rashness, but only when the faith demands it. Those who are not of the faith are leaving in the midst of danger. But the priests and nuns and Brothers remain, not as challenges to the Communists, but as living testimonials to Christ! Hard indeed is their task, but maybe it is no harder than that of those who stay at home, except that they are fulfilling better their vocation. We priests who stay at home are called to be saints; the missionaries who leave home are called to be martyrs, at least in will.

The victory over death and evil was not within three days of the Transfiguration, when Christ's body did shine as the sun, but within three days of Calvary, when His flesh hung from Him like purple rags. The conversion of Communist-infected lands may be closer when we worry about martyrs than in the hour of their safety and peace. These missionaries are staking their lives on the future of each of these pagan lands. They are weathering the storm so that finally, when the clouds blow away, the people may realize that they bore their ills and suffered their infirmities. The missionary even starts with a *social martyrdom,* in the sense that he separates himself from his blood, his friends, and his country. Like their Lord, they set their faces steadfastly toward Jerusalem.

Decisions now made are inherent to an historical crisis, and the steadfastness of the missionaries in the persecuted lands is the greatest harbinger of better days. There is a price on every soul; there is a price on every nation. No blood was shed in evangelizing Ireland, but her apostles shed much in bringing the Gospel to other lands. So there is a price on every country, and though the missionaries may have many setbacks, nevertheless spiritual progress is being made even in defeat. Nations are being bought by the blood of the Lamb and by the heralds of the Lamb. The huts in which the missionaries dwell may be destroyed, but their vocation as missionaries is not being destroyed.

Constant intercession must be made by the Church for these holy men and women, as the Church did for Peter while in prison. They are like the Good Shepherd, and do not flee when they see the wolf of Communism coming. In the midst of persecution, the Church looks

back and recalls how often she sang a requiem over the graves of
those who tolled the bells for her execution. G. K. Chesterton has
gloriously depicted this in his "Ballad of the White Horse":

> That on you is fallen the shadow
> And not upon the Name:
> And though we scatter and though we fly
> And you hang over us like the sky,
> You are more tired of victory
> Than we are tired of shame.
>
> That though you haunt the Christian man
> Like a hare on the hill-side,
> The hare has still more heart to run,
> Than you have heart to ride.

The Missionary a "Witness" to the World

A missionary was never meant to be a "success"; he was meant
to be a witness. The Church for which he labors is going through the
same trials, agonies, and crucifixions as did its Founder while on
earth. The Gospel is the prehistory of the Church, and the Church is
the posthistory of the Gospel. God is forever testing His Church. The
way of the Jews in the Old Testament was not the way of the
Gentiles. The Acts of the Apostles tell us that "in the ages that are
past, he has allowed Gentile folk everywhere to follow their own
devices" (14:15); and again St. Paul is quoted in the Acts as saying:
"God has shut his eyes to the passing follies" of the Gentiles. But it
was not so with the people of Israel, nor is it so with the Church.

There is a suggestion that the multiple tribulations of Israel were
due to the fact that she was a nation chosen by God. As the prophet
Amos wrote: "Nation is none I have claimed for my own, save
you; and the guilt of yours is none that shall go unpunished" (3:2).
God could wink at the transgression of the Gentiles, but His ineffable
holiness and inflexible judgment would chastise Israel if unfaithful.

A truth that no missionary can ever forget is that any judgment or
crisis that comes upon the world starts first with the Church. We have
no less an authority for this statement than the Rock upon which the
Church was built. St. Peter tells us: "The time is ripe for judgment
to begin, *and to begin with God's own household;* and if our turn

comes first, what will be its issue for those who refuse credence to God's message?" (1 Pt 4:17.)

The greater the privileges enjoyed, the greater the obligations entailed, and the greater the guilt incurred when these obligations are ignored. Missionaries who labor in countries where the population is presumably Catholic, but where the practice is not great, may expect a judgment which will begin with the Church. God is far more dishonored by the sins of those who bear His name, than by those who make no profession at all. The privilege of being a member of Christ's Mystical Body is no guarantee of immunity from trial. If we be spiritual Israel, then shall not the justice of God fall upon us for failure to live out the fullness of grace, as it fell upon Israel of old? "And if you cross me still, I will cross you in my turn, punishing your sins seven fold" (Lv 26:23).

Judgment, however, does not explain the total witnessing to Christ. There is also a certain amount of suffering that is intrinsically bound up with the fact that one is a messenger of Christ. Our blessed Lord said that His disciples will be hated until the end of time. They will be blamed for rending cities and homes, dividing populations, undermining family life, and for leading nations astray. They will be called crazy fanatics, enemies of Caesar, disturbers of peace. They will have more bricks thrown at them than other men roses. Their enemy will not just be Satan, but their enemy will be "men." They will have to stand before governors and kings to render testimony and their suffering will help forward that testimony. It is all part of God's plan, and when they are in that hour of passion, the Holy Spirit will advise them what they are to say. Because they remain true to the Word of God in witnessing to Him, the Word will remain true to them.

As missionaries they wander on earth, yet live in heaven; though they are weak, they protect the world; they taste a peace in the midst of cold wars; they are poor, and yet they have all they want; they stand in suffering, and yet sing in prison like Paul and Silas; they appear dead to everyone in the outside world, but they lead a life of faith within; they have been called to the *Ecclesia,* which means that they have been called out from the world in sanctity to witness to it (cf. Mt 10:16–26), as our blessed Lord Himself warned.

5. *Martyrs, Wet and Dry*

The Church probably has a larger martyrology for the past fifty years than for the first three centuries of the Christian era. Whether we be at the end of the present era of witnessing to Christ is hidden from our eyes by Providence. Intense and thorough as the Communist persecution has been, so far it has not been nearly as long as other persecutions. The Moslem persecution was over ten times longer, and wiped out the Church in many areas of the earth. The destruction of seven hundred sees in Northern Africa in the space of two hundred and fifty years tells of the anti-Christian attitude of the descendants of Ishmael. The Roman persecution, too, was longer than the Communist persecution. From Nero to the Edict of Constantine the record of persecution is as follows:

First Century: Six years of persecution and twenty-eight of tolerance.

Second Century: Eighty-six years of persecution and fourteen years of tolerance.

Third Century: Twenty-four years of persecution and seventy-six years of tolerance.

Fourth Century: Thirteen years of persecution out of the first thirteen years.

In all, during the Roman persecutions the Church had one hundred and twenty-nine years of persecution, and one hundred and twenty years of tolerance.

It may be profitable to consider similarities and differences between the pagan and Communist persecutions. The similarities are fivefold: interrogation, arrest, public trial, torture, apostasy.

Interrogation

In both persecutions there was a semblance of legality, namely, an inquiry of the name, address, and occupation of those on trial. A homily of St. John Chrysostom mentions the form of interrogation used at Lyons in 177. It began with inquiries about name, place, occupation:

"Quid vocaris?"

"Victor."

"Cujus conditionis es?"

"Professor sum romanarum litterarum, grammaticus latinus."

"Cujus dignitatis es?"

"Patre decurione Constantiniensium: avo milite, in comitatu militaverit."

When St. Theodora was led before the judge, she was asked:

"What is your state?"

"I am a Christian."

The judge asked: "Are you slave or free?"

Theodora answered: "I told you I am a Christian; therefore, I am free."

It often happened that both accused and accuser sought a different sense for the words. One judge asked:

"What do you desire?"

The Christian answered: "I desire my salvation."

The judge asked: "Does that mean you wish to sacrifice to the gods?"

At Lyons, one Christian answered all questions saying: "I am a Christian." This reminds one of the Chinese priest who kept repeating the Creed during the months of trial and finally died with it on his lips. St. John Chrysostom commenting on St. Lucien said, "By speaking thus [as a Christian] he gave at once his race, his country, his profession."

Tertullian protested that Christians were persecuted when they confessed the truth; all others on trial were exempt from torture when they confessed to their crimes. He argued that the purpose of torture was to force an avowal, but with Christians, the avowal brought torture. In the year 249 the Emperor Decius published an edict to the effect that "all Christians were to be prosecuted until they denied their faith."

The interrogations were often preceded by a gathering of information against the accused. The "case against the accused" in Roman days was called the *elogium*. The Christians — Dativus, Saturinus, and others — who were arrested in one city were sent to Carthage, and the accompanying soldiers brought the *elogia* with them.

The missionaries in China tell of how the Communists prepared to "frame" them with false evidence. In China, a bowl of marrow was used in evidence against a nun to prove she killed babies. The Communists also dug up the bones of children to prove that the Sisters "murdered" the orphans; or planted guns in the homes of the missionaries to "prove" that they were "imperialistic spies."

Just as Judas felt obliged to preface his betrayal of our Divine Lord by a kiss, so all persecutors felt constrained to use legality as a cloak for rascality. The interrogation and "confession" gave to the courts a seeming air of offended majesty. There seems to have been in both persecutions endless interrogation. The incessant night trials in Russia and China had their rehearsal in the early days. St. Cyprian said that one confession of faith was enough to make a martyr, but the "Christian is dragged out of prison endless times" to confess Christ.

Arrest

There were two and possibly three kinds of arrest in Roman persecution. There was the house arrest or *libera custodia* in which the Christian was under the eyes of guards. St. Cyprian was guarded in this way in Carthage. Opposed to house arrest was *custodia publica*. Eusebius mentions that in the year 380 an imperial order demanded a monthly inspection of all under arrest. In Rome the prison was largely preventive. The object of a prison under Roman law was to detain a prisoner, not to punish him. This was generally observed in relation to all martyrs during the first two centuries. But in the later persecutions, the purpose of arrest was punishment, in order to induce the accused to apostatize. He would then be in irons for months and even for years.

St. Paul awaited his trial before Nero almost two years. But he was under a different kind of arrest, *custodia militis*. For a time, both jailer and prisoner lived together in an apartment rented by Paul. Then came the desertions, such as Demas who wanted an unimperiled life, and others like him; the only one who remained faithful was the unobtrusive, cultivated physician, Luke.

These three types of arrest prevail in the Communist persecutions in China. The length of imprisonment seems to be long in all persecutions, as if the judges hoped that continued isolation would break down the constancy of the faithful. Many missionaries in China were in jail from periods of several months to several years. In Roman days, under Decius, there is a record of Moses the priest who was imprisoned nine months and eleven days. Under Diocletian, Pomphilius was in prison two years before his martyrdom.

Public Trial

Publicity against the faithful seems to be a constant characteristic of all persecutions. Even our Lord was several times brought before the mob. The Romans erected public platforms in order that all might see the accused. The raised area was called *castata*. St. Perpetua spoke of it: *"Ascendimus in castata."* An early traveler into Palestine said he saw the *castata* where Pilate interrogated our Lord.

The mobs were incited then as now. St. Cyprian says that the citizens beneath demanded death with loud cries and burning anger. One judge said to St. Polycarp: "It is the people who demand your death. It is them you must convince." He then asked permission to convince them of Christianity — which was refused. Public platforms were erected in cities, baths, amphitheaters, anywhere, to attract a large crowd. In the Acts of St. Mamacrius, it is stated that "town criers were sent out announcing the trials, and those who were unwilling to come were forced to do so by officials."

In Russia and in her satellite countries, Communism has made use of the radio and the press in order to propagandize against the condemned. In China, there is hardly a village that has not had its public platform wherein missionaries were falsely accused. In most instances, no one in the community would bear false witness against the missionaries. In that case as it was with Bishop Ford, they were removed to another locality. The Acts of the Apostles speaking of St. Paul and Silas said: "And the people joined in the attack against them." It is peculiar how democratic processes become perverted, and the "will of the people" which is supposed to be the "voice of God" becomes in truth the "voice of anti-God."

Torture

Certain forms of torture are common to all persecutions. The Roman persecutions included civil degradation which meant deprivation of the rights of a citizen in which St. Paul so prided himself. There seems to have been in Roman days, more commonly than today, a choice between apostasy and prostitution. Tertullian in 197 spoke of the choice: *ad lenonem potius quam ad leonem.*

At the beginning of the third century, confiscation of property began to be the general rule in order to swell the imperial treasures. The prisoners were often put in stocks which were called *nervus.* The Roman stock was so constructed as to make it possible to tighten the stock five notches. Some contemporaries state that few ever endured the fifth notch. In addition, there was a pit, or *imus carcer,* which was found in prisons then more often than today. Many of the martyrs of Lyons in 177 were kept in dungeons. Origen spent several months in a dungeon. Burning was also common; so perished the aged Polycarp. Under the Emperor Decius, burning was the most common of all persecutions. At first there were mounds constructed so that everyone could see the death; later on they did away with them, and the martyrs were burned on the level of the ground. The Emperor Galerius in the year 309 found a way to slow down the torture by sprinkling water both on the victim and the fire. Being thrown to the beasts was also a common form of persecution. St. Cyprian tells us how often the beasts refused to touch the faithful who were later beheaded.

Many of these forms have been used by the Communists, but there is one fundamental difference in torture which marks off the Communist from the Roman persecution, which will be discussed later.

Apostasy

Cruelty is associated with any form of persecution, but we must look for the nonhuman or the diabolical to explain the desire for apostasy among the enemies of Christianity. When Vishinsky tried Kamenev and Zinoviev as Mensheviks, or "nonrevolutionary" Bolsheviks, he did not try to induce them to "apostatize" and become Bolsheviks. Beria was under no plea to recant his "heresy." Trotskyites under trial by Communists were never asked to abandon their philosophy to become Communists nor were kulaks or capitalists. But what is the mystery behind the ubiquitous attempt on the part of all anti-Christian persecutors to induce the accused to recant the faith? The early Fathers tell us the object of every magistrate was to induce the Christians to apostatize. St. Perpetua was under the plea for months. Roman judges were even promised promotion if they succeeded in getting a Christian to give up the faith. To secure this, they often made use of equivocations and wrote down many apostates who refused to speak. Tertullian tells us that the lips and the mouths of the Christians were often beaten by guards so as to make the protestations of the faithful unintelligible, and those mumbled words were taken as recantations of the faith.

Communism shows the same impassioned desire for apostasy. In Russia, it set up the "Living Church" as a refuge for apostates. In China, the same technique erected an "Independent Church" in which, if the faithful joined, they would be spared persecution. One Chinese bishop was asked to be "pope" of China under the Communists. With well-disguised humor he told the Communists that he expected some day to be the "Pope of the World." Would the Communists want to ruin his chances by making him pope of China alone? The Communists, not seeing his humor, dismissed him. One Chinese woman apostatized under persecution and then later on wrote to the bishop: "Peter denied our Lord and was forgiven. Will I be forgiven?"

In some instances in China those who were burned were tied to the stake by a tiny thread. The slightest motion of the finger, or even the burning of the thread were taken as a sign of apostasy. The desire of the Communists to pervert the faithful into becoming Communists is understandable. But the desire to make them apostatize without becoming Communists is diabolical. The essence of the demoniac is the denial of God. At this point the human and the satanic are in collusion, though the human elements may not always be conscious of the bond. The hatred of God alone explains the various techniques devised to induce abandonment of the faith. In Rome and China alike, there are even the same pleas. Eusebius tells us some were told: "Think of your youth." "Avoid torture." St. Basil says others were told: "Consent with your lips, but keep your belief." "Sacrifice to the gods, though you have in mind your God." Arnobius tells of another judge saying: "Just deny Christ, that will be all." At various periods of history the devil is given a long rope; whenever persecutors seek for apostasy the devil is off his rope.

Differences

More important than the similarities are the differences between the Roman and the Communist persecutions. These differences may be reduced to five: darkness and light, blood and morals, religion and atheism, physical-psychological, heresy as end and as means.

Darkness and Light

The Roman persecution came out of the darkness of paganism; the Communist persecution has come from a land and a people who have sinned against the Light. Rome did not have the faith before it shed the blood of martyrs, but Russia had had the faith for a thousand years before it completely turned its back on it. Rome persecuted out of fear of what was coming; Russia out of hatred of what had come.

A persecution is much more severe when those who direct it have sinned against the faith. None of the Roman persecutors were baptized, except Julian the Apostate, but he came after Constantine and was given only two years to practice brutality. His callousness is shown in his attitude toward the Bishop of Arethusus who once saved Julian from massacre but was tortured to death. But many of the Russian persecutors were baptized, Stalin having been in a minor seminary for a time. The loss of faith sharpens torture. "If I had not come and given them My message, they would not have been in fault." Though the Chinese Communists are without faith, nevertheless the inspiration for their persecution has come from Russia. Communism itself was born philosophically of a hatred of Christianity, Feuerbach having taught Marx to develop a humanism which would restore to man the attributes which he was presently and foolishly giving to God.

Corruptio optimi pessima. The lily smells the foulest of all flowers when it rots. Those who have been baptized and turned against Christ have always a hatred which surpasses that of those who never came to know Him. Grace that gets into the soul and is rejected, is like ground glass in the stomach.

Communism has been born out of a hatred of the Mystical Body of Christ and is therefore capable of greater cruelty and more intense persecution than that of either the Romans or the Moslems. It may be true, that as the second and third generation of Russians become the world masters of Communism, they will persecute less than the Stalins who have been baptized and cradled in the sacred associations of the Church; only a Judas knew where to find our Lord after dark. If Communism continues for fifty years — which it will not — it is likely that the persecution which it would inspire would become less in Russia, for those who would then dictate its savagery will have been isolated from all Christian associations.

Blood and Morals

A second difference is: the faithful in other persecutions were killed without the persecutors impugning their morals. But today the persecution is ideological as well as physical. Even as late as the French Revolution, the priests were beheaded simply because they refused to take the oath to an anti-God regime. They were merely led from an upper floor to a ground floor, made to pass in front of the revolutionists, and asked to sign the oath. Refusing, they were told to walk out of a door. As they did so, the executioner's ax decapitated them. The skulls of these priests are now in the Institut Catholique of Paris near the tomb of Frederic Ozanam.

The Roman persecutors did assail the principle of Christianity but not the morals of the individual Christian. The philosophy of Christianity was impugned but not the virtue of the accused. The Communists, however, attempt to kill the reputation of the faithful before killing their bodies. The great murderers in history were content when they shed blood; the present murderers slay the goodness of the person with his life. It is not merely the representative of virtue they would exterminate, but virtue itself.

It has long been known even in political circles that the Communists seek to obtain compromising information about an individual, or else they manufacture and invent it. This is then used to destroy the integrity of the accused. One of the common features of the Communist trials of our missionaries in China is to accuse them of vice, immorality, and murder in order that the faith be assailed at the same time the faithful are attacked. Witnesses have been known to be subjected to great tortures for months until they became a tool of the Communists to slander the good names of the priests, Sisters, and Brothers. At Yungchow, China, twelve Catholic boys were told that if they did not accuse the priests of immorality they would be killed. The boys answered: "It would be a lie to say that, but since we have lived the Joyful Mysteries before you Communists came, we are now ready with your coming to live the Sorrowful Mysteries."

Rome thought that liquidating Christians would liquidate Christianity; Russia seeks to liquidate both together. What is new in the technique of the anti-Christ today is the attempt to destroy Godliness with the Godlike, Christianity with the Christian.

Religion and Atheism

A third difference is that the Roman persecution was religious, whereas the Communist persecution is atheistic. The Romans did not persecute because they were antireligious. They believed in Jupiter or some kind of god; the Communists, however, are definitely anti-God. The Christians were told they could purchase their liberty by sacrificing to the gods, or dropping a grain of incense before their altars. For example, at the beginning of the reign of Commodus in the year 180, the Christians who were persecuted at Carthage were asked to "exchange" their religion. Saturinus the judge said to Speratus the Christian: "We have a religion and you must respect it. We swear by the Imperial Divinity and we pray for the salvation of the Emperor. It is a very simple religion as you see. You have a religion which insults our own."

A statement of this kind would never be heard from the lips of a Communist persecutor. The reason is to be found in the fact that Communism is atheistic. There are two kinds of atheism, the intellectual atheism which is commonly found among sophomores in secular universities — an atheism born of reading a textbook on biology, ten pages of Mencken, a popular-science article, and the first fifteen pages of "The Golden Bough." Communist atheism is not of this kind. It is of the will rather than the intellect. It does not so much deny God; as the devil who challenges God, it would destroy God. Bourgeois or intellectual atheism is without force or passion; Communist atheism is militant and active. It is only the reality of God which gives energy to the Communist hatred. If there were no God for them to hate, they would be like Don Quixote, tilting with windmills. Their atheism is pugnacious because there is a God to "atheate."

This new form of atheism is often lost sight of in the modern world. The persistent attacks against the Church on the part of men who profess or say they are religious belong to this demoniac godlessness. So also are such attitudes as that of Dietrich Kerler who wrote to Max Scheler: "Even if it were proven by mathematics that God exists, I would not believe. I do not want Him to exist, because He would set limits to my greatness." Sartre has the same idea when he says: "What is opposite me is non-ego; but what is non-ego is nothingness. I am nothing to someone else; someone else is nothing to me; therefore one must return to nothingness." These are various forms of the atheism of Nietzsche who boasted, "God is dead"; but, he adds, the death of God is willed by man. Such atheism is heir to Prometheus who stood up against God so that man could live his own life.

While the early persecutions were "religious," the modern ones are demonic. Blind, irrational, cavernous forces which have been held in bondage for a thousand scriptural years are now roaming the earth. Goethe once described the spirit of the demonic as follows: "I am the spirit that denies. Everything has value inasmuch as it perishes. Sin, destruction, evil — each is my element." The essence of the demonic is the destruction of the Divine Image in the human, whether this destruction be pictorial as it is with a Picasso, or philosophical as with dialectical materialism, or political as it is with Communism. The force behind them all is the "mystery of iniquity." As St. Paul wrote to the Thessalonians: "At present there is a power (you know what I mean) which holds him in check, so that he may not show himself before the time appointed to him; meanwhile, the conspiracy of revolt is already at work; only he who checks it now will be able to check it, until he is removed from the enemy's path." ". . . and his wickedness will deceive the souls that are doomed, to punish them for refusing that fellowship in the truth which would have saved them."

The devil can make use of religion to persecute religion for his purpose is always duplicity and deceit. In the Roman days he made use of a belief in false gods to impugn the true God and His Divine Son. Even the Moslems make use of a belief in God to destroy belief in the God made flesh, misunderstanding as they do the Trinity because Mohammed learned the doctrine badly from some Nestorian heretics. But in these later days the devil uses antireligion or atheism against religion. That is why there is persecution. It may be said to come from a deeper depth of hell than the early persecutions.

Physical-Psychological

The fourth difference is that the Roman persecutions were primarily physical; the Communist persecutions are primarily psychological. The first attacked the body; the second attacks the mind. The Romans made "wet martyrs"; the Communists make "dry martyrs." Perhaps the Communists remember the words of Tertullian that "the blood of martyrs is the seed of Christians." Resolved to keep the Church from growing, they abstain from planting the seed. Birth control may apply not only to the prolongation of the natural life; the Communists apply it to the supernatural life. They try whenever possible to prevent blood from falling to the earth lest the seed should fructify into another Christian. So fearful are they of martyrs that the Chinese Communists demand the exhumation of the body of Archbishop Jarré because the Church buried him in red vestments. The Communists knew enough liturgy to suspect that this was because he was being honored as a martyr. They demanded white vestments be put on instead, but the faithful raised such a protest that the Communists finally gave way to their pleas. The Reds do not like red when it means martyrdom. They also went to the Bishop of Shanghai in protest against miracles being worked at the tomb of a priest whose life they had taken. They told the Bishop: "We will hold you responsible for any miracles wrought through his intercession."

Their new technique is to kill the soul while letting the body live. Our blessed Lord told us not to fear those who kill the body, but rather to fear those who can also kill the soul. No one ever was tempted to do that on a large scale before Communism. Making use of the idea of another Russian, Pavlov, and his notion of the conditioned reflex, they have resorted to the double technique of brainwashing and brain-changing. This means first the complete wiping out of old ideas and the infusion of new Soviet ideologies. The personality is then reduced to a conditioned reflex, so that, given a certain situation, he will react like a Communist parrot.

A Hungarian psychiatrist working on Cardinal Mindszenty explained that the moment the "soul" leaves the body he would "infuse" another soul, a Soviet soul. Failing in this he shrieked: "Why is it that Jesus could drive the devil out of a man, and I cannot put the devil into a man?"

At first the Communists attempted brainwashing by thorough torture, such as forcing the victim to stand for days and nights facing a blazing light. In China they have developed a new technique which is to make use of natural necessities — such as food, sleep, and relief of nature. The accused is fed only ground or powdered rice which makes the mouth very dry. He is not permitted to drink, until five hours or more after eating. The result is that he eats less and less and gradually begins to starve. The second technique is to keep the prisoner awake for a minimum of seventy-two hours. The prisoner is then told to sleep, but he is awakened after fifteen minutes; kept awake for another twelve hours, he is told to sleep again and is awakened after a half an hour. This process continues for weeks until finally the brain becomes so weakened that it is susceptible to every form of suggestion. The prisoner is then told to write out Communist phrases so that they will sink into the unconscious mind and later come out when properly stimulated. Added to this is the torture of not being allowed to satisfy other demands of nature, and then under the most terrible difficulties.

Not until Communism has persecution ever developed such diabolical techniques for destroying the human spirit. The Soviets so boast of their brainwashing that a Communist judge told the American newspaperman before him: "If God Almighty were there on that chair we could make Him confess to anything we wanted Him to confess." This represents the last attempt of the demonic to destroy personality made in the image and likeness of God, and to create a new one — made in the image and likeness of anti-God.

Heresy as End and as Means

Christianity and its dogmas were never sufficiently delineated in the early days, nor were they sufficiently diffused to enable the early persecutors to make a detailed attack upon them. Communism, having the advantage of coming at the end of the second millennium, is able to use heresy as a basis of attack. It must not, however, be assumed that Communism is interested in making heretics; it is rather interested in using heresy as a means to atheism. The Communist attack is not directed against a doctrine; it rather sets itself up a mystical body of the anti-Christ against the Mystical Body of Christ. It uses heresy as means, not as end. Heresiarchs of the past were concerned about winning minds over to their heresy. Com-

munism has no heresy to espouse; if it asks a Catholic to become a
heretic, it is because it profits by an historical and a psychological
fact concerning heresy. The historical fact is that heresy after a time
evaporates; it takes some time for a branch cut off from a vine to
die, but eventually it does die. Communism knows that heresy soon
becomes unbelief. The psychological fact is that the denial of one
truth eventually ends in the denial of all truths.

That explains why the Communists in China concentrated their
attacks on such fundamental dogmas of the Church as: (1) belief in
the Primacy of Peter; (2) the Eucharist; (3) the Blessed Mother.
The Roman persecutions hardly ever mentioned Mary, but the
Chinese Communists told some members of the Legion of Mary that
"Mary is hiding in Shanghai." One nun was asked if she prayed to
Mary against devils. On receiving an affirmative answer the Com-
munist slapped her face saying: "We are those devils." The Religious
Revolution of the sixteenth century was also particularly bitter against
Mary and the Eucharist and the Primacy, but always in the name of
Christianity. The Communists are against them in the name of anti-
Christianity. A treatise in apologetics is contained in that one fact,
did but the world distill it out.

That brings us to the interesting point. Why is it that the Chinese
Communists, who do not believe in God, nor in Christ, told the
missionaries that they could retain their churches, their orphanages,
their hospitals, on one condition, namely, that they deny the Vicar
of Christ? Communists are smarter than heretics. They know that
once the head is decapitated from the body, the body will die; they
know not through grace, but through diabolical inspiration, that the
Primacy of Peter has a Divine foundation; they know that Christian
sects that split from Peter have withered in their beliefs and some
no longer profess the divinity of Christ; they know that if they can
undermine the Rock, the house will be grounded on sand, and the
wind and the rain and the storms will eventually blow it over. Never
before has the Church had such a strong negative argument for the
Primacy of Peter as it has had from Communism.

Persecutions change with the times. Looking back on three great
persecutions, the early Roman, the Religious Revolution, and Com-

munism, the attack has always been against Christ but from a different point of view. The early heresies of the Church were almost all directed against the person of Christ, for example, heresies about His natures, His Person, His relation to the Father, etc.; the persecutors in their turn were directed against those who believed in the Person of Christ as the Son of God.

During the Religious Revolution of the sixteenth century, the attack was not against the physical Christ but against the Eucharistic Christ. The prolongation of His Death and Resurrection in the Mass was labeled a superstition; communion service was substituted for sacrifice which was the satanic way of preventing the memorial of Christ's death being perpetuated through the centuries.

Under Communism, it is not the physical Christ nor the Eucharistic Christ, but rather the mystical Christ in His Church that is attacked. The Communist persecution is not a heresy, nor a schism; it is a different entity. It accepts neither religion as did the Romans, nor Christ as did the Reformists; it repudiates religion, God, and Christ. We have probably seen the last of the great heresies; from now on there will be an attempt to set up the reign of the mystical body of the anti-Christ. Communism is a totalitarian philosophy and as such claims the total man — body and soul. The Church is fighting not a civil war from within Christian sects which accept a section of the Creed; today the Church is face to face with an invasion — the intrusion of a totally alien force from the outside, of the logic of all the petty little heresies of the centuries.

What is new in the modern persecution are the dry martyrs who have not shed their blood, but who have had their brains washed and have undergone mental tortures for the faith. Certainly any one of them would have found it a thousand times easier to have shed their blood than to have gone through the interminable night trials. But in the strict sense of the term they are not martyrs, for a martyr is one who sheds his blood and suffers death for the faith.

Of our Lord it is written: *"Oblatus est quia ipse voluit."* Of each of our missionaries in China and our faithful in Russia, it can be said: *Voluit;* though no one was an actual *oblatio*. In the strict sense, the dry martyrs are confessors. They are like Christ in Gethsemane where He suffered mental torture; they are not like Christ on Calvary.

In the annals of the Church, special place must be made for them. The dry martyrs have had the will to die, though denied the death. Communism is diabolical enough to deprive them of the act which is the mark of perfect charity. St. Thérèse of Lisieux always had the will to be a martyr, though she never achieved it either by mental torture or by death. As she put it: "Martyrdom was the dream of my youth, and it has grown with the years."

To the credit of the dry martyrs, it must ever be kept in mind that punishment, torture, and pain do not make a person a martyr. As St. Paul said: "I may give myself up to be burnt at the stake; if I lack charity, it goes for nothing." St. Augustine developing that idea said that what makes martyrs is not endurance, but justice; it is the cause for which he dies, not the nature of the torture which makes a martyr. *Martyres discernit causa, non poena.* He then goes on to say that the devil has his "martyrs." We would add that Communism has its "martyrs," but not because they love God, rather because they hate God. Since the trials and agonies do not make martyrs, there is something to be said for those who have passed through the brainwashing of the Communists. Little Maria Goretti who was canonized in 1950 was popularly said to be "martyred for chastity." It means simply, she was martyred for another virtue besides faith.

It remains for the Church to decide whether the Mindszentys and the Stepinacs and the Berans and the Fords and the other missionaries in China have not a special claim to veneration. They may not have shed their blood, but they have been witnesses and confessors to the faith. There was a device written on the walls of a concentration camp of Güsen in March, 1945: *Per crucem ad lucem sine sanguine non fit redemptio.* Our dry martyrs have borne the cross, and therefore they have come to the Light. They did not shed their blood, and therefore are not martyrs in the strict sense. But that is not because they willed not to be martyrs. Our modern crucifiers use Simon of Cyrene not to assure a crucifixion and the shedding of blood, but rather to prevent the shedding of blood and then bar them from Calvary.

To be decapitated for the faith, to be devoured by the lions, to be burned, is a torture of a few hours for which thousands have merited martyrdom. But shall not the Church find a special place for those who have been mentally tortured for months and years without denying their faith? St. Thomas says that the virtue of martyrdom depends not on the sufferings but on the sacrifice of all things, even life itself, in testimony of the love of God. Dying is less important than the disposition of love which affirms the love of Christ and the Church despite all brainwashings. In our hymn of Easter, we say, love is the priest of the sacrifice of Christ. *Amor sacerdos immolat.*

In a diminished degree, we may say the same of all who are witnessing to the faith in uranium and salt mines, Siberian forests, Chinese prisons, and exile. Communism has found a way not to shed their blood, but it has not found a way to prevent their love of witnessing to Christ. We who are their contemporaries must find a way to honor their love which was denied the shedding of their blood. At least, we can say of them: *Martyres sunt, sed amoris.*

6. Sin and the Missions

The world is full of "Night Christians." "Night Christians" are known in two ways: (a) they are afraid of compromising their position in the world, if they are "too Christian"; (b) they reduce Christ to the role of a Teacher and Wonder-Worker, but not a Savior.

The "patron" of the "Night Christians" is Nicodemus, a learned member of the Sanhedrin, who appeared at night on a visit to our Lord lest his reputation in the court suffer by an open association with our Lord. Furthermore, seeking to flatter our Lord and prove himself broad-minded and tolerant, he called Him a "Teacher."

The Light of the World fixed His eyes on the Night Christian and told him what the world needed is not a teacher, but a Life-Giver. Truth there must be, but also a Power that will turn men around, completely change their natures, give them a new birth. Our Lord is saying He is not just a teacher; He is a Savior. Then He foretells the Cross: "The Son of Man must be lifted up, as the serpent was lifted up by Moses in the wilderness; so that those who believe in Him may not perish, but may have Eternal Life" (Jn 3:15).

The meaning is this: the Israelites in the desert who were bitten by serpents were cured of the poison by looking at a brass serpent which Moses made and hung on a crossbar. The brass serpent looked poisonous, but was not. So our Lord said He *must*, that is, in obedience to His Father's will, be lifted up on a cross. Like the brass serpent that seemed poisonous but was not, so He would seem full of our guilt, and yet be without it, because He was God. He must die, because He must save, and He must save because He loves. The cross to Him would not be a humiliation, but an exaltation.

To bring to men Eternal Life, there must be sacrifice; it does not come from listening to a teacher. It has to be bought, not with study but with pain. Our deepest need is for something more than a teacher or pattern; it is to restore in us the Divine Image that was cracked and marred by sin.

Such "Night Christians" profess Christ, but only as a Teacher, and with a great caution lest they embarrass themselves before the world. They may even in a wild stroke of sophomoric tolerance equate Christ with "the other great teachers like Buddha and George Bernard Shaw."

In our mission lands the Hindus are "Night Christians." They will absorb Christ in their pantheon of millions of gods, provided He does not claim to be Divinity Itself. The Moslems, too, will accept Christ with the proviso that He be termed the "last prophet announcing Mohammed." These and the nocturnal brood in our Western World have one thing in common: *they ignore the fact of human sin.* Only when the blind recognizes his blindness does he cry out for the miracle of sight. Only when each man sees himself as having broken a relationship of love, as desiring pardon and cleansing, and above all as craving a new nature which cannot be evolved from within, but given only from without, will he want a Savior and a Redeemer. To understand Christ, we must understand sin. An underestimation of its gravity brings man down to the superficial and impotent conception of Nicodemus, "Thou art a Teacher."

Our missionaries will never win the Eastern World to Christ by merely demonstrating the superiority of Christ's teaching over that of Buddha or Lao-tze or Confucius. Men will generally choose the teacher they have known longest or best. The key to missionary progress among those who already have great teachers is to go into their hearts — not their books; to hold the mirror up to their consciences — not to nature; to point out the blots on the manuscripts of their lives and not the brilliance of the text.

The philosophy of the Eastern World is based on the negation of desire for the sake of unity with the Absolute. The modern philosophy of our Western World is based on the affirmation of the ego for the sake of pleasure and profit. In neither is there a conviction of sin or a consciousness of guilt, and, therefore, a need of purgation. The Oriental believes he needs only to be taught to be saved; the modern Occidental believes he needs only to be psychoanalyzed to be integrated. The saving knowledge of one comes from without, and of the other, from within.

The Easterner is, perhaps, nearer Christ than the contemporary Westerner. The latter may come to the consciousness of guilt only through disaster and catastrophe; the former, never having rejected the message of salvation, may greet it as "Good News," as it was saluted in the beginning. But to be so accepted, it must be preached. St. Paul did not go among the Gentiles as knowing anything but "Christ and Him Crucified." The heretics of the second century, on the contrary, were willing to accept Christ as another Plato as the Moslems now accept Him as another prophet.

Obstacles to the Preaching of the Crucified

Despite the fact that the Eastern World seems to be favorable to the Cross because of the Eastern love of detachment, there are, nevertheless, the same stumbling blocks in the Eastern World as St. Paul found among the Greeks. These are twofold:

a) The heresy of the Eastern World has been the heresy of Gnosticism. Under this title may be included that conglomerate of fantastic speculations concerning the universe, man, and deity. Those parts of the Eastern World that were in more or less close touch with Christianity through heresies sought access to the Divine through mythological, speculative, ceremonial, and mystical modes, rather than through the self-revelation of God to man.

The essence of the Eastern religions, therefore, is that *man goes to God;* the essence of Christianity is that *God comes to man.* Moslemism accepted the tradition that God comes to man through a book and a revelation, but that man has no need of God to purify him; the absolution from sin is effected through his own ablution and not through the blood of the Lamb. There is no priesthood, no mediatorship between God and man, no redemption, because there is no sense of sin.

b) A second reason why the Eastern World is reluctant to accept the crucified Savior is because, though the gods should be worshiped through fitting sacrifices and cults, they rarely interfered in the lives of men. Buddha does mention gods, but with some mixture of good will and irony. The gods themselves are bound by chains of desire and involved in the "wheel of birth." They may be worshiped, but sometimes Buddha is represented as having the gods pay homage to him as the "Awakened One" who is free from the "cycle of births." The idea is release from the cycle of time and birth, not from the chains of sin and guilt. With the Hindus the amelioration of the world is through successive *avataras* but there is never redemption. The penance of the fakirs is not in expiation of personal guilt but to acquire a superhuman power.

Thus, the Eastern World knows no personal guilt, either because man is conceived as achieving unity with the Absolute through his own efforts, or because the emphasis is on escaping the cycles of time rather than release from sin. The concept of "good" and "evil" plays no important role in Eastern religions, as there is no concept of man's fall. Ethics are based on the integration of man into cosmic happenings, but not with regeneration. Buddhism aims at release from the sorrows of the world, not from the sinfulness of man. Japan has been conspicuous for its inability to discern, much less grapple with, the problem of evil. Whoever breaks a rule of Tao commits an error, but he does not commit a sin in the deeper sense. From a psychological point of view, it is interesting that observers say that the Chinese have few "conflicts" such as are studied in the Western World. "Conflicts" such as we know them are related to guilt; the conflicts of the Chinese, if there be any, are between mask and reality.

Given these facts, the problem remains: how can the missionary bring them a crucified Savior who saves from sin? The answer will, to a great extent, depend on a knowledge of the customs, habits, and philosophy of the people to whom the Gospel is preached. But what must not be forgotten is that God trains His missionaries through suffering, sacrifice, and penance in order to atone for sin, and this method must be used today.

How the Jews Became Mission-Minded Through Sacrifice

Before the Jews were sent into captivity, Jehovah was sometimes regarded as a "national God." David prayed that he might not die away from his country. In exile, the Jews asked: "How can we sing a song to God in a foreign land?" Naaman asked Eliseus for "two mules' burden of earth." Naaman, the Syrian, wished to worship Israel's God who befriended him in Judah. He felt that in order to do so he had to pray on Jehovah's own soil.

This narrow concept of God was changed into a universal concept through captivity, sacrifice, and bondage. Once uprooted and forced to acknowledge God in foreign lands, they understood better a *universal God* of *all men*. The missionary ideal was developed through *crisis*.

Jonas was commissioned by God to go on a foreign mission. He rebelled against it, and took a boat to another port, because God was their God, and not the God of the Gentiles. But his concept of God was enlarged through sacrifice, which actually became a symbol of the sacrifice and death of Christ on the Cross, by his being buried in the belly of a whale for three days. Incidentally, it must be noted that he converted the people of Nineveh by reminding them of their sins and the necessity of doing penance. He, Jonas, was converted by penance, and so were the people. The cross was already beginning to appear as dawn in the sky; Israel was missionary to the extent that it was penitential and crucial, and the pagans were converted to the extent that they were impressed with a cross and redemption.

Simeon was ready to sing his *Nunc Dimittis* the moment he saw a Child who was to be contradicted by a cross, and a Woman who was to be pierced with a sword of sorrow. In Simeon's waiting all the Gentile world was waiting, for this Child who was given the name of Jesus or *"Savior"* was to be, not only a fulfillment of the hopes of Israel, but also a "Light to the Gentiles." Once Simeon had a prophetic anticipation of Calvary, he, too, became missionary, as Jonas did in his suffering, and the Israelites in their exile.

Simeon went still further and saw this Child as one set for the "fall and the resurrection of many." It would be so, not because His teaching would contradict other teachers, but principally because Christ would create a strife between good and evil; His very coming would disclose evil in our lives; the closer He would get to us, the deeper would be our conviction of sin, until at times we would feel that a sword was thrust into our souls. If He were a Light, It was to dissipate darkness, not to be another light; if He were *the* Light, It would be to put the Night Christians to flight by revealing the hidden recesses of sin and evil.

Simeon understood Christ better than Nicodemus, for to Simeon He was a Rock of stumbling and offense, a Signal that calls out the opposition of an imperfect nature, a Sword which pierces the soul and divides virtue and vice. Even in His teaching, the thoughts of many would be revealed, for His presence would determine whether our thoughts are good or evil. If we abide in our former ways after seeing Him, we make ourselves more sinful; He imposes high duties on us, the very neglect of which covers us with fresh guilt.

The coming of Christ to every mission in the world is not that of another teacher; it is the occasion for a fall or a resurrection. Ghana is judged by the way it receives the missionaries; Africa decides its future by the mere fact that it sees the Babe, as did Simeon; Japan determines its future by its attitude to the chapels and the schools and the leprosaria staffed by the ambassadors of the Savior. Christ cannot be exhibited before men without trying their hearts.

Nicodemus thought he was praising our Lord when he called Him a teacher; our Lord said He was the Giver of Life — life to those who were dead in sin. Even the very words with which Nicodemus began the discourse that night, "We know," signified that his learned group felt they had a monopoly on wisdom; in that exclusiveness was a denial of the universalism of redemption. As the Jews of old came to realization of God's love for all men through sacrifice and exile, so the Gentile world will come through the preaching of Christ who died for our sins. Even the development of the missionary spirit at home will be accomplished only through the preaching of sacrifice which is the principle behind the Holy Father's own Pontifical Society for the Propagation of the Faith.

But whichever way the Gentiles come to the Savior, there is always hope for the "Night Christians." Nicodemus the timid was transformed into a courageous confessor. When the cross came, He went to Calvary and claimed the body of Christ. He was not there at the Crucifixion; he was not yet brave enough for that. But probably when he heard of the Crucifixion, he remembered the words of our Lord about "being lifted up." From now on he was ready even for martyrdom, as there dawned on him the only truth worth knowing: *Christ is a Savior.*

The missionaries abroad and we at home can work as a unit to convert the "Night Christians." On their side, they must bring home to pagan hearts the need of a Savior; on our side, we must make sacrifices out of love for that Savior, so that we give to the missions, not our gifts alone, but our spirit which is the fruit of the cross. Then shall the Night Christians and the Day Christians know that "God so loved the world that He gave His only-begotten Son," so that those who believe in Him may not perish, but have eternal life.

7. Intercession and the Missions of the Church

No one ever spiritually influences the world who is a part of it. One cannot tie up a package if he goes into it. The expanse of the sea is best seen from the shore, and the politics and economics and social movements of the world are best viewed *sub specie aeternitatis*.

That is why there has always been throughout history, in time of crisis, a detachment and withdrawal from the world. The Stoics withdrew into a kind of an invulnerability or apathy; the Epicureans, into imperturbability. From a war-ridden Indic world, the Buddhists withdrew into immutability or an unruffled calm (Nirvana).

Theirs was a detachment from the world, however, that never went back to it again. It was an asylum on an island rather than a hospital among the sick. The impulse that carried them along was a push of aversion, not of redemption. When men were more intellectual, as in the days of Greece, the liberated sage was one who detached himself from the world to indulge in blissful contemplation; today, the beatniks, juvenile delinquents, and fellow travelers protest against a society which they refuse to save. They withdraw from the world but not to save it.

Withdrawal and return are the temporal phases of transcendence and immanence in Divinity. God is in the world because He is outside of it.

In the Ascension, Christ withdraws from the world, the better to be in it through the mission of the Spirit. As St. Paul says, Christ ascended from the world *"ut impleret omnia"* — that He might fill all things with His Spirit.

"I have taken you out of the world" is the withdrawal part

of the missionary life; "Go ye into the world" is the return after sanctification.

Making this as concrete as possible, spiritual detachment from the world is the condition of every successful missionary enterprise, whether it be in a rich parish in America or a poor parish in Africa. In a prosperous civilization, it is so easy to believe that all missionary activity is dependent upon alms. It is very likely that Judas had much more money in his pouch than any of the other Apostles, inasmuch as he was treasurer; but his apostolic influence through history has been null. What is often forgotten in the Church is the value of *intercession* for the missions. Intercession is withdrawal and return, but unlike the work of the missionaries themselves it influences the world indirectly. The missionaries operate directly in India, Japan, and other mission lands; intercessors work indirectly: they go to God through withdrawal from the world and thus prepare for the return of God's graces in the souls the Church hopes to convert.

Intercession in Scripture

Within the Church itself, there prevails the Communion of Saints, which like a spiritual telephone exchange permits the transfer of merits between the Church Triumphant, the Church Militant, and the Church Suffering. Is there not, however, in the missions another kind of communion, namely, the communion of the saints or the members of the Church with the nonsaints or those who have not yet been evangelized? It is this kind of communion of saints between the evangelized and the non-evangelized which is one of the most potent influences in the mission world.

The Old Testament is full of this idea. No mission land in this world could be as corrupt as the city of Sodom, and yet did not God say that He would be attentive to Abraham and his intercession? "Should I hide my purpose from Abraham, this man who is destined to give birth to a people so great and so powerful?" (Gn 18:18.)

As we members of the Church of the twentieth century look upon China, Northern Korea, Northern Vietnam, Russia, Hungary, and Poland, shall we not intercede to God and say: "Wilt thou, then, sweep away the innocent with the guilty?" (Gn 18:23.) With a strange mixture of humility and boldness, which is the essence of intercession, Abraham asked if God had considered that His plan to overthrow the five cities would involve a sad commingling of both the righteous and the wicked.

The argument is not that Abraham was more tenderhearted and compassionate than God; rather, he was a just man pleading another's case before God. Intercession is not based on the merits of the intercessor. Abraham knew this for he confessed that he was nothing "but dust and ashes" (verse 27) and he felt that God might be angry at a mere man presuming thus to reason with Him.

When, therefore, prayers are asked for the missions, the faithful of the Church in Rome and New York, Brussels and Buenos Aires must not think that God hears their prayers simply because they are just, but because they have an interest in the blind and unfortunate and in sinners. What is interesting to note is that as the bargaining went on, Abraham *ceased asking before God stopped giving*. Abraham stopped at ten just men in the city, but if he had pursued further, we know not at what figure God would have stopped. We do know from another instance that for one man Jerusalem would have been spared.

> Go the rounds of Jerusalem, search the streets of it with hue and cry; and if you find one man there that faithfully does his duty, and keeps troth, then the city shall be pardoned (Jer 5:1).

Did not Judah intercede for Benjamin (cf. Gn 44:18), Esther intercede for her people (cf. Est 8:3), Daniel intercede for his people (cf. Dn 9:11)? Does not God, through Isaias, reveal the necessity of interceding for the nonbelievers?

> I have set watchmen, Jerusalem, upon thy walls, that shall never cease crying aloud, day or night; you that keep the Lord in remembrance, take no rest, nor let him rest either, till he has restored Jerusalem, spread her fame over all the earth (Is 62:6, 7).

The missionaries are, as it were, watchmen set on the wall of Jerusalem. They are to work day and night. Here there may be a reference to the Law which required those who ministered in the sanctuary to serve day and night (cf. Ps 133:1; Acts 20:31).

But all who make mention of the Lord, Isaias continues, are bidden not to keep silence. This includes all the faithful. How powerful this intercession is is to be found in the words of the Vulgate: *Ne detis silentium ei* — "Give the Lord no rest." We are to remind Him of His gracious promises, as Jacob did (cf. Gn 32:12), and, like Jacob, wrestle with Him until we prevail. The same constancy of intercession is found in the New Testament — for example, the Chanaanite woman and the unfortunate widow (cf. Mt 15:22–28; Lk 18:1–8). The Lord of the Harvest is to be given no rest, no peace. We "harass" Him with our pleadings, our appeals for the Moslems, the Buddhists, the Communists! Or do we? The world is wicked, we may object; why intercede for it?

The World

The "world" has various significations in Scripture. First, it may be the physical world in which there is a revelation of the created power of God.

> The God who made the world and all that is in it, that God who is Lord of heaven and earth, does not dwell in temples that our hands have made; no human handicraft can do Him service, as if He stood in need of anything, He, who gives to all of us life and breath and all we have (Acts 17:24, 25).

The "world" also signifies humanity:

> He, through whom the world was made, was in the world, and the world treated Him as a stranger (Jn 1:10).

On the other hand, the "world" may be understood as a "spirit," and here the world and God are in complete opposition, because the spirit of Christ is not the spirit of the world.

> Those others, belonging to the world, speak the world's language, and the world listens to them (1 Jn 4:5).

Furthermore, the world is dominated by the prince of this world:

> . . . now is the time when the prince of this world is to be cast out (Jn 12:31).

It is the spirit of the world that hates Christ (cf. Jn 15:18–19). All those who possess the Spirit of Christ are in the world, but they are not of it.

If the world is understood as being the seat of the power of evil and the enemy of the Spirit of Christ from which we are to be separated, then what relation do the faithful have to Communist countries and to mission countries, which certainly do not have the Spirit of Christ? Can there be any bond between the Light shining in darkness and the darkness itself?

Here intercession enters into an entirely new phase, and the bond between the two is intercession understood as *sacrifice,* not just as mere pleading. The duty of being bound to the mission world by intercession is beyond challenge:

> This, first of all, I ask: that petition, prayer, entreaty and thanksgiving should be offered *for all mankind,* especially for kings and others in high station, so that we can live a calm and tranquil life, as dutifully and decently as we may (1 Tm 2:1, 2).

But the communication between those who have Christ and those who have not Christ has a deeper dimension, and it involves an intercession related to the sacerdotal prayer of Christ. Nothing better expresses what our intercession should be, in relation to the mission world, than the fifty-third chapter of Isaias and the words of John in reference to our blessed Lord:

> Look, this is the Lamb of God; look, this is he who *takes away the sins of the world.*

Here we have set in contrast darkness and Light, the sin of the world and the absolute Innocence of the Lamb of God. What is the bond between the two? It is the sacrifice of the Lamb. It is the death of the Innocent for sinners. The forgiveness of sins during His mortal life, the expulsion of the devils — even seven of them from one woman — reached its climax in the missionary prayer from the cross: "Father, forgive them for they know not what they do." At the Jordan and on Calvary there is the taking on of the burden of guilt of others, which is a higher form of intercession than Abraham knew, until he had the dim vision of it in the command to sacrifice his son.

Too often we throw off the words "prayer for the missions" according to a set formula and without much thought. We who are committed by pontifical appointment to the work of soliciting alms shrink from the mere material side of the missionary task, knowing that our task is not fulfilled in overflowing coffers but in some incorporation to Jordan and to Calvary, to Africa and to Asia.

Both Spiritual and Physical

Prayer for the missions, therefore, does not mean a pious *Hail Mary* said in favor of others. It is not a pious monologue of the Church with itself. There is something profoundly corporal about it. This we find in St. Paul's Epistle to the Romans:

> And now, brethren, I appeal to you by God's mercies to *offer up your bodies as a living sacrifice,* consecrated to God and worthy of his acceptance (Rom 12:1).

It is not just the lips and common worship that bind the Church with the missions. The body is the common denominator and the means of reconciling the Lamb of God with the sins of the world and the Church of the faithful with those who are walking in darkness. Intercession is not uniquely a spiritual thing; it is not just vocal prayer, as the sacrifice of our Lord was not uniquely a spiritual act. Intercession is both spiritual and physical; it belongs to body and soul and is confirmed by the sacrifice of one's life for a neighbor.

The Greek word that is used by St. Paul in the preceding verse is the usual one for the *presenting* of sacrificial animals at the altar. Our bodies are here specified with probable reference to the bodies of victims which were offered in the old ritual. Our sacrifice, however, differs from them in that it is a "living sacrifice." This means that the body is the agent by which we offer ourselves, after the example of Christ, to bring the non-Christian world to redemption. Furthermore, it is to be a rational or *reasonable sacrifice* in which the intercession is not based solely upon the thing offered, but upon the act of offering; it is not just a ceremonial or external plea for the mission world, but rather that of a devoted life. As we read in Sacred Scripture, "the body is for the Lord," and the Lord's purposes are for the salvation of the world.

Because of a purely canonical approach to their faith, Catholics are too apt to think that their spiritual relationships are solely with one another. Intercession, on the contrary, places the faithful and the Church between God and the world. Hence, we read: "This, first of all, I ask: that petition, prayer, entreaty and thanksgiving should be offered *for all mankind,* especially for kings and others in high station, so that we can live a calm and tranquil life, as dutifully and decently as we may" (1 Tm 2:1, 2).

Here is a missionary concept at its height, namely, the presence of the Church in the world, intervening for the world before the throne of God who has loved the world so much that He sent His only-begotten Son. St. Paul puts this kind of intercession first and foremost. St. Chrysostom tells us that the early liturgies of the Church bore this idea: "Every day, both in evening and in morning, we offered prayers for the whole world." The literal acceptance of this would mean that we would have to pray for Communists, for Queen Elizabeth, for the President of the United States, for African kings, and for heads of tribes in New Guinea. The role of the Church Militant is not just to battle against evil or those who are totally unredeemed, but rather to do battle that we may spiritually bring others unto the sweet yoke of Christ.

St. Paul explains:

> Such prayer is our duty, it is what God, our Savior, expects of us, since it is his will that *all men should be saved,* and be led to recognize the Truth; there is only one God, and only one Mediator between God and men, Jesus Christ, who is a man like them and gave Himself as a ransom for them all (1 Tm 2:3–6).

Responsible for All Men

The Church Militant does not fulfill its duty merely by sanctifying those who are already sanctified or by educating those who are already baptized, essential as these be, but also by extending some kind of sacrificial intercession to those whom our blessed Lord said He would draw to Himself by being lifted up on the Cross.

> Yes, if only I am lifted up from the earth, I will attract all men to myself (Jn 12:32).

The missionary language used in this passage is in contrast to the restrictiveness which would ignore what St. Paul suggested in the Epistle to the Colossians, that it should be our aim "to present *every man* perfect in Christ" (Col 1:28). This intercession cannot be renounced even when the political authorities are the declared enemies of the Church and persecute it. St. Peter at the close of his life asked that the king be honored, and here he referred to the very one who would crucify him upside down. The men who exercise authority may be wicked, but the authority itself comes from God. The words of our Lord rest unaltered:

> Love your enemies, do good to those who hate you, pray for those who persecute and insult you, that so you may be true sons of your Father in Heaven, who makes his sun rise on the evil and equally on the good, his rain fall on the just and equally on the unjust (Mt 5:44, 45).

Intercession for the missions is more than an Our Father, a Hail Mary, and an invocation to St. Francis Xavier every day. It is something that involves our body, because of the supreme truth that Christ died for *all men*. As He used His body as the instrument of Redemption, so we in a lesser degree, and through the power of His grace, use our bodies for the extension of that Redemption. If prayer involved only the mind, it would not involve sacrifice; but inasmuch as Redemption was accomplished through the body, our missionary intercession involves the body. Though we may not go to foreign lands, nevertheless our body is offered as a reasonable sacrifice to God that sin may not have dominion over those who are outside of the fold. An unconcern for those outside of the Church is to forget the high priestly prayer of our Lord the night of the Last Supper, when speaking to His heavenly Father, He said:

> . . . So that *the world* may come to believe that it is Thou who hast sent Me (Jn 17:21).

8. *The Spiritual Approach to Vocations*

The institutions of the world in all their forms are committed to making a success of the human experiment in egocentricity. The purpose of the Church, on the contrary, is to bring man to repentance and hope. The very evils of the world today are a proof of the transcendence of Christianity since these evils increase as civilization opposes Christianity. The exile of God is followed always by the tyrannization of man. The business of the Church is not to build a social order on an unregenerate humanity, but rather to give men another birth and thus beget a new social order. The primary function of the Church is not to improve human nature, but to redeem it; the commission given to the Church by the Divine Master was not to make men better in the natural order, but to elevate them to an order which is more above the natural than the life of a rose is above the existence of the stone.

A second principle is that *regeneration is to be accomplished through the minority, not the majority.* It was the majority that condemned our Lord before Pilate; it was the minority of only one hundred and twenty souls who awaited the Spirit on Pentecost, and then converted the Roman Empire. The great error of Communism as well as of a democracy that loses its Divine roots is to think that the masses or the majority make civilization. Lenin held this view at one time, but later abandoned it, and came to the idea that if the world is ever to be won to Communism, there would have to be a revolutionary *elite* who would guide the stupid masses; thus they would be made to choose their own enslavement. This vision of a revolutionary core at the center is actually a perversion of the

254

Christian idea of an apostolic elite. Lenin stole the idea of vocation from Christianity, but instead of making men disciples of Christ, he made them disciples of anti-Christ.

The problem of vocation has thus been put into an entirely new light by the fact that the whole world outside the Church has become missionary.

1. *Communism is missionary.* It has its own propaganda; its foreign-mission field is the world; its mandate is "Going therefore teach ye all nations, communizing them in the name of Marx, Lenin, and Stalin"; it trains its disciples in the rigid seminary of the Kremlin, and its sole purpose is to rebuild Babel with a hammer and cut down the Wheat of Life with a sickle. Suddenly the Church is face to face with a countermissionary activity. We needed vocations before because we had to call the heathens to Christ; now we need them because, not lands, but souls, have become the prize of both the Church and the anti-Church. Communism wants lands, but not like the colonialism of the past century. It seeks *minds first,* and then lands; first propaganda, and then economic slavery. Christianity is challenged for the first time by a world power seeking immortal souls, as Satan seeks them; it behooves the Church to concentrate on vocations as never before. Communism and Christianity are both seeking souls but for purposes as different as God and Baal.

2. *Secular governments are missionary.* They are offering help to the socially disinherited people of the world. The United States has given billions of dollars to the foreign peoples of the world, for relief, rehabilitation, and recovery. Religious leaders often ignore the value of this generosity on the part of our government, but there had to be a tremendous leaven of Christianity to produce such an outpouring of sacrifices within one world power. Sacrifices indeed they are, though they are called grants and subsidies, because they have come from the pockets of the American people, who think of other people as well as themselves.

Shall the secular forces of the world against which we sometimes protest outdo us who are pledged to charity? Shall their technical assistants, who are a kind of missionary, be the only ones in the foreign field? The Kremlin takes possession of minds by propaganda, while our government is trying to heal famished bodies and untrained minds through alms. Shall the Church lag behind? With propagandists from Russia, technical assistants from America, what about vocations from the Church?

The missionary problem is not now what it was in the nineteenth or any other century. We now have to combat the atheism of Communism and the secularism of the United Nations. Physicians are more needed in a plague than in seasons of health. Vocations are needed more when governments take over souls in one instance, and in the other reduce spiritual problems to social welfare. The Lord calls, but in addition to the call from above we now have a call from below, that is, from the people themselves. The new vocation will not only have to save the pagans *for* God; it will have to save them also from secularization.

Why Are Vocations Lost?

Our blessed Lord once explained why vocations are lost. The first reason is that volunteers for the missions forget that the missions are a sacrifice and not a romance. When the young man, without counting the costs, told our Lord that he would go wherever He wanted him to go, our Lord asked him if he was prepared for discomforts. "The foxes have holes, the birds of the air their nests, but the Son of Man hath nowhere to lay His Head."

The second reason why they are lost is worldliness, that is, a refusal to give up consolations. The second young man asked our Lord to bury his father before going on the missions but our Lord suggested that following Him meant leaving the world; let the spiritually dead bury the physically dead; but the spiritually alive are needed for the living. Forget your home or your diocese or your country and follow Me.

The third reason why vocations are lost to the foreign missions is because of a desire to stay at home, and the consequent refusal to become one with the people we are to serve. When called, the young man asked our Lord permission to take leave of those at home. Farewells must be said, ties with home must be strengthened, the heart must be strengthened in its domesticity. But our Lord said that the foreign missionary life was social martyrdom. It is no better to defer a vocation for the sake of the living than for the sake of the dead. Today is golden and tomorrow is silver.

Specific Recommendations for Increasing
Foreign Missionaries

Religious societies will secure more vocations if they give a certain number of their members to the missions, either domestic or foreign. The spiritual law here applies: As we give, so it shall be given unto us. If a community of Sisters send their Sisters only to the parishes where they are well paid and well housed, and in one instance have the walls of their cells decorated, and refuse to send them to the poor missions where there are no returns except the souls they save, the community will find that their vocations will decrease. One community known to us sent six Sisters on a poor mission in the South. The superior took them out and transferred them to a "good parish" in the North. That year the community lost ten young Sisters, six by death, and the Mother Superior immediately dispatched Sisters to the poor missions of the Church. There is a deep spiritual lesson hidden in the fact that today the greatest increase of vocations is either in the contemplative orders or in the mission societies. Young people are looking for sacrifice. It is not just their wool they are willing to have sheared; they are also little lambs of God ready for sacrifice.

Date et Dabitur. There are two ways to look at giving: whether the gifts be materiality or personality. The first is the mundane way: what we give we lose. If I give half my apple to the foreign missions, I diminish my possessions 50 percent. The second is the Divine way: "Give and it will be given unto you."

This is an aspect of the *stultitia crucis,* where the Divine arithmetic is the inverse of that of the world. Ananias was the first "practical" lay worker of the Church. After all, he had to look after his own needs, and this business of supplying the Apostles like Thomas and James who were ready to start out for India and Spain seemed a waste. Divine Justice does not act so promptly today on the "practical," but the Divine Displeasure remains the same.

Nature itself suggests that there be a sharing before a possessing.

The right and left side of the heart have no communion with one another. The blood that flows from one side of the heart has to pass through the entire body and its cells, before it comes back to the other half of the heart. In like manner, a parish, a diocese, a religious community never enters into the fullness of its own life until it has passed its plasma of spirituality and its blood-giving missionary activity through the entire Mystical Body which is the Church.

Educating priests in mission lands. Admitting the advantages of diocesan seminaries, their multiplication can injure the more Catholic spirit which is essential to the Church. Seminarians are educated *in* the diocese, *for* the diocese, and *with* the diocesan clergy. Their vision from the first day is to a great extent circumscribed by their dioceses, and the missions are looked upon as a work of supererogation, or an ideal which must be presently deferred. The great increase of diocesan seminaries, to some extent, may develop a parochialism and a narrowness of view, which is inconsistent both with the political and the religious outlook on the world. Unity is desirable but not uniformity. This was the great error of Dr. Conant of Harvard in opposing religious schools. He would destroy the difference of opinion resulting from that which is essential to the functioning of democracy. In like manner, unity is the mark of the Church, but to have all the men in a diocese educated in the same way, by the same teachers, with identically the same outlook on Probabilism and Physical Premotion, is to forget the diversity of threads that makes up the seamless garment of the Church.

The Church in America would prosper more if, in addition to educating young men in our diocesan seminaries, provision was also made to send some abroad to study. The European seminaries are well known, but some students could be sent to the seminaries in India or Africa. Their courses are on a par with any of our seminaries, and in some instances are better. The bishop would then have priests who thought of the Church in the *world* rather than the Church in the *parish*. As a result, the diocese would be blessed by priests educating the faithful about the world and by awakening the young to vocations for the "ends of the earth" where apostles were sent to bear witness to the Divine Name.

Recognition by the bishops that they belong to the world. The bishops of the Church are first sent to the world; only for jurisdictional reasons are they given certain areas. They are first missionary; they first have the circle of the world and then are assigned to a segment; they are called for a communion with other bishops first and then to their title; they are of the world before they are of the diocese. As they pay tribute to the universal mission, God will bless their jurisdiction. The paternity of a bishop and the priest is not American; they are neither American nor African, neither English nor Indian; our fatherhood is beyond "flesh and blood" and resides in those higher regions of the spirit of those who received the Spirit of adoption. Few there are who can claim the same love of souls as did Bishop Grandin, but none who will fail to admire him in his detachment: "I have never bought an episcopal ornament; on many circumstances money has been given me for my personal use, but I always give it to the missions. It is only after twenty-five years of the episcopacy that I have all that was required for pontifical ceremonies, and I would not have had these ornaments if they were not given."

As the bishop is not secondarily missionary but is first summoned to preach Christ to unregenerate humanity and then to a diocese, so the priest is committed to universality. As priests we are committed to Christ who in the drama of Reparation permitted Himself to be stripped of all His garments, that He might not be localized in time or in place, nor belong to any nation, or race, or people. In imitation of it, all the priests of the world in renewing Calvary may never dress so as to identify themselves with their nationality or their people. They are like *universals* in philosophy, stripped of all individuating notes to remind them that the sacrifice is for the world. During the Mass the Church tells the priest, as he lowers the chalice in the Offertory, to swing it over the corporal in the four directions of the earth; thus his heart, his faith, and his love go out to China, India, the Eskimos, and the Russians as he says: *Totius mundi salute.* Thus he is separated from that narrowness of vision which would make him think of the sheep only in his own pasture, and make him ardently yearn for the day when the blood of Christ will be the laver of regeneration to the one billion one hundred million pagans in the world.

Parents should encourage love of the missions in their children.
The Christ who says to the child, "Give Me your heart," also says
to the parents, "Give Me your child for the missions." The parents
are but trustees of that wealth. The child has come from them, but
not for them. He is an arrow put into the quiver of a home, but its
target has been set by God for all eternity. Nothing so speeds the
arrow to that target as spreading the love of Christ in pagan lands.

"The harvest is great and the laborers are few." Through prayers
and encouragement, the youth of America can be induced to join
many of the mission-sending societies, to follow what the Holy
Father calls a "sublime vocation." America in the economic order is
the pantry of the world; in the military realm it is the arsenal of
democracy; in the domain of the spirit, it must become the nursery
of the future apostles to lands that are older in culture but still unborn
in the faith.

9. *America Needs a Modern Saint*

America needs a saint, an American saint. After three hundred years of Catholic life, we cannot point to one saint who was born in this great land, who was educated in our schools, and showed in crisis how an American Catholic can relive the life of Christ crucified. We have the greatest Catholic school system in the world, the widest forms of charity work, the most compact army of teachers and religious, but the niches of our churches are empty.

Our dollars are cleansing lepers, digging wells for Moslems, setting up chapels in Nigeria and orphanages in Japan, but we must be more than hewers of schools and drainers of dollars. We must give to the world more than our gifts. We ought also to present it with a saint — a saint to prove we are not as materialistic as some believe; a saint who would be a priest, and preferably a bishop, to prove that sanctity in a nation must begin with the bishops, then the clergy, and finally the faithful; a saint who needs must be born here but need not die here to prove that the "melting pot" of America bubbles over in its love of humanity and pays back the debt of immigration that made us great; a saint who might have been so American as to have gone to school in Brooklyn — for what city has such a ring of Americanism about it; a saint who would have served the Church in other lands, for though we want a saint *from* America we do not want a saint who was only *for* America. We ought to present the world with a saint so American that his grandfather might have fought in the Civil War and his uncle might have lost his life when the *Merrimac* sank the *Cumberland,* whose father might have been the first newspaperman to publish a paper with a circulation of a million, whose grandfather, on his mother's side, might have driven one of the first trains into Des Moines, and whose parents might have been married by an American bishop. We need a saint so American that as a boy he would, like all American boys, make fun of anyone with a foreign accent, and then prove that he meant it in such good faith that he would take the message of the Gospel into foreign lands. In a word, we need a saint so American that he might have the same name as one of our automobiles.

Saying that we want a saint like this is not to say we have one, or will ever have one, but we believe we have a candidate to submit to the Church for her decision in our great American missionary to China, Bishop Francis Ford.

Francis Ford walked the streets of Brooklyn and New York; his confessor was the former Archbishop of Brooklyn. When he was twelve years of age, he heard an Italian missionary lecture on his work among the lepers. He gave a nickel in the collection which was much for a boy in those days and still is highly valued in some congregations. What stuck in his heart were the last words of the missionary, "My one ambeesch is to die a martyr." He kept repeating them over and over again; false ambition seemed squelched in the accent, but true ambition was satisfied in a Communist jail, as the accent now became Chinese: "My one ambition is to die a martyr."

One need never throw a log into a stream to see which way the current is flowing; a straw will tell us just as well. The little things of life more often indicate a character than some great burst of heroism or affection. It may very well be that a turtle and a wounded bird were the preface and the postscript to his episcopal motto which in its turn was the prophecy of his life. In his late teens just beginning to study for the missions, he wrote a little note to his superior: "I don't like to annoy you, but would you ask someone to let my turtle free. I left him near the pump and had not time to attend him." . . . Years pass and as a bishop in China, he one day was carrying a box through the yard to put over an outdoor crucifix. He saw beneath his feet a wounded bird. Under the image of the wounded Lord, the bishop stopped to heal the creature with the scarred flight, but it died in his hands.

In between the turtle and the bird incident, he was consecrated a bishop and what motto would this great missionary be expected to choose other than the one word which summed up his reaction to the turtle and the bird: "Compassion." Written across his episcopal shield was the word *"condolere"* which he took from St. Paul's description of the great High Priest and Bishop of our souls: "Who can have compassion on them that are ignorant and that err, because He Himself also is compassed with infirmity."

The superior could release the turtle out of compassion, but the Lord in heaven would not release Bishop Ford from a Communist cell. The wounded bird the Bishop could not restore to life, even under the eyes of the crucifix, but the Savior, who would not release him from captivity because He willed that "he should be compassed with infirmity," will give healing to his wings and one day raise him to new life in the Resurrection of the just.

Late in 1950 as the Communist police began to close in on the mission and as the news filtered in of the arrest and persecution of priests, Bishop Ford's reaction was like that of his Master on the occasion of the visit of the Greeks. As the seed produces new life only by falling to the ground, so now he sees the Communist persecution as the Cross-condition of China's Easter: "We may lose a few lives, but that is what is needed to convert China." As some of the Sister catechists were arrested, he said: "Remember the Church is not only a triumphant Church, but also a suffering Church; with Christ you may expect not only joy, but sorrow, but He is with you."

One often wonders why, with all the details in the life of Christ, only one man is mentioned in the Creed, and that is the representative of Caesar: "He suffered under Pontius Pilate." Judas is not named, nor Caiphas, nor Herod, nor the Pharisees, but only a political figure. This is not only to record an historical fact, but also to be a prophesy of how the mystical Christ in various rehearsals through history, and then in the final conflict of the forces of good and evil, will go to His death, "suffering under Pontius Pilate," suffering under the power of the omnipotent State.

"Thou art not a friend of Caesar" has echoed back from the balustrade of Pilate's court and now rings through Eastern Europe and China as the devout followers of Christ are accused of under-mining Caesar.

To be like the Savior, and to be a model of resistance in this totalitarian era, it was fitting that Bishop Ford should be charged with "harboring Kuomintang agents and Kongsi landlords, and of slanders against the People's Government." When Caesar becomes God, then a new crisis arises, the crisis of believing in God who is not Caesar. As the Communists often said to the missionaries: "Do you not know the devil is the head of our government?"

As the Lord started the procession to Calvary, the Cyrenian and the pious women consoled Him while the crowds buffeted and mocked Him. Bishop Ford has his consolation in the shopkeepers and their families who bowed low to him as he was led bound from his mission at Kaying. But there were also those who spat at him, threw stones and offal as some boasted: "I gave him a good wallop." To show that the curtain never goes down on the drama of Calvary, but merely has new actors, instead of the sarcastic banner carried before Christ bearing His name and His alleged crime, there was the sarcastic banner carried before Bishop Ford reading, "The People's Government welcomes the spy, Bishop Ford." While all this was going on, Bishop Ford was seen blessing and making the sign of the cross, as best he could with his handcuffed hands.

Many a missioner in China when asked: "Why do you not ask God to help you now?" answered: "I would not ask Him. I prefer to suffer for Christ." Another, when asked "What can your God do for you now?" answered: "He can teach me to forgive you." Our divine Lord is never without witnesses in every age of His passion and death. But how sweetly Providence watches over those who heralded the cross in their lives. Out of all the prisoners in jail, no one was given bread and wine except Bishop Ford.

> Too weak to stand, he leaned against the prison wall,
> His hair was long and white, his beard matted,
> His face emaciated and pale from torture.
> On his lap was a tin tray for an altar stone,
> His own burnt eyes were the candles.
> His unconscious servers, fellow prisoners,
> His Cathedral, a prison,

His *cathedra,* a cold cement floor,
His vestments, a black padded Chinese gown,
His mitre, a stocking cap,
His music, the groans of the suffering,
His missal, the memory of Calvary,
His sanctuary bell, the death knell about to strike.
But what Mass in a Gothic Cathedral
With forest aisles of stones,
Sunset panes and rose windows,
With chant, bright robes, and candles,
Could equal the Golgothian splendor of that prison Mass,
As Bishop Ford moved his fingers over the tin tray
Saying, "Qui pridie quam pateretur."

If the Mass be the memorial of the death of Christ, then this was it *par excellence.* The great High Priest whose death was being renewed in the lower room of a Chinese death cell was inseparably Priest and Victim. Hence our Lord on the cross was upright as a priest and prostrate as a victim. We who, possessed of His powers, call ourselves priests, never call ourselves victims; yet, in us, as well as in the Master, the two are meant to be inseparable. Who shall deny that Bishop Ford at this moment was both priest and victim; priest because he was strong enough to make oblation; victim because he was too weak to do it standing. Tremendous is the significance of the words of the Consecration when pronounced in circumstances such as these, for how deep must have been the identification of Bishop Ford with the words of the Consecration, "This is *My* Body; this is *My* Blood." . . . No parasite was he on the Mystical Body of Christ! Here was a new body and new blood for Christ to live and die . . . and be born again.

The murderer returns to the scene of his crime. I wonder if anyone in history has ever speculated about the idea that Judas might have hanged himself on the naked cross of Calvary after our Lord had been laid in the sepulcher? It would seem the fitting place for him to avenge in himself his crime. What is particularly interesting in the life of Bishop Ford is that the chief of police who supervised the investigation, a certain Tsong K'i Yao, was a vacillating indi-vidual who became a Red because it paid off. He knew Bishop Ford well, was acquainted with the good repute he enjoyed in the mission field, how he aided the poor, started pagans in business, taught the young, solaced the sick, and buried the dead. But as a Communist, he persecuted the Bishop. All of this must have been done with the consciousness that it was wrong, just as Judas knew he was wrong in betraying. Bishop Ford finally died as a dry martyr in February, 1952. One month later, the chief of police committed suicide. . . . Where? Of all places, he went back to Bishop Ford's room, and there hanged himself, as his bowels burst asunder.

America needs a saint, a saint who scratches initials in our school desks, who is ordained here, who *seems* just like the rest of us; a man popular with everyone who knows him well, unpopular with a few who think they know him better; a saint who mingles sanctity with humor, a mixture that is indispensable to holiness from our American point of view; a saint who brings American methods to the missions, and yet who is American enough to love all nationalities and who seeks to build up native clergy for the Church and prays that his successors may be Chinese.

America needs a saint who has done more than most priests and bishops will ever be called upon to do, namely to die for the faith, but who thus will always make us humbly realize how far short in all successes we fall from the ideal to "take up the cross daily"; a saint who dies outside our shores as our Lord died outside Jerusalem to prove

> It was not life alone he gave,
> But country up for man.

We are not saying that Bishop Ford is a saint, for in this we must wait upon the judgment of our Mother, the Church. But in any case, he comes closer to being a saint than we know ourselves to be in the honesty of our hearts.

We Americans are good administrators, but lest our love for counting, for statistics, and for buildings makes us forget that we are shepherds, and that the temple we must build above all others is the Temple of the Holy Ghost, we need the example of a man who so combined Americanism and the faith as to make us love them not as irreconcilables, but as father and mother.

Lest our offering be thought to be only material, may God give us a saint that we can give to the world, that the world may see that American progress and methods are not obstacles to sanctity, that the good-natured, free, easy, and comfortable lives we live in the routine of our priestly existence do not make us any less prepared for martyrdom than those to whom charity means a long face on top of a hair shirt.

It would be wonderful if this American Bishop, who prayed that he might be "ground underfoot and spat upon and worn out" as a doorstep in the King's Highway "to China," might also deign to become the stone on which our faithful, our clergy, might climb to such a spiritual eminence, that other nations, who now take our money, may take our holiness and learn that America has another "business," the business of the salvation of souls.

10. The Whole World Lives on the Eucharist

Tension and conflict are among the basic laws of the universe. St. Augustine describes them in terms of the struggle between the city of God and the city of man; the Apocalypse is the battle between the Woman and the dragon, and the Gospel is those on the cross and those beneath it. It is the purpose of this chapter to describe a conflict of the forces of good and evil in terms of the Eucharist.

The whole world lives on the Eucharist. Those who have the faith and are making sacrifices to spread the Church in mission lands are living on the Body and Blood of Christ. Those who persecute the Church and hinder its missionaries from bringing salvation to the benighted pagans are also related to the Eucharist in the sense that they prolong the death of Christ. St. Paul, speaking of those who receive unworthily, asks: "Would they crucify the Son of God a second time?" Communism behind the Iron Curtain and Communism behind the Bamboo Curtain is living on the Eucharist. Communists are crucifying Christ in His priests, in His Church, in His missionaries, as He is "delivered up" anew to other Pilates. The sickle for the wheat of good souls and the hammer for the press of grapes of men of goodwill are the principal instruments of recrucifixion.

There are two ways of taking the Eucharist: one unto the life of the New Testament, the other "eating and drinking damnation, not recognizing the Lord's Body for what It is." Both these manners of eating and drinking the Bread and the Cup of life began at the Last Supper when eleven Apostles took the Eucharist unto the fruits of the Passion and one, Judas, as the death food for self-destruction.

These two ways of taking the Eucharist endure through the whole history of the Church. Everyone in the world lives on the Eucharist; everyone either crucifies the Body and Blood of Christ or else he lives by That which was crucified. In a very remarkable passage by Catherine Ann Emmerich, it was revealed to her that the enemies of our Lord said to Pilate: "He promised He would give us His Flesh to eat and His blood to drink." Pilate, looking at the torn and bleeding body of Christ, with His flesh hanging from Him like purple rags, and reading the wrath and anger in their hearts against the tortured prisoner, answered: "It is true, you have already eaten His Flesh, you are already drinking His Blood."

Take, for example, the testimony of Doctor Thomas Dooley in his book, *Deliver Us From Evil*. He claims that there had to be more than wrath against humanity to account for the Communist atrocities that he witnessed in Southeast Asia:

> As the weeks passed I found myself increasingly puzzled, not only by the growing number but by the character of Communist atrocities. They seemed almost to have a religious significance. I was accustomed by now to patching up emasculated men, and women whose breasts had been mutilated, and even little children without fingers or hands. But more and more, I was learning that these punishments were linked to the refugees' belief in God.
>
> I saw a man lying on a bamboo stretcher, writhing in agony, his lips moving in silent prayer. When I pulled away the dirty blanket I found that his body was a mass of blackened flesh from the shoulders to the knees. The belly was hard and distended and the scrotum swollen to the size of a football. I gave him a shot of morphine, and inserted the large needle in the scrotum in an attempt to draw off some of the fluid.
>
> The old woman said that the man was her brother, a Catholic priest from a little town now within Communist territory. The Viet-Minh had told him he could hold only one Mass daily, at 6 A.M., the hour when everyone had to gather in the village square for a daily lecture on "new life!" When he persisted in saying Mass secretly at night, the Communists decided that he needed re-education. They hung him by his feet from the rafters of the Church, so that his hands just barely touched the floor and beat him with bamboo rods concentrating on the genitalia. How long this went on he could not remember but early the next morning the altar boys found him hanging there and cut him down.
>
> They lashed together an arrangement of bamboo poles that could be carried on a litter and floated as a raft. They hid the old priest near the river bank. Then after dark, they swam down stream towing

the raft and carried him to his sister's hut in a still free zone . . . on
another gruesome day there came to my hospital tent seven little boys
and an emaciated young man who was barely conscious. The children
looked like zombies, thick pus was running from their ears and a few
of them still had queer looking things protruding from their heads —
chopsticks!

We pieced together the story. The Communists had caught a school
teacher leading his class in the Lord's Prayer. They made him repeat it
for them, line by line, and made a mockery of their words.

"Give us this day our daily bread." Then they said to the children,
"Who gives you bread? God? No! The state!" When the lesson was
ended, they led the pupils into the schoolyard and taught the pupils
a different kind of lesson. Two Viet-Minh guards held a child by the
arms and another grasped his head, then the leader rammed the chop-
stick deep into his ear, splitting the canal and shattering the inner ear.
When all seven children had been "treated" the guards turned to the
teacher; they drew forth his tongue with pincers and sawed it off with
a blunt bayonet.

Men — if they can be called men — who do these things do not
regard God as a phantom. Communists are not the atheists of the
Western World who have no enthusiasm for their atheism. The Communists *believe* in God not as the saints believe in God but as the
devils believe; they believe to destroy. No man today raises his fists
against Caesar or Napoleon or swears revenge at the grave of Alexander. These men are dead but the intense hatred which the name of
Christ invokes among the Communists is in itself a testimony of the
reality of Christ Himself. Communists are not fighting against phan-
toms and figments of the imagination. They know that their tyranny
over hearts can never become supreme unless they master the
regnancy of Christ in human souls. If they did not have the Body
and Blood of Christ prolonged in His Church and in His priests and
in His faithful, they would have no object for their scorn. It is the
very reality of That which they attack which gives them their
diabolical fury.

A Russian Orthodox lady who recently returned from Shanghai
gave this testimony in favor of those whom the Eucharist sustains
in the face of those "who would drink and eat judgment unto
themselves."

I am not speaking only of those who are rotting in prisons but also
those at home in so-called liberty. There is a constant surveillance not

only by the regular police but also by that special type of police that is made up of civilians — of a given quarter or of a particular street — who to save their own skins are obliged to inform on others. Every least gesture and the most inoffensive word are run through the sieve. Day and night the so-called free people may have a visit from the police; day and night they may be subjected to endless interrogations, or they may be forced to attend accusation meetings. If they are unwilling to accuse their Bishop, there is nothing left for them but death by starvation. I know entire groups who are living in extreme want because they refuse to give a signature which they think would be blameworthy. I am not a Roman Catholic, but I assure you that I did all I could, unhappily very little in fact, to alleviate the sufferings of these poor people. How is it that such a thing is possible in the twentieth century?

Another witness who recently returned from Shanghai said:

Humanly speaking, the situation of Catholics is a desperate one: chased as they are from schools and universities, without the possibility of finding the least employment because they are classed as anti-revolutionaries. I really do not know how they can survive for long periods; many of them are walking skeletons and I know many who are spitting blood. In spite of this, they are obliged to assist at meetings that last for ten consecutive hours, sometimes for whole nights. They are there crouched on a small bench, like stones without stirring. This very motionlessness, this refusal to take part in the acclamations, this refusal to accuse, is in itself a crime.

In our modern world the area of indifference is narrowing. Communism is forcing men to take sides. The great lesson of Calvary reappears, that it is the cross that unifies — not only friends but enemies. It unites the friends, particularly in the Eucharist, "For they who eat One Bread are one body." But what is forgotten is that it also unites the enemies. It melts away all the lesser differences between men and combines them into the unity of hostility. Caesar and the people who were enemies were united in the condemnation of Christ. Pharisees and Sadducees, who despised one another for opposite doctrines, united in the crucifixion. Caiphas and Judas, Pilate and Herod all threw themselves into one another's arms because they found a greater hate. It is Christ who makes men forget their trivial divergences in order to concentrate their common differences or even hatred against Him.

Socialists, progressivists, liberals, freethinkers, like the characters that figured in the Passion, now cease to be conflicting personalities and unite in coalition against the Body that is the Temple of God. The hatred of the Communists against the Church has been whispered to them by the very demons who asked our Lord: "Art Thou come to destroy us, Jesus of Nazareth?" Indeed, He had come to destroy the evil thing that disquieted the mind of man or tampered with the souls of nations. Evil is always hypersensitive to the presence of good. Satan pours out his unpentecostal spirit to make the evil cease dissipating their energies against innocuous opponents in order to make a final stand on Calvary or at the Communion rail. The indifferent people of the Western World are not thinking about the Church; they never avert to it, never dwell upon the sacrifices of the missionaries. But the Communists are thinking about it; they never take their minds off it, as the demons never take their eyes off a soul.

Our blessed Lord still permits Himself now, as then, to be delivered over to His enemies. The Gospel constantly speaks of His "being delivered" to us, either for resurrection or damnation. Our blessed Lord Himself said: "He will be delivered into the hands of the Chief Priests and Scribes who will condemn Him to death; and these will give Him into the hands of the Gentiles who will mock Him and spit upon Him and scourge Him and kill Him." From that day on to this, Christ is at the mercy of the world. He "delivers Himself" unto us either to be the food of our soul or else the poison, if we reject Him.

We have thought of the Eucharist as being only for those who have faith, or are in the state of grace, or are members of Christ's Mystical Body. But the Eucharist is for the world. Our Lord knew it was for His enemies as well, when He said: "Destroy this Temple and in three days I will rebuild It." But He was speaking of the Temple of His Body. Would there ever have been a Eucharist if there had not been a crucifixion? But if there is a crucifixion will there not be those who will modernize for our generation and our times the death that is commemorated in the Mass?

Running through the universe there is a law: "We live by what we slay." The gangster and the criminal live by murder, but in the normal way the vegetables that enrich us, the meat that gives us strength, have all been slain; plants have been torn up from the roots of the earth and subjected to fire; animals are submitted to the sacrificial knife and the shedding of blood. In the supernatural order: "We live by what we slay." It is our sins which crucified Christ; those who are His friends live by what they slay, and those who are His enemies live for their brief hour by what they slay, tearing at the Flesh and drinking of the Blood of Christ.

Our problem, therefore, is not a material one of aid; it is a problem of hastening by our prayers and our sacrifices the glorious days of the Resurrection for mission lands:

. . . when Tibet will bring its lotus flower to the Wounded Brow in tribute to the fulfillment of contemplation they love so well;

. . . when Japan will see its Rising Sun spelled "Son" and mean the Righteousness that conquers death;

. . . when China, with its crimson architecture and now its blood-crimsoned cells, will seek forgiveness in the Red Blood that fell from Wounded Feet;

. . . when Oceania, dripping with the waters of the Pacific, will ask to be bathed again in the laver of regeneration purchased by the cross;

. . . when Africa will lift up black hands in adoration of a Eucharistic Lord; and

. . . when the whole world will see the Eucharist as the bond of all peoples in unity and peace, for they who eat One Bread are one body.